A Scorpion in The Lemon Tree

Mad adventures on a Greek peninsula

(Third book in the Peloponnese series)

By Marjory McGinn

A Scorpion In The Lemon Tree

Published by Createspace Independent Publishing Platform, 2016.

ISBN-13: 978-1534782303.
ISBN-10: 1534782303.

Text © Marjory McGinn 2016.

The rights of Marjory McGinn to be identified as the Author of this Work have been asserted by her in accordance with the Copyright, Designs and Patents Act, 1988.

All rights reserved. This book is sold under the condition that no part of it may be reproduced, copied, stored in a retrieval system or transmitted in any form or by any means, electronic, mechanical, photocopying, recording or otherwise without prior permission in writing of the author Marjory McGinn (info@bigfatgreekodyssey.com). A CIP catalogue of this is available from the British Library.

Cover illustration and design by Tony Hannaford. (www.anthonyhannaford.co.uk)

Editing, book design and author photographs by Jim Bruce. (www.ebooklover.co.uk)

About the author

Marjory McGinn was born in Scotland and brought up in Australia, where she became a newspaper journalist. Her features have appeared in major Australian publications, including *The Sydney Morning Herald* and *The Sun-Herald*. In 2000, she returned to Scotland and worked as a freelance journalist, with stories appearing in leading British newspapers, including the *Daily Mail*, *Daily Telegraph* and Scotland's *The Herald*.

A youthful work/travel year in Athens inspired a lifelong fascination for Greece. In 2010, with her partner Jim and their crazy Jack Russell dog, Wallace, she set off on an adventure to the southern Peloponnese that lasted four years and became the basis for her three travel memoirs: *Things Can Only Get Feta*, *Homer's Where The Heart Is* and this book. In 2018, Marjory published her first novel, *A Saint For The Summer*.

Marjory writes a blog with a Greek theme on the website www.bigfatgreekodyssey.com and she can be followed on Twitter www.twitter.com/fatgreekodyssey and Facebook www.Facebook.com/ThingsCanOnlyGetFeta.

She is currently based in East Sussex, England.

Dedication

For my parents, John and Mary, and Euphamia.

Note – Modern Greek

Modern Greek is a complex language and some word forms may confuse readers. Basically, articles, nouns, adjectives and most pronouns change according to gender, number and their position in a sentence (whether subject or object).

The noun *xenos*, for example, meaning foreigner or stranger, in the masculine form, sometimes appears in the text in plural form xenoi, or feminine singular, xeni.

Masculine names that end in 'os', 'as' or 'is' will drop the final 's' in the vocative case (when addressing someone directly). The name Dimitris, for example, will change when you say: "Dimitri, are you listening?"

Author's note

This book is based on real events and characters. While I have kept the real names of villages and other locations, I have changed the names of most characters to protect the innocent ... and the guilty know exactly who they are.

Stop beside the still lake, passer-by,
The curly sea and the tormented ships
The roads that wrapped mountains and gave birth to stars
All end here on this broad surface
— **George Seferis**

Contents

Map of the region ....page 8
Preface ....page 9
Chapter 1: Big fat calamity ....page 11
Chapter 2: Critter jitters ....page 23
Chapter 3: Only Koroni ....page 37
Chapter 4: Gone with the anemos ....page 46
Chapter 5: Foteini – famous at last! ....page 64
Chapter 6: House in the olive orchards revisited ....page 73
Chapter 7: Wallakos goes large ....page 86
Chapter 8: What lies above ....page 96
Chapter 9: There's a grasshopper in my underpants .....page 110
Chapter 10: I should be souvlaki ....page 120
Chapter 11: A man needs a little madness ....page 129
Chapter 12: Socks and the city ....page 138
Chapter 13: Pear group pressure ....page 150
Chapter 14: Things get worse before they get Feta ....page 157
Chapter 15: What's it all about, Alfa? .... page 173
Chapter 16: The Hand of God Tree .... page 182
Chapter 17: Knowing your arse from your omega ......page 190
Chapter 18: The Lotus Eaters ....page 200
Chapter 19: Too old to conjugate ....page 211
Chapter 20: Life on the rogue carpet ....page 219
Chapter 21: Walls with a view ....page 227
Chapter 22: In the lap of the dogs ....page 234
Chapter 23: No money, but plenty of Monet ....page 246
Chapter 24: Day of lost souls ....page 258
Chapter 25: I was born under a wandering star .....page 263
Chapter 26: Margarita's inheritance ....page 271
Acknowledgements ....page 277
The prequels ....page 278
New novel ....page 282

Map of the region

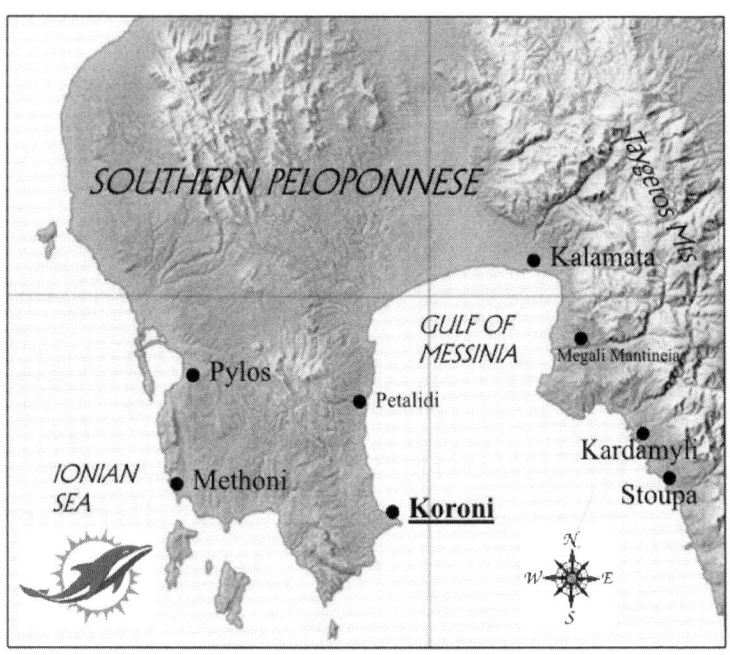

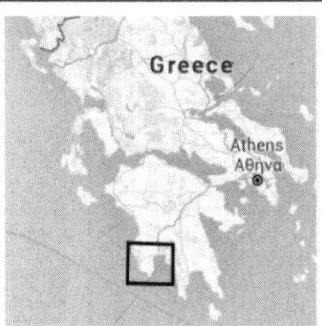

Preface

EVERYONE needs an odyssey at least once in their life – and in our case, at least twice. The second time around proved that while you can try to replicate the first one down to the fine details, it will never go to plan – especially in Greece!

Jim and I started our odysseys back in 2010, when we left our Scottish village for the wild and beautiful Mani region in the southern Peloponnese, together with our famously mad Jack Russell dog, Wallace. What had been planned as a year's mid-life adventure turned into three. We moved to the hillside village of Megali Mantineia and set about integrating with the rural community, with many funny and challenging outcomes.

It was here we met the inimitable characters who would feature in my first two books, *Things Can Only Get Feta* and *Homer's Where The Heart Is*. The most memorable of them was the goat farmer Foteini, who we met on our first day in the village as she rode home on her donkey, Riko, piled high with a chair, a beach umbrella and much more. She is a unique rural character, who shared the stories of her life and endeared herself to many readers in the process.

It was Foteini who first christened me Margarita, and Jim became Dimitris. It was to become one of the most unusual friendships of my life that would continue for the next three years, despite us living in different locations – and would lope into this latest escapade as well.

At the end of 2012, we returned to Scotland after living through the worst year of the Greek crisis up to that point, with a raft of swingeing austerity measures, which some commentators described as a "slow death for Greece".

Fortunately, this hasn't happened but the country continues with political and economic uncertainty.

In 2014, we followed our nomadic destiny and set out on another long odyssey in the southern Peloponnese, ending up this time in a peninsula we didn't choose, in a house we never thought we'd live in, with schedules riffing to a spontaneous Greek beat. How this happened is our continuing story.

And while a slew of animals and critters insinuated their way into this odyssey, for reasons that remain a mystery, none was manhandled in researching and writing the book. If only that were true for the scorpions ...

1

Big fat calamity

AS we neared the western fringes of Kalamata city, the robotic voice on the car's satellite navigation box became shouty. It told us we were approaching the *"Calamitous Coronary Road!"*

"What?" we both said, staring at the screen on the black box in disbelief as a pink arrow jerked forward like a sluggish blood flow, up the map towards our destination at the remote tip of the Messinian Peninsula. Jim was driving and wiped a finger over the sweaty sheen of his forehead. The sat-nav's female voice repeated the directions.

"Why's she talking about a Calamitous Coronary Road?" Jim said.

"Or Heart Attack Highway perhaps?" I offered, laughing, getting into the spirit of the daft sat-nav commentary that we had been following for hours.

Okay, it had been a very long, tiring day after an early-morning arrival in Greece on the ferry from Ancona, Italy. It had also been unseasonably hot for early April.

"We've just driven from Patras – on a stretch of road where Greek drivers are plotting suicide, driving in the middle of the road, talking on mobiles, drinking frappés with both hands. No way are we approaching the Heart Attack Highway," said Jim.

But sat-nav woman kept punching it out over and over. "After 200 metres turn left on to the Calamitous Coronary Road."

"It's mental, isn't it?" moaned Jim, keeping his eyes trained on the road ahead, as a battered pick-up truck with a goat tethered in the back swung from side to side while the driver seemed to be leaning over the passenger seat trying to retrieve something – a mobile perhaps!

I sat for a while pondering the sat-nav. "It's her Greek pronunciation, isn't it? She's just mangled the words 'Kalamatas-Koronis' road and made them sound like a health condition."

This was the road that connected the city of Kalamata to the town of Koroni, where we were heading.

"That's a relief then. We're not about to fall off the twig any minute," said Jim.

We lapsed into exhausted silence for a moment. That's when I became aware of the frenzied slurping noise from the back of the car. I swivelled round and saw Wallace, perched up in his dog bed on a tower of suitcases. He was worrying his paws in a fit of compulsive grooming, the air humming with the aroma of wet feet and dog breath.

"Wallace is going stir-crazy back there."

Jim wasn't listening. His brain was apparently still wired into sat-nav woman.

"I get what you're saying about the duff pronunciation, but why does sat-nav woman put the extra 'S' at the end of each word? Why can't she just say Kalamata-Koroni Road?"

I sighed. "Greek grammar, Jimbo. She's using the genitive case, with 'Ss'."

"The what?"

I started to explain but he was suddenly disinterested.

"It's too late in the day for Greek grammar. Too late in life for it as well," he said, sighing.

Poor Jim has suffered, trying to learn Greek from our early days in the Mani region in 2010 after we decided to rip up the normal template and have a mid-life adventure, living in an old hillside village. Since then, he has struggled with the language, like a man trying to prise the lid off a sealed jam jar with his teeth. As someone who had started learning the language decades earlier, I had sympathy for his plight.

Jim could get by now, more or less, but he only spoke in the present tense. The 'past', to mangle an aphorism, was another language, as well as another country.

"I've become Greek. I only live in the minute," he liked to say.

While we drove the last peaceful stretch of our journey, in the late afternoon sun with a clear view of the Messinian gulf on our left-hand side, the ambience was marred only by sat-nav woman punching out her coronary predictions, so we finally switched her off. She'd been a minx from the start – France, Switzerland, Italy, Greece – and she'd messed up in every language, so much so, that several times along the way, we had missed turn-offs because we couldn't understand her pronunciation.

It was all Wallace's fault really.

For this journey to the Messinian peninsula, the left-hand of the three that hang down from the southern Peloponnese like pulled roots, we had decided to buy the sat-nav to help mainly in finding our 'pet-friendly' hotels on the route from Calais to Ancona. The hotels offering to take dogs were usually miles from motorways, out in the sticks and at the end of farm tracks. We had also planned a two-day stopover at Bellagio, on Lake Como, in northern Italy. We were just getting to grips with sat-nav woman's odd Italian pronunciation when she played an outrageous prank on us late in the afternoon. To get to Bellagio, we were directed down a narrow road that runs along one side of Lake Como, with a string of villages we'd never heard of before.

"We've been driving for ages now and I can't see a sign for Bellagio. This is odd!" Jim said, rubbing a hand over his tired eyes and commanding me to check the destination in our massive European map book, like the co-pilot I was supposed to be. As if! Women *can* read maps, of course we can! We just don't have the urge to do it. My fingers trailed about the page, along the narrow road that looked like a spider vein skirting the lake's edge.

"I can't find Bellagio on this road. It must have been abducted overnight by aliens."

"This is no laughing matter, Margarita. Keep looking," said Jim, with a sigh. Jim calls me by my 'Greek' name as a term of endearment but also when he wants my undivided attention. A moment later, however, sat-nav woman directed us towards the lake itself, down a steep road to the water's edge.

"Are we supposed to drive on water now?" said Jim, stopping the car and whipping the map book away from me. He glared at the outline of Lake Como, bunching up his brows, forcing air noisily through his lips, all of which is default male behaviour for dealing with female inadequacy, particularly map-reading dysfunction, which I have been guilty of on a few occasions. I lapsed into weary silence, desperate to get into the hotel, showered and then out again to a nice Italian restaurant for a cartwheel pizza and a glass of chianti.

Jim suddenly jerked his head out of the book. "Hell's feckin' bells! She's taken us to the wrong side of the lake, Margarita!"

To retrace our journey and get to the correct side would take a good hour. It would be dark soon.

"Why did she do that?" I asked.

"Who knows, but I just wish we'd never bought the bloody thing!"

"Maybe she's thinking like a woman, lateral, you know. Maybe we're *supposed* to be here... to em... catch a *ferry*," I said, emphatically, pointing to the small wharf nearby that Jim seemed to have overlooked during his strop. And there was also a 'ticket office' of sorts.

Jim squinted at the building. "This is peculiar. But look, you take Wallace for a piddle break and I'll check it out."

Sure enough, a ferry was due soon, the last one of the afternoon for Bellagio, where we had booked a room in a fashionably old hotel at the top of a hill overlooking the lake, a small indulgence on our long trek to Greece. The sat-nav was taking us on the most direct route, and probably quickest, from this side of the lake to the town, directly opposite.

"She could have told us what was going on, the minx!" said Jim, as we drove on to the ferry, with the whole car deck to ourselves.

Lake Como was a delight and after two days of relaxation and Italian cuisine we were on the road again, driving south through Italy, with its frenetic motorways full of macho speedsters, while sat-nav woman ramped up the anxiety with more language gaffes. Increasingly, we had to rely on the map book, with me humiliated by bouts of map-reading under-achievement. But men can't always reign supreme in a motor vehicle.

When we drove on to the ferry at Ancona, poor Jimbo got a lesson in eating humble pie from one of the Greek parking crew dressed in a bright orange industrial onesie. Parking on this car ferry, we discovered, even on our first long drive to Greece in 2010, is a crazy, seat-of-the-pants undertaking, aimed at squeezing as many vehicles in as possible on the car decks to maximise the dosh.

Jim was commanded by the orange suit to *reverse* down a steep ramp to the lower floor, a manoeuvre we'd never encountered here before. With typical impatience, the Greek worker shouted directions: "Right, left, more right, more left, no, not like that, *panayia mou* (holy Virgin)!..." And so forth, and with the usual colourful gestures: forehead slapping, and arms flung out in frustration as cars were log-jamming on the upper car deck, waiting their turn to descend. Jim was getting rattled and couldn't sort his left from his right. I tried to help, by repeating the instructions.

"Shh, Margarita, I can't listen and drive at the same time."

That's a peculiarly male complaint which explains why, whenever Jim is doing a normal reverse park, he always turns the radio off. Orange suit was working up a real head of steam now and nearby Greek truck drivers were laughing and offering big windmill arm gestures of amusement. It was all very entertaining, until orange suit suddenly yanked the driver door open.

"You go, I do it!" he shouted.

Jim was plucked out in an instant, like an escargot from its crusty shell. He stood at the top of the ramp with his shoulders wilting. The Greek leapt in and took the wheel. Wallace barked at the territorial intrusion, sending blasts of rancid breath about the car, but the driver was like a man possessed.

He pitched the car backwards down the ramp at great speed. I screamed and Wallace howled, like two big-dipper rookies. Then we were further imprisoned in the car, shaking, while orange suit did dozens of fast, back-and-forth movements in a ridiculously small space between two parked four-wheel drives, until we were jammed in so tight, I couldn't open the passenger door and had to crawl over the driver's seat to get out.

Jim had to walk the ramp of shame down to the car and it took a plate of moussaka in the dining room later and a bottle of Nemea red for him to get over his worst encounter with Greek machismo.

When we arrived in Patras, on the west coast of the northern Peloponnese, we didn't really need the sat-nav any more. We'd been on this road to Kalamata before, but somehow we'd become drugged by the robotic drone of sat-nav woman and we just forgot to switch her off. Embarking on a car journey to Greece, for another long odyssey, had not been our preferred mode of transport, even though we had great confidence in the small Fiat car we'd first bought in Greece and took back to Scotland with us in 2012. We knew it was up to the trip. But was lovable Wallace, a Jack Russell with a penchant for thumbing rides along the crazy spectrum?

When we decided on this second adventure in Greece in 2014, we realised that taking Wallace with us would ramp up our difficulties with travelling and finding rental accommodation, though leaving him behind was never an option. The situation had been similar when we first went to the Mani region, situated in the middle peninsula of the southern Peloponnese, four years earlier. For that journey, we had chosen to do things the hard way, and not just because we had Wallace with us.

Unlike many expats, we didn't own a house in this part of Greece, or even know anyone who did. Apart from a short holiday in the Mani once, we didn't even know that much about the region. We rented a holiday house for a month near the sea and that was all. Beyond that, we had no idea where we wanted to live, only that it should be in a fairly traditional village away from tourist sites.

Having Wallace of course narrowed our choices of decent rental properties and we were just days away from a premature return to Scotland when a Kalamatan estate agent came across the small stone house in Megali Mantineia in the foothills of the Taygetos mountains, where we stayed for a year and where the English owner was fine about dogs. For the following two years we lived on a rambling property near the sea, owned by a warm-hearted Greek family. We always landed on our feet.

We had returned from our three years in the Mani in December 2012. It had seemed like a sensible move, with family issues to sort out back in the UK, and also Greeks warning us the country was facing more economic chaos, with no telling how much hardship that would cause.

During our last year in the Mani, I had also been writing my first book about our experiences, called *Things Can Only Get Feta*, and at the end of 2012, two publishers were interested in seeing the completed work. I felt it would be easier to secure publication while back in the UK. The book was eventually published in July 2013 by a small London publisher and got off to a flying start as the timing was just right for a book set in the Greek *crisi*, crisis.

Possibly because of the excitement of the book launch and the promotional work involved, it meant our lives inevitably revolved around Greek issues and we started to feel a distinct longing to return.

Jim had returned temporarily to journalism as a sub-editor on a Glasgow tabloid, a job he didn't relish. At the same time, he had started his own freelance business as a book editor, which was a perfect vehicle for his journalism skills, even though he had little desire now to be part of the mainstream profession.

The newspaper industry had contracted and changed during the previous five years, to the point where we both felt it was not as lucrative or secure as it once was. We had both worked in Australia, where I was brought up, on popular Sydney newspapers. We had lived through the heyday of journalism, when it was more glamorous and certainly more fun − but those days had gone forever.

After 10 years in the Scottish newspaper industry as well, we had been relieved to sidestep journalism. Now that we were both involved in the book publishing world we were able to work anywhere as long as we had our laptops and internet access.

Restless for the lifestyle and the warmth of Greece, we made plans to go back for a while. This time, we took the more radical decision of selling our apartment in Scotland, so that we would feel unencumbered in case we decided to stay longer than just the summer, or even to buy a bargain holiday house, as there was said to be an over-supply of property on the Greek market due to the crisis.

As was the case in 2010, friends and family thought we were crazy. To have one mid-life break is okay, but two in quick succession was quite another matter. One friend in Scotland, with a difficult job and a couple of kids, was downcast when I told him we were off again.

"Where is our mid-life odyssey?" he said. "When can we do what you're doing?"

I felt for his predicament. "You can do it one day if you really want it badly enough" was all I could offer him. But it did become our stock answer to the unexpected comments we received, because that statement had been true for us from the beginning, and continued to be, despite Greece still being deep in crisis. Once again it took a massive amount of planning. Our 'to-do' list before we left was several A4 pages long.

We planned to return to the Mani, to continue where we had left off and to see the Greek friends we had become fond of during our time there. I also wanted to write another book, the sequel to *Things Can Only Get Feta,* and thought it would be so much easier to do it there, steeped in the beauty of the place, the heat, the aromas, the crazy unpredictability of life.

But I was about to discover that this was a creative whim that the Greek gods would toy with, like a Jack Russell with a lamb bone. As a Greek once explained to me: "*Otan o anthropos kanei schedia, o Theos yelaei.*" When a man makes plans, God laughs." Oh boy, was God chortling that year!

However, as we drove down the peninsula towards Koroni, I had to firmly remind myself why we were heading there at all, when we had our heart set on living once more in the Mani. We didn't even particularly like Koroni that much, based on a day trip we had taken from the Mani in 2010. There had been no particular reason why. It was a laid-back harbourside town, and picturesque, enclosed by high cliffs on each side and an old castle on top. But it was remote, near the southern-most tip of the Messinian peninsula, with the gulf on one side and the Ionian Sea on the other. It was as close to an island as you could get without it being an island. So why Koroni?

While we were in Scotland planning this adventure, we had approached it much as we had the first, by trying to secure a holiday let first and then worrying about the rest of the plan once we got to the Mani. This time, however, we couldn't get past the first hurdle. Even after weeks of checking the internet sites of estate agents for a holiday villa and sending emails to friends and acquaintances for help, we had come up with nothing. Even in the middle of the crisis, it seemed no-one was renting out properties.

After weeks of searching, nothing suitable turned up in the Mani, or even close to Kalamata. In the end, there was only one group of villas, in Koroni, on the opposite peninsula, that were in a pleasing location and, most importantly, where the Greek owner was happy to have the dog. Time had just run out.

"Okay, we'll book it for a month and use it as a base," Jim had said. "Then we can blitz all the local agencies we couldn't check online, and call some more of our old friends for help. Something will turn up, it always does. In the meantime, we'll have a nice chill-out break."

However, from the 'base' it took almost an hour-and-a-half to drive to Kalamata, where we would need to go regularly for serious shopping, the vet, and other professionals, and it was nearly two hours to north Mani. But, what the hell, we had to start somewhere!

Half-way down the road to Koroni, we stopped for a while so I could take over the driving for the last stretch. We parked by the road, opposite a pebbly beach, and walked up a dirt track to stretch our legs and let Wallace have a rest from dog grooming. It was good to be walking on Greek soil again, taking in the aromas of the late afternoon: the smell of the sea, the scent of wild spring herbs. By the side of the track, wild *marathos* (dill) was growing abundantly. I snapped off a tall sprig with its light fluffy top and the aroma filled the air. How good it felt to be back in Greece, a place where the simplest things caressed all your senses at once. How I had missed it.

The drive to Koroni was not unpleasant, apart from the winding road and the crazy drivers of course, but the traffic thinned out as we neared the end of the peninsula. We turned into the wide car park at the main supermarket just outside the town at 6pm, where we had arranged to meet one of the villa owners.

Yiannis arrived a few minutes after us and picked us out straight away from the pile of suitcases in the back and Wallace, staring mournfully out the side window, like a prisoner in a van being hauled off to a secure unit. If we hadn't been sure about Koroni, we liked Yiannis immediately. He was a thin, lanky guy in his forties, with big soulful eyes and a casual, almost hippy style about him. He was wearing a psychedelic T-shirt and wide stripy trousers and sandals, like a laid-back paddy-field worker. He had an amiable smile and, speaking in passable English, asked us to follow him.

We bumped along a narrow track through olive groves, past a few discreet holiday villas, and finally, a ramshackle farm on one side with tethered goats, dogs on chains and a few people sitting on a collection of wobbly chairs under a fruit tree with a Greek flag fluttering nearby, hoisted on a bit of a pole. The group were talking loudly and drinking coffee. This was more like the maverick Mani style we had become used to in previous years. All that was missing was women on donkeys and young guys shooting out road signs with hunting rifles.

We turned off the main track, just beyond the farm, where a bumpy concrete drive wound up past a collection of villas on various levels, the last three villas standing on top of a hill, where we parked the cars. Yiannis took us first to the edge of the garden, where we leaned on a wooden fence to admire this peaceful eyrie with its uninterrupted view of the Mani peninsula opposite, the spine of the Taygetos mountains running like a big dipper all the way to the bottom.

Right in front of us, beyond a green expanse of olive orchards, was Koroni harbour and the town, built in tiers down the amphitheatre shape of the cliff-face. The town looked like it was nestling in the crook of an arm, with the sturdy battlements of Koroni Castle above. The view from the balcony of our villa was no less dramatic and was shaded on one side by several large olive trees and a vibrant lemon tree. The villa was clean and pleasant and promised a comfortable stay. With Greek Easter coming up, it was likely to be peaceful as well, with few tourists around so early in the season.

"We'll probably never see another tourist up here for a while. We'll have the hilltop to ourselves until after Easter," said Jim, rubbing the palms of his hands together with glee.

But if there's one rule in life it's got to be this: whenever you say you'll hardly ever see a certain thing, it arrives, larger than life, mostly in droves, like 20 British buses, none of which is going your way.

2

Critter jitters

"COME quickly, Jim!" I called out from the kitchen, where I was busy preparing breakfast. "What is it," he said, rubbing sleepy eyes.

"Look! There's a naked peeping tom outside, holding binoculars!"

"What?"

I pointed through the window that overlooked the side garden with its dozen or so olive trees. A man was standing beside the tree closest to us. He was naked except for a pair of boxer shorts, his pot belly hanging over the tight elastic. It was bright red, like his chest, from a bout of reckless sunbathing, no doubt. He was training his binoculars towards some distant point. He hardly moved, hardly flinched a muscle.

"What the bloody hell is he doing?" said Jim.

"Some kind of madman, I think. And that's our week of peace over with, I guess."

The first week we had seen no-one up on the hill except for Yiannis, who came and went with towels and other provisions, and a white van driven by a cousin of the family, who had a field next to the villa complex with a high fence. There were rows of grapevines inside, a flock of sheep and goats, and a 'guard' dog, which the cousin came regularly to feed. It was a powerful spotted spaniel cross, with big, long ears like tortilla wraps. We named him Pluto, since he most resembled the Disney bloodhound character. He was cute but no-one's fool and we had respect for his hunting skills when we saw him catch a massive brown snake one morning and flung it about like a toy before he killed it. He was now barking at the man with the binoculars, who seemed oblivious.

"Go out and ask him what he's doing. This is our bit of garden after all," I said with proprietorial nippiness. "Better still, let's send Wallace outside. That will scare him off."

As if he understood he was being summoned for impromptu mischief, Wallace bounced into the kitchen, tail wagging, tongue lolling.

"Okay, he needs a piddle, in any case," said Jim, opening the door.

Wallace raced ahead of him and right round to where the man was standing. Wallace did one of his rare handstand pees, on his front legs, pee shooting out over the trunk of the olive tree behind him, narrowly missing the man's legs. It was one of Wallace's funny habits from puppyhood and was much commented on in our conservative Scottish village. Age had taken some of the verve out of the manoeuvre, but it always got a laugh. The man wasn't laughing, however.

With the binoculars hanging now on their leather strap over his belly, he had his arms crossed over his crotch. Then Wallace stepped up the anxiety and unleashed his distinctive screamy bark, which had also arrived in his youth, along with the pee trick. Pluto added to the mayhem, bounding backwards and forwards along the fence line. Peaceful hillside, be damned! I watched from the window as the man stood with his back against the olive tree. He looked terrified.

"That's the remedy for peeping toms," I muttered to myself.

I could hear Jim quizzing the interloper who, after a few minutes, scurried back to one of the villas behind us, as if he were being chased by a rhino.

Jim came back in, shaking his head. "He's a twitcher. He's spotted some kind of rare coloured parrot or something."

"I hope he's not going to slink about olive trees every morning."

"Wallace and Pluto scared him off."

"British?"

"Yes. A couple, and they're here for a month."

"Oh lordy! A month of birdwatching?"

"Afraid so. He seems serious about it. And his wife. They've brought their bird books of Greece along and plan to be around the villas a fair bit."

Just our luck, I thought. But we planned to be out a lot in any case, exploring more of the town and the surrounding area and eating out in local tavernas. Most of the tavernas in the town were slowly opening up before Easter and were situated on the *paralia*, the long road along the harbour front, where by early summer the outdoor areas at the water's edge would all be operating and the place would be swarming with visitors.

We quickly found our favourite taverna, which also happened to be one of the first to open for the season. The Parthenon had a wide outdoor space near the water and the kind of scuffed, roll-down plastic sides you see everywhere in Greece. Although it was hot during the day, it was still nippy at night and at first we ate inside with an eclectic group of diners.

The inside was cavernous, with floor-to-ceiling windows and an open kitchen at one end. It was a homely set-up, with a TV propped up high at one corner, and usually there was a table of old Greek guys in the centre, smoking and drinking ouzo, eating from small plates of *mezedes* arranged in the middle of the table. These were raucous symposia: loud conversations, arguments over politics, jokes and wind-ups. They were simply enjoying their 'Greek life' because in a few months they would have to move to other haunts in the backstreets of Koroni, where they wouldn't be disturbed by the tourist hordes. I can't say I blamed them. When the TV was off, there was always popular *laiki* music playing from a hidden sound system. It was a lively place and reminded me of tavernas I had been to years before on trips around Greece. The place was run by a very genial woman called Oreanthi (beautiful flower), whose family had run the business since the 1970s. These days her son Spiros served and various relatives helped with cooking. It all had a nice vibe.

One evening, when the weather was slightly warmer, we ate outside at a corner table, cocooned by plastic walls, and ordered a plate of seafood with a Greek salad and a carafe of local wine. It's only when you eat outside that you slip back into the sensuality of being in Greece, enjoying simple wholesome food and ambience. As usual there was a steady stream of locals passing along the road: kids on bikes, priests strolling, hawkers selling new season strawberries. All of life in Koroni passed down this *paralia*, so it was in a way the heart of the town, or its jugular at any rate.

We tried all the other tavernas as well and one night in a pleasant place up a side street we came across the twitchers, Jed and Delia. We knew it had to happen sooner or later. They were sitting in the corner of the front terrace, half-way through their meal. We waved and sat a few tables away, to give them space, imagining Jed would still be embarrassed about our first encounter.

We hadn't seen much of Delia until now. Perhaps she had the midnight bird watch, waiting for small brown owls to appear. She was a slim woman with thick blonde hair that stood up at the top and sides vibrantly. She was wearing a bright floral dress and I rather fancied, in a dull moment while I toyed about with the menu, that she looked like a pretty South American parrot. Side by side in this setting, they were both birdlike. I had only ever seen Jed outside, wearing sunglasses, but now I noticed he had big attentive eyes and combined with his usual beetroot sunbather's chest, he looked like a large robin redbreast. They were starting to resemble the objects of their obsession.

We enjoyed our dinner, a massive brick of moussaka and chicken souvlaki, while other punters slowly drifted away for the evening. At one point, we saw Delia get up and hover over one of the empty tables, where a family of Greeks had left mounds of food on their plates and the waiter hadn't bothered yet to clear it up because there was a crucial sports event on the TV inside. Jim and I exchanged quizzical looks in her direction. She seemed to be dithering over a plate of lamb chops. Had she not had enough for her dinner? Next minute, Delia picked up the plate of meat and carried it past our table and out of the taverna. Jed ambled over, red-faced, bending towards us and whispering like David Attenborough in the wilderness.

"The wife is soft-hearted. She has a thing about cats, you see. She comes to a taverna and then at the end, when people have left food, she gathers it up, takes it outside and scrapes it on to the ground for them. She can't bear to see a cat starve."

Then he bent in a bit closer. "When you look at what some of the Greeks leave on their plate, you ask yourself: 'What crisis, eh?'" Then he winked.

Jim and I frowned at each other. What can you say to people who come to Greece but only see animals on their radar screen, worthy though that is. Just as they were leaving the restaurant, they both stopped at our table a moment. Jed suggested we get together for a drink one night, so we could tell them about our Greek adventures, then they flew away for the night.

"It's your fault for tempting fate and saying we'd be on the hillside alone," I said to Jim when they were well out of earshot.

"I suppose they're up at dawn feeding all the birds as well."

They were genial enough folk, but all the same we were beginning to see the downside of living in a tourist complex.

We would have to start looking seriously for a long-term rental as soon as Easter had passed.

◎◎◎◎◎

That Easter, to get into the spirit of things, I suggested we should have an ecclesiastical marathon to pass the time and go to every evening church service of the *Megali Evdomada*, the Holy Week, as most Greeks do, and which we had never quite achieved before. It's the best way to get a feel for Greek Easter, as each daily service advances the story bit by bit towards the resurrection on the Saturday. Also, there's never a better way to gain some insight into the character of local Greeks than during church services, as we found while living in a hillside village in the Mani.

We tried different churches too, from the main church in Koroni's *plateia*, Ayios Dimitrios, to smaller ones in the outlying villages. It was a not unpleasant kind of marathon, except that Jim developed what he thought was a new and devious medical problem, EKS, or Ecclesiastical Knee Syndrome, because there is so much standing up and sitting down during Greek services, and at night the churches were rather chilly.

We made it to Holy Thursday, though, and once you're there you can be lulled into thinking the longest part of the week is over and the best is yet to come, with the pomp and ceremony of the popular Friday service, when a flower-decked bier is carried around every town and village in Greece, to the famous Saturday service, with candles, singing and fire crackers for a rousing resurrection finale. But the Thursday service we discovered was the one that sorted out the mice from the minotaurs. It was, frankly, a revelation.

We had heard there was a new young priest in the lovely church of the Panayia Eleistria (dedicated to the Virgin Mary), perched on a cliff at the rear of Koroni Castle and overlooking the long beaches of Zaga and Memi, far below. We had heard the *papas* had some new and different ideas, so off we went to the Thursday service to find out. We were not disappointed.

The service is excruciatingly long and harrowing, even for the Greeks, and follows the trial of Christ, and finally his crucifixion and death on the cross. The service started at 7pm, the climax of which is one of high drama. The lights were dimmed and the priest carried a large wooden cross around the inside of the church, three times. The cross had three lit candles and it was a tricky business to navigate it around the hanging oil lanterns and banners without setting the place on fire. Accompanied by a retinue, including the deacon and hyperactive choir boys, the ritual was complete and suitably dramatic, with the young, fresh-faced, slightly tubby *papas* singing the traditional and very reverent 'crucifixion' hymn that went with it.

The rest of the service was longer than I ever remembered any to be, full of Greek I couldn't decipher, and as I glanced around the church I saw many Greeks looking pale and wilted, with many of the men discreetly slipping outside for a quick cigarette in the cool evening air. As foreigners we felt the need to stay, and endure, lest we be considered slightly soft or disinterested.

Nine-thirty came and went in a strange agony of chanting, incense and a babble of high Greek. After a while I welcomed EKS, and every opportunity to stand up and feel my legs, like an economy passenger on a long-haul flight to Australia, which is what it all began to feel like. As we nudged up to the three-hour mark, Jim and I exchanged looks. Jim had a pained smile and I wondered if he wanted to leave finally, but we tacitly agreed to stay on because it's one of those peculiar things in life that after you've endured something for a long time, the balance is tipped over and it becomes sheer lunacy not to go the final hurdle. Children were squirming in their seats and I was full of admiration for the painstaking way Greek kids are reared. If British youngsters had to sit for three hours in a church, there would be mayhem on an industrial scale.

Most of all, I had reverence for the ancient thin women, dressed in black, sitting motionless in the high-back chairs placed around the walls, their gaunt, tired faces like the ghosts of Easters past. If you want to see how Greeks cultivate stoicism and survive economic crises, the church is the go-to place of study.

And still the service continued. My mind was flagging. Why does the Orthodox Church make this particular service so damned long, I asked myself, longer than I had ever remembered a Thursday service to be. Why does it have to be so excruciating, full of heavy, lugubrious chanting, endless passages of scripture. Couldn't it be shortened? I felt my mind flaking, my patience withering like a salt-doused slug. Then I finally got it. Those cunning Byzantines, what guys they were! They deliberately made this a long one to simulate the agony of Christ, the final hours. I felt every inch of it. My head was throbbing and my stomach was starting to gurgle loudly, as we had decided to wait until after the service and have a late meal, not thinking it would be this late.

Just when everyone seemed to be at the point where a mass walk-out might have been on the cards, the *papas* did something cheeky. He was standing at the central arch of the *iconostasis*, holding a massive gold-plated Bible. As he read from it his voice got louder and more emotional as he described the last moments of Christ's life. I could also sense the people around me sighing with guilty gratitude, knowing the end was nigh.

The *papas* suddenly slammed the Bible shut with a mighty resonating 'thwack' that echoed around the church and made everyone jump. I heard an old woman nearby gasp for air and invoke the guidance of a slew of saints. The *papas* then shot into the sanctuary, leaving us all in mini-shock and silence, looking from one to another.

I guessed this was not in the usual script and it seemed to have riled some of the patriarchs of the congregation, who made their way out of the church huffing and puffing. But Jim and I were well pleased that our long wait had been worth it after all. I hadn't remembered Greek church being quite this dramatic ever. With that one gesture, the *papas* had put us through the whole Easter agony — and didn't we know it!

We came back to the same church for the Friday and Saturday services, wondering what kind of rabbit the young *papas* might pull out of his *kalimavchi*, black stovepipe hat. But the services conformed to the usual drama and euphoria, ending with the mighty clamour of Saturday night, and the resurrection: bells tolling loudly, fire crackers exploding on the periphery of the church yard, like mortar fire. There was, as always, a feeling that something new and exciting was about to begin. I hoped that was right, most especially for Greece.

The week after Easter, we explored more of Koroni, as we reckoned that while we were here we would make the most of our time. Koroni was originally called ancient Asine (Ασίνη), a colony of the town of the same name in Tolon in the northern Peloponnese. Many of its citizens fled from here after they refused to fight against the Spartans. They built an acropolis (meaning citadel) on the high cliff where the castle now stands. The original town called Korone had been established in 369BC by Epimelides from Thebes, but further up the peninsula in present-day Petalidi. Proving that nothing was simple in Greek history, when the citizens of Korone were also forced out by bands of marauders, they moved south to Asine and took the Korone moniker with them.

This peninsula suffered innumerable invasions over the centuries: the Franks in 1204, then in 1207 the Venetians, who extensively rebuilt Koroni Castle and turned the town into their power base alongside Methoni, on the other side of the Messinian peninsula. Methoni also had a sprawling castle on a rugged promontory, and together they became known as the "Eyes of the Venetian Republic".

In 1500, Koroni was captured by the Ottoman Turks, who banished many of the locals to the Ionian islands. In 1532, a fighting force led by famous admiral Andrea Doria, from Genoa in Italy, briefly captured the town, but was later ousted by infamous Turkish pirate raider Barbarossa. In 1685, Koroni was seized by Francesco Morosini for Venice again, with a massacre of Turkish defenders. But the Turks fought back and retook the town in 1718 and remained until the French liberated it after the Greek War of Independence in 1821-27. When the Venetians controlled Koroni it became an important trading port for wine, fruit and olive oil and was settled by wealthy traders and businessmen.

The outcome of these historic invasions was that Koroni was continually bombarded by cannon fire from the sea and the castle took the brunt of it, which is why there is only a skeletal shape of walls left. In the narrow zig-zag of Koroni streets, originally laid out in medieval times and rebuilt and embellished mostly by the Venetians, you can still sense the town's chequered history. Every invader has left layers of culture like a deep geological core sample.

Inside the castle grounds is the lovely monastery of Timios Prodromou, which has three churches and several small chapels. The Byzantine church of Ayia Sophia is built over an ancient Temple of Apollo, and a nearby castle wall incorporates fascinating pieces of marble carving, taken from the temple and from the ancient site of Asine.

We explored the backstreets of Koroni, finding churches, a well with an ancient spring, old *kafeneia*, *ouzeries* and *artopoieia*, traditional bakeries that have been owned by a few families for generations, as have most of the other old houses and businesses in this town. It is a place where everyone is connected either by the plight of history or by the businesses they engage in. The more we discovered about Koroni, the more we began to like its vibe. The most surprising thing of all was that we had come across very few British expats, as it was the Germans who had mostly colonised this peninsula from the 1960s, buying houses, opening tourist businesses in the town. But whether their entrenched lives were suddenly less easy because of the crisis and the increasing anti-German feeling was difficult to ascertain.

By early May, it was warm enough to sit on our villa balcony for a couple of hours in the morning, unless there was a strong sea breeze from the Ionian. It was a glorious eyrie for watching the ever-changing colours of the gulf, the swathes of wildflowers in the orchards below, the sight of farmers grazing newborn sheep and lambs, and the arrival of the swallows.

Occasionally we saw Jed lurking in the garden, binoculars fixed on some fluttering creature. There was so much to choose from now in the ornithological spectrum and nests were springing up each morning around the eaves of the villas. For the most part, we just ignored Jed's antics. He was harmless enough. One morning, however, I had my laptop on the glass-topped table outside, that had quickly become my 'study'. I was writing emails when Wallace came roaring outside, head thrown back, engaging in a round of his 'screamy' barking. There was a skittering behind me in the garden. I turned to see Jed in shorts and T-shirt, his binoculars focused on the lemon tree that hung over the balcony, just where I was sitting. I felt annoyed at the intrusion.

"Jed, what are you doing? There are no birds in this tree, or cats for that matter," I said with impatience.

"Ah, yes, but there's a big fat scorpion. I'm looking right at it."

"Jesus!" I leapt up from the table, knocking it and a coffee cup, sending a small wave of liquid over the glass top, but just missing the keyboard.

"Where?" I said, standing well back from the tree, not knowing whether to curse Jed, or be grateful.

"There."

Jed was beside the tree, pointing to a branch that hung lower over the balcony railing.

"It's a *big* 'un, too."

Well, yes, it wasn't hard to miss, a big black thing with big pincers and the tail lolling behind. It seemed to be asleep. It was our first scorpion sighting in Koroni – and unfortunately it wouldn't be our last.

I called Jim outside and he came armed with a sweepy brush. We had encountered a few scorpions in our years in the Mani and we never got used to the sight of them. With the crab-like pincers and eight legs it was easy to see how they were related to other arachnids like spiders, but after that they were crossed with the devil and given a pitchfork tail. It was no surprise to learn that ancient Spartan foot soldiers had a giant scorpion painted on their shields to scare the enemy.

"I'd leave the scorpion if I were you," said Jed, letting his binoculars flop over his belly. After many trips to Greece in pursuit of birds, Jed was nevertheless something of a scorpion expert.

"There will be plenty more of them under the house; a colony, now that it's spring and they're out of hibernation. You can't do much about it."

Underneath the slightly elevated villas there were bits of abandoned rocks and masonry from the build. It's a peculiarity of Greeks that they leave this stuff lying around houses, long after they've been finished. And I was reminded of the ancient proverb: "Look for a scorpion under every rock."

"Did you know that the female scorpion carries her young scorplings on her back? Some species have up to 100 scorplings."

"Scorplings? Did you make that up?"

"No Jim. That's what the babies are called," explained Jed, with a haughty jolt of his chin.

"Oh, too much information, guys!" I squealed.

Jim finally gave the scorpion a whack, pinging it off the branch. It landed on the ground not far from Jed's sandaled feet, and he hopped about like a man on razor wire. I smiled to myself. Served him right. He poked the thing with a bit of stick and stared at it.

"It wouldn't have done you any harm, really. They're shy creatures. They're more harmful to each other actually," he said, sounding like a PR officer from the Scorpion Protection League. "They have been known to sting their own offspring. And they can be cannibals, too."

"Excellent idea, Jed. It will keep numbers down," I said.

"Look, mate, we'll perform a requiem mass for your scorpion later, okay?" said Jim, sweeping some debris off the balcony in Jed's direction, to give him a hint perhaps that we were growing tired of the critter tattle, and expats stalking around the villas.

I couldn't help but wonder how many lesser spotted Hoarywarblers on the wing he'd missed while he was dithering around with arachnids, or how many cats had sloped past, begging for lunch.

Jed hadn't quite finished with the subject, however. "Well, I just think it's very odd to see one in a tree, and they usually don't like citrus trees at any rate. I knew an expat in Greece who used to put lemon leaves around the house to stop the scorpions coming indoors."

With that, he ambled away, as Delia called him for lunch at their balcony table. I sighed with relief. I probably wouldn't even have noticed the bloody scorpion if he hadn't drawn my attention to it, I thought, as I mopped up the spilt coffee around my laptop. And I didn't need to be reminded there might be colonies of them nearby. I sat down at my laptop again, while Jim fired up his own machine.

"I've heard that black scorpions are rarer on this peninsula. So it's not a good sign, is it? A black scorpion on a lemon tree. The gods are not smiling on us," I said.

Jim looked at me over his laptop screen. His lovely green eyes, that I always thought resembled Greek olives, had become thoughtful. "Not so fast, Margarita. I say, bring on the scorpions, whatever the colour. It's part of the adventure, right? When things go askew it will just remind us that we're here in Greece, not sitting at home or having a spa weekend at the Dorchester."

"Yes, please! I'd like the Dorchester."

"You don't really mean that, do you?" he said, wagging a finger at me.

"No, you're right, Jimbo. Let's…em…embrace these pesky arachnids."

I would think about this conversation quite a few times during our odyssey when more scorpions started to arrive – and problems of a different nature scuttled in as well.

3

Only Koroni

ONE morning we received an email from a Greek friend who had kindly been sourcing rental property for weeks among her friends in Kalamata.

"I think I've found you something. I'm sure you'll like it," she wrote, including a link to a website with pictures of the property.

We had managed to see a few other houses since Easter, handled by local agencies, but they were all in the Messinian peninsula and mostly quite run-down and unsuitable for a couple with a dog. This particular house was in Verga, south-east of Kalamata, on the western slopes of Mount Kalathio in the Taygetos.

Verga was a sought-after area because of its views of the gulf and Kalamata. It also had a higher outpost, called Ano Verga, near the top of Mount Kalathio that only a sadist would want to live in because of the vertiginous, zigzag road ascending to it. The lower Verga had once been a simple hillside village, but was now slightly over-developed, with huge and expensive summer houses for wealthy Athenians and Greek celebrities, as well as nightclubs. It had a lot of cachet for Kalamatans but not much pull for us in our constant search for authenticity in southern Greece, especially as there was very little of the original village left and few 'locals'.

However, at that point it was the only house on offer and the internet pictures at least showed amazing views and a quirky, rustic house clinging to a mountain ridge. Of course, we had to see it. The owner was a businessman from Kalamata, whose wealthy, professional family had used the house for several decades as a weekend retreat. He gave us instructions on how to find it and we were to meet him there.

The road up was full of switch-back bends and the first real drawback soon became apparent. There was no parking at the house. It meant leaving the car on the main road, if you could find a park in summer. We left the car in a parking bay as the owner had instructed, and started the trek along a footpath, past holiday houses, hunched up beside old wrecks, and I broke out in a sweat wondering how we would lug shopping along here in high summer.

The house was a boxy, three-storey plaster and wood construction built into a rock face at the back with balconies at the front. The garden was small and terraced, but the view was by far its best attribute, looking straight down the mountainside on to the whole city of Kalamata spread out below, and its long city beach in front. It was like looking out of an aeroplane window.

"How amazing is this?" said Jim.

We stood at the side of the house, unable to take our eyes off the view, when Vassilis the owner turned up. He seemed in a hurry, slightly flustered. Instead of opening the front door he did something odd, he knocked first. The thick wooden door creaked open, and a woman who sounded Eastern European answered it, with a vacuum cleaner hose in one hand. Ah, the hired help!

"Is it okay to come in?" Vassilis asked the woman.

That set off a few alarm bells. I looked at Jim and he arched his eyebrows. Inside it looked as if she'd been engaged in a frenzy of cleaning, which seemed a bit extreme unless there were things hoovered up they preferred that we didn't see. My brain was working overtime: scorpions came to mind, or snake skins, spiders, dead rats?

You get a feel for a house the minute you walk in: an odour, a sensation, a chill in the air. It was the latter here, a chill, despite it being a hot day. It felt cold and musty, partly because it was built into the rock face on one side and some of the rock was left exposed here and there, which gave the house a subterranean feel. It also felt tired, with old windows sagging on hinges and gaps that would be an easy entry for critters. Vassilis was a pleasant enough guy, however, and there was no pressure. He let us wander round the house while he made calls on his mobile.

We stood on one of the front balconies, looking down on Kalamata like two minor Olympian gods.

"Summer would be lovely here," I said to Jim, "if you could forget about the long trek from the car. But what about winter?"

One of our criteria for a house was that it should be a good winter house, in case we wanted to stay longer. Jim craned his neck towards Mount Kalathio behind us.

"It'll be freezing up here in winter with the winds from the snow-capped Taygetos roaring down the mountainside."

The main source of heat would come from a pleasing old fireplace in the sitting room and a few reverse-cycle air-conditioners, but it didn't feel like it would be enough with the layout and the rock walls. It might feel as if we were living in a cave house, like Fred and Wilma from *The Flintstones*. Just as we were mulling things over, a great chute of water came hurtling down from the upper balcony as the cleaning woman emptied a bucket of dirty liquid on to the terrace below.

"Bloody charming!" said Jim.

"Why all this manic cleaning?"

"I have no idea, Margarita, and I don't want to know," said Jim with sudden decisiveness. "Let's go – this isn't for us, is it?"

I looked down at the view, the only thing about the house I coveted, but there's more to life than a view.

"I agree, Jimbo. It's not for us," I said, wondering what was.

We went home that night feeling despondent. It was the last house and no other options had arisen. Jed and Delia had been following our rental search with interest. They constantly asked us how we were getting on, offering us advice, sometimes for a bit of a wind-up.

"Why don't you ask Yiannis if you can have one of the old houses down there? God knows there's plenty of them," Jed said, jerking his thumb to a row of empty village houses on the lower level of the villa complex that looked like they were ready to become renovation projects, or in the midst of it. One had the shell of a swimming pool at the back and a foot of winter rain.

"We're not planning to stay in Koroni," Jim told Jed. "We're not planning to rent one of those either."

"I've had a look down there and there's one new build among the old stuff that seems pretty ready. Could be a possibility," said Jed with a shrug.

"You seem to know a lot about what goes on here," said Jim, though that wasn't hard, as the couple were always sloping about the hillside, twitching.

"Well, it's like this, Jim. We've been thinking of doing the same as you two, to be honest. I've been checking out the Koroni area. Maybe next year, we'll come for six months."

My heart sank slightly.

Jim suddenly pointed to the sky. "Oh look, Jed, you've just missed a brown eagle up there. It's just gone behind a cloud."

Jed wheeled around. "Are you sure? Damn! Where's my binoculars."

He dashed off towards his villa without a parting word. Jim winked at me.

"Did you really see an eagle?"

"Course not. Don't be daft."

Only Koroni

That night, over our favourite plate of seafood and a carafe of wine at the Parthenon, we talked over the rental situation as waves slapped gently at the sea wall on the other side of the roll-down plastic. We were the only people eating outside. Coming from Scotland, the weather in the Greek spring always struck us as tropical. We had had one of our first swims that morning on the little beach at Zaga that sits under the Eleistria church, where we had been at Easter. The water was bracing, the waves a bit gutsy at times but there was always something about the Greek sea, and the first swim of the season that anchored our affection for this country and cleansed us of all our frustrations and doubts. That was just the way it was. It also firmed our resolve to find suitable accommodation so we could stay a while.

The Mani still had a strong pull on our imagination after the years we'd spent there. I had already called some of our Greek friends in the village of Megali Mantineia to see how they were and to tell them we were back, though we hadn't had time yet for a visit. I hadn't managed to raise our old farming friend Foteini, however, because she rarely answered her phone, due to slight deafness. Yet the hope of living again in the Mani was fading with every passing day, unless we were prepared to take on some dingy heap or, conversely, over-stretch ourselves with a large holiday villa, of which there were a few empty ones, often owned by expats.

"Maybe we'll have to stay in *this* area. How do you feel about that?" asked Jim.

I sighed. "It's not ideal, is it, despite its fabulous setting. We seem too far from everyone we know and the drive to Kalamata's a bit tormenting."

Jim rubbed his hand over his chin. "The longer we leave it, the worse it will get as the summer season wears on. Villas are becoming more and more expensive."

I thought again about our chat with that shrewd old birdy, Jed.

"Let's talk to Yiannis soon about his other two villas below, or the row of old houses, and see if any of them would be suitable for us."

Jim agreed that the sooner we sorted something out, the better, as we couldn't organise our work lives without a proper house. I had done very little writing on the second book since we'd been in Greece. There were few tables in the villa suitable for a laptop and when the mood took me I would simply sit on the sofa with the computer resting on my knee, or outside on the balcony.

A couple of days later, Yiannis knocked on our door bearing gifts: towels and a bag of spring onions. These kind of Greek gifts always made me laugh because of their crazy pairings. It was something we had experienced before with our Greek landlords in the Mani, who would bring us peculiarly paired items, like broccoli and mouthwash, or sweet peppers and oven cleaner.

We had grown to like Yiannis. He was a genial guy, who seemed quite sensitive and thoughtful, perhaps owing to a health problem that meant he had to make regular long trips to Athens for private treatment. Nothing much bothered him, except he didn't know what to make of Wallace. When he knocked on the door, Wallace would scoot out to meet him, barking and tapping his paws on his knees. It was a refinement of his previous puppy behaviour in Scotland, rushing at visitors and kneecapping them before they could get inside the house. Yiannis would always brush his trousers afterwards, as if Wallace had contaminated them with his dusty paws.

"Why does he bark every time he sees me? Doesn't he know me by now?" Yiannis asked, with doleful eyes.

"It's his way of saying 'hello'," I told him.

Yiannis would shake his head in confusion and it occurred to me that although he tolerated dogs on site, it didn't mean he wanted them around all the time, and that might put the kybosh on our bid for a long-term rental. But that wasn't our only problem. The day he brought us the towels, he looked slightly ill at ease and before we had a chance to raise the question of rentals, he handed Jim a white envelope.

When we first arrived we had asked if we could use the villa address for any mail that might be sent on from the UK by Jim's father. Instead, Yiannis gave us his family's post office box number in Koroni. Most of the established families in the town had their own blue box at the post office. Most of the *xenoi*, foreigners, had their mail heaped up on one end of the counter, where everyone could riffle through it and where the majority of mail was unpaid utility bills.

"I apologise, Jim, that your letter is open. My father has picked up the letters today and opened your one here by mistake," he said with a grimace.

Jim looked at the re-directed letter and noticed it had 'Sussex Police' stamped on the envelope.

"Bugger! What's this now?"

Yiannis was eyeing us curiously as Jim took the letter out, read it quickly and explained.

"It's a speeding ticket. Can you believe that? I must have been caught on camera a couple of days before we left England. I was clocked doing 37 miles an hour in a 30 zone. They're telling me I could have a fixed penalty or I might have to go to court over it. Ridiculous!"

"Is there a problem?" asked Yiannis, who hadn't understood all our conversation.

Jim explained it again more slowly and I had a go in Greek for good measure. I imagined that when the letter arrived and Yiannis's father opened it, and showed it to him, with the police stamp on the back, there must have been a frisson of alarm. Who could blame them? Here were two people turning up for an indefinite stay, their car packed to the rafters with possessions, their crazy dog in tow, and now a letter from the police. Were they wondering if we'd committed a serious crime and fled the country? We tried to laugh it off.

"You can't imagine what the UK is like," I told him in Greek. "Too many rules. Very strict. *Grafeiokratia* (bureaucracy). *Trela*. Madness!"

He laughed at that. It appealed to his Greek sense of maverick rule-breaking. But still he seemed wary.

"Your father probably thought we were a couple of *figades* (fugitives), didn't he? Bonnie and Clyde," I told him.

I wondered if he'd seen that film. He must have, because he laughed heartily at the joke.

"No, no *figades*. No Bonnie and Clyde," he said, but the look in his eyes told me something different.

We didn't think it was the right time to discuss long-term rentals and after Yiannis had gone, Jim sent the Sussex Police an email telling them he was in Greece and he would pay the fixed penalty.

A few days later Yiannis returned with a bottle opener and a bag of lettuce from his nearby *kipos*, garden, where he spent a lot of his time, and we were relieved that he seemed more relaxed. I made some coffee and we invited him inside for a chat. He was the one who now raised the issue of how long we planned to stay. We told him we'd had no success with a long-term rental.

"We thought you might like to rent out one of your villas to us for the summer, maybe longer," Jim explained.

Yiannis threw out his hands and shrugged majestically. He told us it was impossible, as all the villas were booked out, more or less, from the beginning of June through the summer. And one of the villas on the lower level, that looked slightly disused to our mind, turned out to be rented all year round by an Austrian woman. Lucky her!

"I will speak to my sister Stavroula. She will be coming from Kalamata soon. She knows a lot of people with property."

Okay, that was hopeful at least because our plans for this second odyssey, even in Koroni, were looking dodgier by the day. To quote a colourful Aussie journo friend called Kevin, whom I once went on a challenging media travel trip with: "Geez! We're up the Barcoo in a barbed-wire canoe." Kevin was referring to a remote outback river in Queensland, once the unsavoury haunt of tropical diseases. It's an expression that I've found will happily cover all vicissitudes in life.

4

Gone with the anemos

"YOU'VE forgotten me already, Margarita, *koritsara mou*," Foteini shouted down the phone, calling me 'my girl', one of her usual terms of endearment. Then a loud barrage of village Greek followed which, as usual, I found hard to fathom, especially on the phone.

After many calls to her village home, I had finally managed to speak to Foteini. Back in Scotland, I had often called her on her village number. It was always a strange experience, not just to hear her barking comically down the phone, or the sound of goat bells in the background, or village motorbikes backfiring. It seemed strange to be ringing this woman at all. From the day we first met her, riding her donkey on the village road, I marvelled at the fact we had become friends at all because, on the face of it, we had absolutely nothing in common.

The ensuing friendship had been one of the strangest and most challenging of my life, and it was probably true to say she was one of the main factors in me writing the first book. The times I had spent with her, the stories she told me, were simply unique, and had inspired me. It had been Foteini who christened me Margarita on the first day, and it quickly became my Greek name, one that I felt comfortable with, that linked me to the place forever more.

She was pleased to hear we were back on Greek soil but mortified that we didn't have a house to rent yet.

"And you're where?" she screamed down the phone.
"Koroni?"
"KORONI! What are you doing in Koroni, Margarita?" she said. To Foteini, Koroni was not just on another penin-

sula, but was another country entirely. She had only been there once. She had rarely been out of the Mani and had never left southern Greece.

"When are you coming to see me?" she asked.

"I don't know, Foteini. As soon as we have sorted a house. As soon as we can. Maybe not until June."

"JUNE!" She cursed like a navvy under her breath. It made me smile. I promised to call her again soon with an update.

"If I hear of anything in the village to rent, I'll let you know, Margarita."

I had given her my Greek mobile number but I didn't expect her to call me very often, as it would be more expensive, and to a poor farmer like Foteini, every *lepta*, cent, was precious, or as my funny Scottish grandmother Euphamia would say: "Every penny's a prisoner." Foteini certainly didn't have a mobile herself. Once she had tried to use mine to ring a farming friend, and I smiled at her attempt to punch tiny keypads with her breeze-block fingers.

We hadn't even considered trying to find another house in or near Megali Mantineia again. After living there for a year in 2010, we had searched high and low for another, slightly more comfortable, property – and had found nothing.

In 2011 we had moved to the village of Paleohora, a short drive away by the sea, where we lived for the next two years. We had also thought of trying to find a property in that village and had been in touch with our previous landlords there, Andreas and Marina, who were now spending a lot of time at the Paleohora house, rather than the Kalamata apartment they shared with their two old mothers. We suspected that the mothers were driving them mad and this was a retreat from them.

I had called Andreas once to see how the couple were getting on and to sound them out about the possibility of renting their house again. He seemed vague about it, for reasons I couldn't fathom.

"We wait till we see you and then we talk," said Andreas. "Many things have changed here, Margarita, because of the crisis."

@@@@@

When we left the Mani in the winter of 2012, the crisis had just gone through its most intense period, with violent demonstrations and strikes over austerity measures, particularly the new taxes and cuts to jobs and pensions. But other issues had been severe, like the lack of medical help for poorer families and a dearth of essential drugs. In October 2012, the government, led by New Democracy's Antonis Samaras, in coalition with the socialist party Pasok, and other smaller parties, passed a 13.5 billion euro austerity plan in order to receive the next package of bailout loans from the EU and global lenders. In 2013, to save more money, the government carried out one of its most audacious cuts in closing down the popular government broadcasting organisation ERT, which had a raft of provincial TV and radio stations throughout the mainland and on the islands.

Although Samaras in late 2013 had predicted a return to growth in the coming years, this proved to be wildly overoptimism, with unemployment at 28 per cent, and 60pc for young people. There were already signs of greater changes in the wings when the radical left coalition party Syriza, led by Alexis Tsipras, was placed first in the election to the European Parliament in May 2014, with 26.6 of the vote, showing a strong groundswell of support for anti-austerity parties in Greece after six years of recession and swingeing cuts by the Troika (the European Commission, European Central Bank and International Monetary Fund).

Greeks had become increasingly dispirited, knowing that despite the 240 billion euros of bailout funds the country had received through negotiations with the Troika, the economy was in no better shape than in 2010, and economic growth had nose-dived. It had been calculated that only 10 per cent of the money from the bailout funds had gone directly to the Greek people. And the total Greek debt had surged to 323 billion euros, with money owed to the IMF, ECB, Greek banks, foreign banks and Eurozone nations, of which the biggest creditor was Germany.

The outcome of all this was a mindless situation where money was flowing in from lenders and going back out to more or less the same organisations in interest repayments, while Greece dug itself into a bigger debt hole. One Greek friend had explained it to me using the popular expression: *"Yiannis kernaei, kai Yiannis pinei."* John treats you to drinks and then helps himself to all of them.

While the southern Peloponnese, strongly based in agriculture, oil and olives, was less affected than other parts of Greece, what we noticed when we returned to the region in 2014 was that businesses had suffered and many had closed. Many people were now out of work and had lost hope for their future. Children were forced to depend on their parents for financial help, and many were leaving to study and work abroad, including the children of many of the friends we had made while in Greece.

※※※※※

By mid-May, the weather suddenly improved – it was warm enough to swim whenever we wanted. And most mornings we sat on our villa balcony in T-shirts and shorts, soaking up the warmth and aromas of late spring, admiring the view across to the Taygetos mountains opposite, surprisingly still snow-capped on their highest peaks. The slight remoteness of this peninsula began to please us more and more. Some might have called it a pleasant backwater but it had the laid-back, unstructured feel of old Greece, in which I had rambled in my youth.

I had settled into a routine of sorts, even without a study, and spent the mornings outside, working at the computer, trying to get ahead with the second book, of which I had written about a third, and also writing articles about *Things Can Only Get Feta* and our Greek adventures for several publications and website blogs. The book had sold very well and had sparked a huge amount of interest in Greece, due to an interview I had given to the editor of the bilingual Greek newspaper *Neos Kosmos* in Australia the previous August, after the book came out.

The interview for the English edition had a straightforward angle on why we embarked on our mid-life odyssey and had chosen to live a Greek kind of life in a remote hillside village. But when the interview was reworked by the editor, for the Greek edition of the paper, it had an altogether different slant. Sotiris Hatzimanolis had seen something in the story that for me was still slightly under the skin but the headline said it all: "An Australian journalist is besotted with Greece". It revealed that I had been in love with the country since I first set foot there in the 1970s and that my love affair with the place had continued, even during the economic crisis.

The Greek feature had been picked up by a major press agency in Athens and subsequently by most other media outlets in Greece. Sotiris had obviously plugged into the Greek psyche at that moment in a way I hadn't and the timing was perfect. The story he wrote struck a chord with Greeks suffering through the crisis. There had been so little written during the crisis in the international media that wasn't blaming and insulting, with an emphasis on corruption and work-avoidance in Greece.

With Sotiris's story, most media outlets promoted it as a "good news" piece and a stream of interview offers arrived in my email inbox from newspapers and TV stations, all wanting me to talk about my passion for their beleaguered country and why the world's media had somehow got things wrong. Many ordinary Greeks also linked to our website, with thousands of hits in just one day, and many visitors left thank-you messages for being positive about Greece. One of my favourites simply said: "For your information, Greece loves you back." I also had several dinner invitations from different locations around Greece. It was the closest I would probably ever get to a media frenzy.

Not all the interview requests reached fruition but it was a heart-warming experience and I liked the fact that, if nothing else, my small Greek memoir had made a lot of Greeks feel good about themselves. And it had a further consequence in making me think more deeply about my own feelings for Greece in a way I hadn't perhaps before, which consequently set the tone for the second book. Greece and I did have a history together and yet I had skirted around the issue of my affection for it most of my life, keeping it to myself. I had generally found that other people feel uncomfortable when you confess your love for a country, especially one that isn't your own.

By May 2014, I was still happily promoting the book while getting ready to offer the first 10 chapters of the second book to my London publisher for consideration. We had vaguely discussed the sequel before I left Scotland and while he was happy to look at a submission there was a certain reticence about the project that, given the success of the first book, I found mystifying.

I would have to wait a few months to discover what lay behind it. Sadly, cracks had begun to appear in my relationship with the publisher, Sir Ambrose, a rather austere British 'aristocrat', a baronet, who was often tardy in returning emails and calls, and had also forgotten to pay my first round of royalties, which had created an understandable coldness in the relationship and which took a lot of reminding on my part for him to put right. An experienced author friend and mentor in Scotland, when I confided my publishing experience in him, urged me to join a certain professional authors' society in London, which I did. It was the best piece of advice I was ever given in my fledgling book-writing career.

With so much work to do, we quickly discovered that the wi-fi was an issue in this part of Greece. The villas had a row of masts up on the hillside, with the broadband signal relayed via a router in Yiannis's father's house in Koroni. It was a crazy system that could only exist in Greece, not because their telecommunications company was set in the Dark Ages, it wasn't. The problems stemmed from the geography and the remoteness of outlying areas, with no telephone landlines. In many other ways, it was easier to set up broadband or iron out problems because, unlike in the UK, there were offices in Kalamata with real people you could talk to about your phone and broadband issues. Whether they would be happy chaps was another matter.

When we first lived in the Mani, we had been told by our English landlord at the old stone house in Megali Mantineia that while there was a phone line, if we wanted broadband we would have to visit the government-run OTE company in Kalamata to set it up, and it would take around a week.

At OTE, we elbowed our way around a throng of people in a troublesome Greek queue until a small irascible-looking man in a glassed-in office beckoned us. He spoke good English and we told him what we wanted. He started to fill out the relevant stack of paperwork, which he didn't seem to relish. At that time, the public sector in Greece was overstaffed and had been earmarked for staff pruning and wage cuts under the terms of the Troika bailout.

Of course this worker wasn't happy with the state of play – but we didn't expect mental health issues. Mid form-filling, he put his pen down and rubbed his tired dark eyes.

"I've just come back from a wonderful holiday on the islands. Now I have to put up with this job for months and months, maybe years and years. *Panayia mou!* Holy Virgin! I feel so depressed." He put his head in his hands. Jim and I locked eyes and grimaced.

The man finally raised his head. He looked pitiful. "I feel like I'm going to go mad!"

I felt my palms becoming sweaty. The broadband had almost been ours. But this was no time to give up.

"We understand your predicament, but please don't go mad today," I said, with a pleading look, nodding towards the paperwork still to be completed.

I anticipated a mental strop, but he just threw his head back and laughed – maniacally.

"Okay, my friend. I try not to. But it's hard." And he scribbled away at the remaining forms.

We sighed with relief. This is what you had to go through with government officials in crisis-ridden Greece. But despite the despondency, the broadband was connected in a week. And that's the miracle of Greece. Things always get done in the end, one breakdown at a time.

The wi-fi situation at the villas was a harder issue to solve because of the relay distances and the fact that when it wasn't working, we had to ask Yiannis to get his father to reset the router at his house. It would have been easier to put in a phone line for the villas, or so we thought.

"Ten thousand euro to bring a line up the hillside," Yiannis had told us. "Who has a spare 10,000?"

We were given strict instructions from Yiannis to call him on his mobile if there was a lapse in transmission and he would call his parents for the router wiggling. So that's what we did. We called him so often that all we had to say was 'wi-fi'. In fact, sometimes we didn't have to say anything. We rarely called him for anything else.

One morning, while we were working at our laptops on the balcony table, Yiannis arrived with another letter from Sussex Police. This time, the envelope was still sealed and he stood beside us while Jim ripped it open.

"Why can't they just email me back," said Jim, reading through the letter and running his hand nervously through his hair.

"They want me to prove that I'm living in Greece," he said.

Yiannis made a big windmill gesture with his arm.

"That is easy. You write and you tell police you have no money, that you spend your time going to government offices, the wi-fi is not working right and you are feeling very much the *anisihia* (anxiety). And then they know you live here."

We all laughed over that.

"If only it were that easy, Yianni, but they want me to send them a Greek electricity bill, or another bill with my name on it which, of course, I don't have yet. They want proof that this isn't some trick to get out of paying a fine, or having a court appearance, if it should come to that," said Jim.

We tried to explain about UK bureaucracy and how we were merely hapless victims of the system. I think he was beginning to wonder at the insistence of Sussex Police.

"Bonnie and Clyde for sure!" he said, his big soulful eyes creasing at the edges with amusement. "Don't worry. We have *grafeiokratia* (bureaucracy) too in Greece. I think we invent it. Yes? And silly *kanones* (rules). We have to wear the *kranos* (helmet) on motorbikes and if we do not, we get a fine, 400 euros. That's what a life is worth here? But we just ignore. We don't trust rules. We take the *kranos* and fix to the handle of the bike and if police come by we put it on," he said, laughing heartily.

We later discovered that maverick Yiannis had crashed his own motorbike once, an ancient 1950s BMW model that stood off-road gathering dust at the villas, with no desire on his part to go through the endless formality to get it on the road again. It was typical of the Greek mentality to want to dodge a rule wherever possible. To a Brit, it was one of their endearing features, even if it sometimes made life difficult.

One day in May we had gone on a short excursion to the village of Logga, outside Koroni, because we had heard there was an ancient temple of Apollo nearby. That's an invitation in Greece to lose yourself on a hillside, where temples will be hidden in long grass, and the road signs will be facing the wrong way, which is what happened here. Later we ended up in the village itself, where the main road had been pedestrianised and yet cars were parked along it. We parked there as well but when we locked the car and started to walk away, I felt guilty and asked an old guy sitting on a stool outside his shop if it was okay to leave the car where it was. He gave me a sad, sorry look and said: "*Stin Ellada tora, o kosmos kanei o,ti thelei.*" "In Greece today everyone does what they want." Then he shrugged vibrantly.

The letter from Sussex Police this time seemed to be less of a worry for Yiannis than before. Whether or not he thought we were bank robbers on the run, clearly we appeared pretty harmless. Yet for us, the police letters were the start of long, drawn-out line of communication as Jim attempted to prove our existence in Greece. With a possible court appearance hanging over his head, Jim was relieved that finally, in the summer, the police dropped the whole issue because it had all become too hard. A touch of Greek *logiki* (logic) perhaps, and in the end our protracted woes with the cops endeared us to Yiannis, as it roused his rebellious streak.

Yiannis had agreed we could stay in the villa until the end of May, which was just a few weeks away. He was now definitely hooked into our anxiety about hunting down a long-term rental.

"Don't worry. I will call my sister Stavroula tonight and explain. She will be here tomorrow at the villas and you will tell her what you need, if you want to stay in Koroni."

We nodded, creeping closer to the realisation that we might have to stay here for the longer term.

"There is one house. I think it is good for you," he said, kissing the tips of his fingers in the way Greeks do to convey perfection. We felt excited now. The Greek cavalry had arrived. We were not facing homelessness and an ignominious return to Scotland.

We assumed he was alluding to a place on the lower level with its row of old houses. These belonged to Yiannis and Stavroula's family, but would once have been inhabited by the extended family as well: grandparents, uncles and cousins, going back a few generations. This area was like a small village, with orchards for olive farming and enclosures for keeping goats and hens. The family still worked their olive groves and their father Anastasios had helped his children by giving them a swathe of land to build their rental villas. Stavroula was more interested in the older houses, however, having something of a flair for renovation and interior design, and she had worked in real estate in Kalamata.

We discussed the matter after Yiannis left and decided the house he had in mind was the new one that Jed had sussed out already. Perhaps he had earmarked it for his own Greek sojourn the following year. In the past week we had seen workers there every day in a buzz of activity — painting and hammering and churning up rivers of cement for the wide driveway at the front. Every day it looked more liveable.

"Let's go and check it out now. The workmen have gone home," said Jim, rubbing his hands together with anticipation.

The house was white, with that look that new dwellings have in Greece, freshly plastered and almost powdery like a lightly sugar-dusted cake. It had a stylish roof with brown pantiles and a broad L-shaped balcony running down the side and along the front, which was its best feature, with fantastic views over the orchards and the Messinian gulf beyond. It had earned its name, Villa Anemos (Windy Villa), due to its position on the edge of the hillside, where it caught all the winds converging from the Ionian Sea and the gulf.

"Surely there would be bookings for the summer though? That would be more lucrative than a long-term rental," I said to Jim, starting to feel doubtful.

"Well, I can't see what else Yiannis was alluding to when he kissed his fingertips. The rest of the houses here are pretty minging. Unless we've missed something," said Jim, pulling a face.

The old house right behind Villa Anemos was a case in point. It was a traditional Koroni rural house, solid and squat, with white walls that were scuffed, and old blue shutters, some of them broken and hanging askew. The house had the local design quirk of blue metal poles along the balconies instead of columns. It would have been nice once, surrounded by trees: sweet orange, grapefruit, figs.

The biggest window at the front of the house had its shutters pinned back and you could clearly see inside, into the main room, with a kitchen and bathroom at one end and a load of rubbish and junk in the middle. It looked like it hadn't been lived in for years. I couldn't figure out why it had been left like this, with a chic new villa in front. It was an embarrassment, like a drunk and dishevelled relative slumped in the corner of the marquee at a posh wedding.

But none of that concerned us as we marched about the balconies of Villa Anemos, admiring the view at the front. Through a side window we could see the open-plan sitting room with a kitchen across the far wall. It had gleaming new blue and white tiles and smart appliances.

"Are you sure this is the one?" I asked Jim, racked with doubts again.

"It has to be this one. Nothing else is fit to live in."

"Yes, of course," I said. That had clinched it. There was nowhere else we could go.

As we walked back along the narrow road that wound up to the top villas, we checked out the other old houses on the way. One had a rusting fridge on the balcony and a mess of ripped-out wood and an ancient air-conditioner pinned on the outside wall. Some had rotten shutters and crumbling balconies. These had all been earmarked for future renovation, though a controlled explosion might have been a better way forward.

The next day we were feeling chipper. Yiannis's sister Stavroula knocked on our door and introduced herself and we followed her down to the lower road. She was the opposite of Yiannis in colouring, with fair hair and grey/blue eyes, and with a very considered, yet genial, demeanour. She had very good English.

"Yiannis has told me you are looking for a long-term rental here."

We nodded.

"I have a house in mind. Come with me now and we will see it."

Jim winked at me as she walked ahead, leading us to the top of the driveway at the new house. We were joined by Yiannis, who had earlier been trailing about in his garden.

"The house I have in mind for you is here," she said.

"We know. We've seen it already. It's lovely," I told her.

She gave me a quizzical look. "Which house do you mean?"

"Villa Anemos."

Her eyes flickered towards Yiannis for a moment and back again.

"No, it's not that one. That one has bookings already for June. Come, I will show you the house."

Jim and I exchanged worried looks, but Yiannis was smiling and kissing his fingertips again, which only increased the mystery. But as we walked down the driveway of Villa Anemos my stomach did a queasy cha-cha. Stavroula stopped and turned to the right, towards a set of uneven stone steps that led straight on to the front balcony of the old white house with the blue shutters.

"THIS one?" I said, my eyes darting towards Jim. His shoulders were hunched. He had a face like a sunken soufflé.

So, we were not destined for the new villa after all. Why was I not surprised? Greeks are the kindest people I've ever met but they are nothing if not shrewd and business-minded. And who could blame them in an economic crisis.

"But this house is a wreck. And we need to move out of our villa by the beginning of June. Isn't that right, Yiannis?"

Yiannis was looking anxious now. "Yes, my friends, you do, but I promised we would help you ... "

Stavroula charged in. "*Paidia*, guys. Don't look at the cottage as it is now. Forget what you see. It is *hamos*. A mess. But we will fix it. You will be.... You will be...."

She rattled around for the word. "You will be *astonished* at what we will do with this house."

'Astonished' would be too weak a word for it, if they could actually turn this mouldering heap into a habitable dwelling. Or were we to be the hapless participants in an extreme home makeover show for Greek TV? What I wanted to do with the old pile at that moment was to blow it up, along with the other wrecks on the road. But we trailed after Stavroula to the wooden front door, which seemed to have been made for another house because none of its sides fitted squarely into the frame, with gaps everywhere. She unlocked the door but it wouldn't budge. Yiannis put his slim shoulders to it, but it still wouldn't give, then Stavroula tried it. Finally, Jim heaved into it, and it gave way with a crunch and the painful grinding of wood over rubble on the hard flooring.

We all stood at the front door, peering into a dusty, reeking space filled with old furniture and bits of rubbish pulled into the centre. It was worse from this angle than it appeared through the window. Yiannis and Stavroula moved further inside, and even they looked a bit dubious. The floor was covered in dirt and dust, with dead beetles and slugs and the debris of indeterminate critters. They explained that the house had been like this for three years since the previous long-term tenants had scarpered, leaving it in a filthy state.

Stavroula quickly sensed our anxiety. "*Paidia*, we will take out all the old things. We will paint it all white inside and clean the floor. It is marble. Very old. It will be lovely. We will put in some new furniture and replace some windows and shutters. You will not recognise it."

Oh yes I would. I would recognise this house in a hurricane on a dark night with a paper bag over my head. Jim and I exchanged weary looks and I kept thinking about Villa Anemos – how sweet and fresh it had looked, how normal. We had lived in a few challenging environments in our years in Greece, but this one was in a league of its own.

"What the hell is that old thing?" I asked, pointing to the corner of the main room, where a rusting drum sat on the floor attached to a metal chimney pipe. The front of the drum was missing.

"It's an old wood-burning stove," said Yiannis with a rueful smile.

Is this how Greeks lived in years gone by? I thought.

"This has been here for years. It's going to go. Do not fear, Margarita," he said.

"It will be a lot of work for you to do in just a few weeks," I said.

"I know, but this is a very sentimental house for us," said Stavroula, who was going to project manage the whole thing. "This house has been in my family for more than 100 years, maybe longer, we don't know. In the old days people didn't register their houses. Many houses are much older than we think. We always called it Yiayia's House, my father's mother lived here and her parents before that. We played here when we were children. *Yiayia* put in many of the trees you see, and the rose bushes. It's very special and it will be good to have a reason to fix it up now. You are inspiring me to carry out this project. And you will have a house for as long as you want."

Yiannis nodded enthusiastically. Stavroula described in more detail what she was planning to do and waited outside while we wandered about the old wreck. The bedroom was an odd shape, with just enough room for a small double bed under the window. The second bedroom was by far the best room in the house, even though it was tiny. At least the window overlooked the olive groves and an almond tree that had flowered a few weeks earlier. The air had been thick with its sweet, exotic smell.

It was hard to imagine what the family could do with this house in just a few weeks, but at that point we didn't have an alternative property to view. This was it. Jim gave me a grave look.

"What do you think?" he asked.

"I don't know. We can either take it, or go on another scouting mission for houses in the Mani. Or go back to Britain."

"After coming all this way?" said Jim.

We stood for a moment gazing out the window towards the nearby olive groves, lost for words. I felt the adventure slipping away from us. This was the second time we had come to Greece trusting in serendipity. The first time we had landed on our feet. Now we were about to have a crash-landing on our bums.

We went outside and told Stavroula we weren't sure about the house. We couldn't quite visualise the make-over. She was a sensitive woman, though, and was quick to allay our fears.

"Okay. We will fix the house anyway, because it's time, and if you don't like it in the end there is no obligation to take it, or if you take it for a month and don't like it, again you don't have to stay. There is no pressure. You can call me tomorrow and let me know what you decide."

We walked back up the hill and discussed the matter over dinner on the balcony.

"Honestly, what a right pair of twats we were, thinking we'd get sparkling new Villa Anemos," I said.

Jim laughed. "It's Jed's fault. He should've just kept his attention focused on lesser-spotted Hoarywarblers."

But we agreed Stavroula's proposal was generous and the monthly rent she quoted was reasonable and it meant we could afford to stay longer than the summer if we wanted.

"I just don't see how Stavroula and the work crew can turn that place into a liveable house in a few weeks, do you?"

Jim sighed. "Well, we know that Greeks can work like navvies when they put their minds to something. They are masters of brinkmanship."

I remembered the 2004 Olympics and how the world's press had gone into a jeering frenzy at the number of venues, including the main stadium, that were still incomplete, with just weeks to go before the opening ceremony. And yet the Greeks had finished every last building on time. I had often seen this with Greeks, how they can be slow to fire up, but once they have, they move faster than Jack Russells with the scent of a rabbit.

"And the most important issue here is that we don't have a choice, Margarita."

"Okay, we'll tell Stavroula we'll take the house, but we should also try for a back-up plan. Let's go to Megali Mantineia soon, call in to see Foteini, of course, but also Andreas and Marina in Paleohora, and see what the story is with their house."

I hung on to this slim possibility.

Gone With The Anemos

The house in Paleohora had been comfortable enough, even though it needed some modernisation inside. There had been a rabble of mad cats, chickens and the big dog Zina, that Wallace had finally become friends with. It was a slightly eccentric set-up. We had to share the grounds with the couple, as they came every other night and at weekends to fix up the old *spitaki*, stone house, in the corner of the property. But it had all worked out well and we had become good friends with the family, and had plenty of escapades there.

"I'll give them a call soon and we'll arrange to see them and suss things out at Paleohora in case Yiayia's House turns out to be a lemon," I said.

Yes, a big fat Greek *lemoni*, with a few scorpions fizzing there for good measure!

5

Foteini – famous at last!

I HAD rung Foteini the night before we planned our trip to Megali Mantineia. There was no answer. I began to doubt that Foteini ever heard the phone in her village house. Neighbours had tried to attach it to various kinds of amplifiers but with no success and it remained a 'techie' thorn in her side. When we lived in the Mani, I rang her often. Very occasionally she picked up the phone. She would always say: "I haven't heard from you, *koritsara mou*. You've forgotten me already."

"But Foteini, I've called you so many times."

"Really? Well, so you say, but how would I know if I can't hear the phone?"

And on the conversation would go, in ever decreasing circles. It was always difficult to argue with her peculiar rural logic. In the end you gave up. We planned to call by her *ktima,* farm, in the late morning before visiting Andreas and Marina. I just hoped she'd be there.

It was a curious thing, driving into Megali Mantineia for the first time in about eighteen months. We took the same route into it that we had taken the first time we went there in 2010. Nothing had changed and it brought back the memory of excitement and trepidation about having an odyssey in Greece at the beginning of the crisis. Nothing much had changed at Foteini's *ktima* either, we noticed, as we drove past and parked in a vacant lot nearby. It was still a mess of wood piles, plastic chairs, stray cats in various stages of craziness. The fact that Riko the donkey was tied up in the *ktima* meant that Foteini was there.

Foteini has the uncanny ability of remembering everyone's car and when we drove our white Fiat past her main gates she must have seen it and came rushing from the far end of the compound, as if afraid we'd drive on by. She met us at the metal gates, dressed in her usual mismatched layers: an old plaid shirt and blue trousers with the bum patched and sewn. She was wearing her outsized straw hat, the same one we'd seen her wearing the first day we'd encountered her, riding Riko towards the village.

She was shouting excitedly: "*Kalos irthate, paidia!*" Welcome, children! She hugged me first and I caught the familiar aroma of goats, herbs and something else I could only describe as 'fresh air', the smell that washing has when it's been hanging out all day.

"*Yeia sou, Margarita, koritsara mou*! Hello, Margarita, my girl!"

After she'd hugged and kissed us, she stood back to look us up and down with a squinty expression, as if she wasn't sure if we were real or not. Then she led us into the *ktima*. Riko was keeping sentinel over his usual industrial-sized feta tin, brimming with water. I gave his ears a rub and he recognised me at once, nuzzling my hand. The sweetest, most stoical beast I had ever come across.

When Foteini wasn't looking, I slipped him a bit of carrot I'd secreted in one of my pockets. If she saw me doing this she'd go mad, as she had a few times before. To her rural mind, donkeys don't eat tasty vegetables, they just eat the cremated pods of the venerable carob trees that overhang the road. These blackened relics, collected every year, are hard and dry and will keep until hell freezes over, or the national debt of Greece becomes a trifling amount.

Riko munched while Foteini raced on ahead, down the dirt-covered stone steps towards her *kaliva*, shed, where she was about to make us coffee, a ritual we had indulged in many, many times. Jim and I stayed for a bit under the shade of the olive trees.

"You know, I'd love to ride Riko one day, around the *ktima*. It would be great fun, wouldn't it? It's one of the things on my Greek wish list."

"I don't think she'll let you. She loves that donkey."

"We'll see," I said, sizing up the donkey's height and the heavy wooden saddle that was on him, ready for Foteini's afternoon ride back to her village house. I had ridden horses for some years in Scotland and thought it would be a snip to ride such a small, compliant beast. But I put it to the back of my mind for now. We heard Foteini calling from her *kaliva* and made our way towards it.

"*Elate, paidia*. Come on and sit here. I won't be long," she said, pointing to the scuffed plastic table and chairs under the fig and mulberry trees.

It was no more than a patch of dried ground with old banana skins and empty yoghurt tubs scattered as usual around the periphery. We had jokingly christened this place the *kafeneio,* though it was like no café on the planet. There were red-legged hornets and bees, droning around the fruit trees and hovering over the refuse. Once, while living in the village, I had boldly asked her why she threw so much rubbish about her *ktima*. She looked at me, her blue eyes wide with indignation.

"*Ti les,* Margarita? What are you saying? Why should I worry what's thrown about here. This is not my home, is it?"

That was her rural logic. This wasn't where she lived, so what did it matter? In many ways, this statement summed up one of the things that was definitely wrong with Greece; the inability of people here to take responsibility for the environment, or anything that occurred beyond the perimeter fence of their own home. It was why there was so much rubbish left at bins: furniture, appliances, dead dogs and cats, old mattresses.

There was no point in arguing over these things with Foteini and I definitely didn't have the urge that day. We sat quietly at the table while she made coffee. The *kaliva* was something I had only been in once on a cold winter's day, when she practically blew it up by manhandling the *petrogazi*, gas stove. I never went in again.

It was the beginning of June now and very hot with the typical indelible blue sky of this month, with just a few puffs of cloud that promised steady heat all the way to September. The air seemed to be sizzling, not unless there was another misadventure inside with faulty gas rings. Cicadas were ramping it up in the undergrowth, making a noise like electric castanets. Swallows swooped overhead. There was such an aching familiarity to the scene here: the hill not far from the main road with its 18th century castle of Trikitsova and its coronet of ruined walls; and on the outer flank of the Taygetos Mountains, a tall cave like a flame-shaped gash in the pale expanse of rock. This was the same cave that Foteini once told us she had spent many summer hours, sheltering the family's flock of goats that she'd walked from the village of Altomira, deep in the mountains. It was pleasant just to sit a while and allow the heat and the familiarity to overtake us.

The peaceful moment was broken, however, by the sound of a heavy drawer being pulled open and raked over; the clinking of cups and spoons and Foteini cursing under her breath about some lack of a domestic accoutrement that I couldn't quite catch the drift of. Jim and I smiled at each other.

"It's not Costa's coffee shop, is it?"

"No, and thank God for that, Jimbo."

Finally, she appeared carrying a battered tray with a *briki*, pot, and three little white cups. Once Foteini had poured coffee and sat down on an overturned plastic bucket, I brought out the cakes we had picked up on the way through Kalamata. It was a box of small, round, cream-filled cakes with chocolate icing that I remembered she loved so much. When I undid the box, she peered inside and her eyes flickered with child-like anticipation.

There were six cakes, bedded down in pink, pleated casings. She put one of her big hands in and drew a cake out, the paper casing fluttering to the ground, where it sat unremarked upon. She held the cake up and looked at it in wonder, as if she'd never seen one before. She turned it this way and that, admiring it, I imagined, for its confectionary charm. Then she went further and sniffed it several times. This was one of her endearing peculiarities and I had seen her sniff many food offerings in my time.

I started to giggle, as I always did when Foteini ran the gamut of rural eccentricities. Jim and I winked at each other. And then she did something I'd never seen her do before – she crammed the whole cake into her mouth in one go, munching it quietly, her cheeks puffed out like a boa constrictor devouring a football. I laughed then, I couldn't help it. Jim started to cackle as well. She watched us but had no facial slack left for smiling. Her eyes watered by way of response and, finally, she swallowed.

"*Poli nostimo*, Margarita. Delicious!" she said, wiping her cream-caked lips with the back of a sweaty hand. She downed another one, licked the ends of her powerful fingers and declared herself full for the rest of the day. We gave her the last two cakes to take home and she quickly picked up the box, fastened the lid and transported it to the depths of her cool *kaliva*.

"Do you still have mice?" I asked her.

"Yes, Margarita. Mice in the shed, and snakes in the olive groves. Big ones," she said, holding her hands apart a couple of feet.

I shuddered, and that's when I remembered Cyclops. How could I have forgotten? He was the one-eyed cat we had given Foteini as a farewell present before we left the

Mani in 2012. We gave it to her because we didn't want to leave Cyclops at the mercy of wild cats and feisty young roosters at Andreas and Marina's Paleohora property.

"Where's Cyclops?" I asked her, looking round the yard.

She pulled a face and muttered something under her breath that I couldn't catch. I still had trouble with her rural accent and her habit of chopping the ends of words or running words together.

"Ach, the cat disappeared one day and never came back," she said, with a grimace of indignation, as if I'd given her a delinquent to look after, instead of a proper mouse catcher.

"When was this?"

"During the first winter after you left. It was cold. Maybe it found somewhere more luxurious to live," she said, with a cheeky grin.

Jim asked me what we were talking about when he heard the word 'Cyclops'. I relayed the conversation.

"Gone somewhere more luxurious? Well that's a no-brainer, isn't it?" he said, looking around the coffee corner and kicking a rotting banana skin out of sight under his chair.

I felt sad for Cyclops. It was an old scruffy thing that had lost its eye in a youthful dust-up with another cat. I had tried my best to feed it and keep it away from the other greedy cats in Paleohora. It seemed like an old soul and I wanted it to be a survivor, just like Greece itself, but now it had gone. And maybe there was no help for the country either. It would certainly feel that way in the following year.

I would never know what had become of Cyclops, apart from the fact that probably Foteini never fed it and it was too old to catch a wily Maniot mouse. It had simply gone away to die.

"We made a pact, Foteini. You promised to look after Cyclops if I promised to return to the Mani, and I kept up my end of the bargain."

She looked down at her dusty, decrepit wellies and poked her tongue into the side of her mouth, rolling it up and down, making her cheek ripple. She often did this when she was embarrassed.

"Ach, don't say anything, Margarita. I've got goats to look after. I can't be worried about cats. I'm sorry."

That had always been her response when she didn't have time to do something, or go somewhere. Always the goats. Even the villagers in Megali Mantineia were amused at her attachment to these animals. One feisty matron told me: "Why does she need the goats? They don't bring in much money." But when farmers are as poor as Foteini, a little money is better than none.

But I had cheerier things to share with Foteini that day and took a copy of my book *Things Can Only Get Feta* out of my bag and gave it to her. I had already told her several times in letters and on the phone about the book and her part in it, but she hadn't quite understood – until now. I tapped the lovely cover illustration, a scene reminiscent of the first day we'd met her.

"That's you and Riko on the road outside."

She grabbed the book out of my hands and stared at it in wonder, turning it this way and that and, yes, she even sniffed the cover, with its still pungent printing aromas. She touched the image of herself, dressed in layers in her big straw hat.

"Is that really me, Margarita?"

"Yes, Foteini, you and the donkey."

Her expression was one I don't think I'll ever forget. One of awe, and a lot of pride as well. It brought a tear to my eyes. Such innocent joy! Having a book published is a great enough experience, but watching Foteini grip her own copy of the book she had inspired so much ranks as one of the most satisfying moments of my life.

"*Fili mou, eyines diasimi tora.* My friend, you are famous now," I told her.

"What, me?" she said bashfully.

Okay, I ramped the fame up a bit, but what did any kind of fame mean to Foteini? She has no concept of it, or celebrity, or social media. The modern world was another planet. How could I explain to her that people were reading about her, and her tough life, not in their millions, of course, but in enough numbers to make her a minor Greek heroine at least.

"People in Britain have read about you, America, Australia, everywhere."

Her eyes widened at each continent, yet she couldn't quite get her head around it.

"Some people have written to me to say they've come to the village just to see you riding your donkey."

"Really? Come to see me? Do you think I should ask them in for coffee in my *ktima*?"

"No, no. You don't need to go that far," I said. Why frighten off readers? was my first thought, laughing to myself.

It was hard to know what Foteini really thought of it all but when I asked her if I could have a photo of her with the book, standing beside Riko, she was happy to oblige.

"But I'm in my old work clothes," she said, showing an uncharacteristic streak of self-consciousness. Foteini had two distinct sides: the farmer and the village woman. For work, she wore her dusty, diverting layers; for church and social occasions she scrubbed up well, in smart outfits with modest jewellery and a handbag hooked over her arm. She was almost unrecognisable in this incarnation. But in the end, she didn't care about the farm clothes and had a photo taken with good grace.

"Bring me a copy of the photo, Margarita. Don't forget," she asked me at least six times before we left for the day. "And come back soon, eh?"

I promised we'd make the journey again but reminded her how long it took.

"Ach Koroni!" she said, waving her arm towards the opposite peninsula, as if it were the Gulag Archipelago. "Why did you pick Koroni?"

"We haven't yet. We're still searching." Well it was more or less true.

When she waved us goodbye, she was standing at the main gate, still holding on to the book, looking down at it now and then and caressing the cover with her breeze-block hand. It was a memorable moment.

6

House in the olive orchards revisited

WE stopped for lunch at the Klidonas taverna on the sea road at Akroyiali, one of the villages close to Paleohora. It was a place we had gone to often while we lived for two years at the house in Odos Elaionon, the Road of the Olive Orchards. The taverna was a small place, nothing special, but with a cool terrace covered in grapevines, and the food was always wonderful, cooked by the owner Vangelis's wife. There was always a basin of freshly caught fish in the fridge as well, covered with a tea towel, that you were obliged to look at before making your choice.

Vangelis was a character, with a laconic sense of humour, who had been delighted when we stayed in Paleohora for two years. We were by far his most regular customers. Vangelis always sat at a small table outside, beside the open kitchen door, with a small glass of ouzo or Greek coffee by his side. When we saw him there that day he waved. It was as if we had never been away, as if we had lived in this part of Greece all our lives. He bear-hugged us and wanted to know all our news.

"Why are you staying in Koroni?" It was the common refrain. We told him our problems. He took our mobile number and promised to call us if he found some place suitable to rent. We ate fried *kolokithokeftedes*, courgette fritters, fresh *sardelles*, sardines, and a Greek salad and some of his home-made wine, with its melony, honey flavours. The food was delicious.

"Your wife's still the best cook around," I told him.

"Shh, don't tell her that. She'll want bigger wages!" It had been his regular joke. One of those markers in a relationship that is a cue to being a bit silly and having a laugh.

After our meeting with Foteini that morning and now this lunch, I started to feel a strong tug towards the Mani again and hoped we could still find something here, especially as I knew the old house that Stavroula was renovating would be finished whether we were there or not. Maybe Andreas and Marina would be willing to rent again. That was my hope.

Later we drove to Paleohora and up the winding road to the house. It was still horribly steep and badly concreted, with hairpin bends. I had once stalled the Fiat on a slow ascent and was forced to reverse back down the hill again and into a field to avoid a collision with a massive sewage truck. But like all imperfect things in Greece, it was a road that eventually took a little piece of our hearts, with the view of the gulf from its top reaches, the fig trees laden with fat purple fruit growing along its verges, and the gentle paths that snaked off it into the olive groves.

We had missed the big rambling house, and Andreas and Marina, with whom we had shared many crazy and sad moments as the economic crisis had intensified from 2011. We were looking forward to seeing them and all the animals. But the big dog Zina wouldn't be there. Despite having great stamina for an old dog, chained outside most of the time, she had died in the winter of 2013.

Marina had told us they had a new dog now, which they got as a puppy when no-one else wanted it because it had only one eye, showing a distinct tendency for this region to create one-eyed animals. This one was called Ares, after the mythical Greek God of war which, we would soon realise, suited it perfectly. The minute we parked in front of the property at the big sliding metal gates, Ares came roaring up to them, barking and leaping about. It was now an adult and a big brute of a thing, with thick unruly fur and the one pale eye looked menacing. It was a mongrel mix, like a cross between a collie dog and a husky. I pressed the intercom buzzer on the gate post. A female voice answered, slightly unfamiliar.

"It's Margarita. Is that you, Marina?" I asked.

I couldn't understand the reply through a crackling reception, and Ares barking, apart from: "The gate's unlocked. Drive in."

I went round to the driver's side window and conveyed the message to Jim.

"The only problem is the dog looks feral. And when I roll back the gates, he'll rush out," I said.

"I'll do it, if you like. You can drive in."

But my female pride kicked in.

"No, I can manage," I said, in a thin voice.

I don't like big dogs much. As I'm small and slight, they make me feel like a ten pin about to be scuttled into the bowling alley gutter.

"Margarita, you'll have to be quick. We can't park out here, remember. We're blocking the road."

There were several properties further up the hill and the one person I didn't want to see again was grizzled Orestes, the old farmer who lived next door and had a penchant for shooting at things, especially thrushes in his almond trees, and possibly *xenoi*, foreigners. I started to pull back the gate. It was heavy and sat on rollers, and the grinding sound ramped up the dog's fizzy behaviour even more. No way did I want to get tangled up with that thing. I changed my mind and rolled the gate shut again. I saw Jim unbuckling his seatbelt, about to get out, and I held up my hand to stop him. I rang the buzzer again. The same voice answered and I explained the problem.

"Don't be silly, Ares is fine." All the same, the woman told me she was coming down to sort it out.

A few minutes later an elderly woman I didn't recognise ambled towards the gate. She was wearing a kind of work dress, with her hair in strands around her face. Did the couple have lodgers now?

"*Kalos irthate*, welcome," she said, "Marina and Andreas won't be back for a while, but you can wait inside, Margarita."

I rubbed at my chin. "Do you know me?" I asked her over the top of the dog barking.

She gave me a quizzical look. "It's Iphigenia. Don't you remember me? Marina's mother."

I gasped, shocked that this woman at the gate was the same one who had come to the house once in box pleats and a smart straw hat and stirred the unctuous mixture that was olive oil soap, and talked to us about her Maniot childhood. The last couple of years hadn't been easy then.

"Are you visiting today?" I asked her.

"No, we live here now. Ach, it's a terrible story. Come in and I will explain."

"But the dog. He's scaring me."

She laughed. "*Den einai agrio, to skilaki*, Margarita!" He's not wild. But as if he was on a mission to prove her wrong, he came bounding up. She put her arm out to quieten him, but it made him rear up on his back legs, like a small brown bear. She shrieked and turned towards the gate, grabbing the handle and pulling it away from the perimeter wall. No way did I want this gate to open and the crazy dog to get out.

I grabbed the metal spars and pushed it closed again. She squared up to me with a determined look and rolled it open again. She was strong for a woman in her seventies. I rolled it shut. She opened it. I don't know how many times we did this, and yet the gate never progressed further than a foot or so. I was breaking out in a sweat. I began to understand the Myth of Sisyphus for the first time: the poor guy who had to roll a stone up a hill, only to have it come crashing down again. I looked back at Jim for some assistance but he was smiling benignly. Didn't I look terrified enough?

Just then, a car pulled up behind the Fiat, the driver rapping his fingers on the steering wheel and watching the tug-of-war scene with irritation. Greek drivers are not the soul of patience. We rolled the gate a few more times back and forth. The driver was on the horn. Jim poked his head out the window.

"What's going on?"

While the gate was in its shut position for the umpteenth time, I turned and bolted to the car, throwing myself in the open passenger side and slamming the door.

"Couldn't you see I was having a problem, Jimbo? Iphigenia was trying to let that damned dog out and I was trying to stop her."

"That's Iphigenia?" he said.

She finally got the gate open all the way and we drove in while she dragged the God of War by the collar to the underneath of the house, attaching his collar to a long chain that snaked over the cement floor. Some things hadn't changed. The 'basement' area was open on all sides and still stacked with piles of olive wood and bits of reclaimed furniture, one of Marina's arty hobbies.

I had a feeling this was going to be a long afternoon. When we finally got out of the car we were greeted by Maria, Andreas's mother, whom we had only met a few times but had always found her to be vivacious and entertaining. The house had once been Iphigenia's home, but when her husband died she moved to Kalamata to live with Andreas and Marina. The place had been full of family possessions and memorabilia which Marina had cleared away when we rented the house. Now it was all back again, filling every shelf and flat surface. It didn't feel like the house we'd once lived in.

While Iphigenia went off to make Greek coffee, we sat on the front balcony that we had loved so much, with its sweeping view of Kalamata and the Messinian peninsula across the gulf. At least the balcony felt right, and it was sweet that the family had kept it as it was, with our pots of herbs still thriving and our collection of sea stones perched on the balcony walls.

I ran my hand over the smooth grey and white stones. The feel of them brought back such intense memories of long, carefree summer months spent on the nearby coves where the stones were gathered. I had such longing for those days, for that particular adventure, that I felt a lump gather in my throat. I also remembered the baking hot nights we had sat on this balcony with the TV rigged up here so we could catch a sea breeze. It was here we had watched so much of the economic crisis unfold on late-night news programmes, along with every other Greek family gathered on their own balconies until the early hours of the morning.

Iphigenia came up behind me, rattling cups on a tray, and finally broke my train of thought.

"So, you're living here now?" I asked her.

"And Maria too," she said, her eyes flickering towards the older woman, who crossed herself several times. She spoke first.

"There was a fire in our house in Kalamata, but we don't know what started it. It was a heatwave and maybe it was a faulty electrical wire. We were in bed having a siesta. The children were over here feeding the animals. The fire was in the kitchen and at first we heard nothing and then I smelt something and got up. *Panayia mou,* when I saw the fire, I ran downstairs, opened the front door and shouted to people passing by. They came to help me. They called out the fire brigade." She crossed herself once more.

"That's a terrible story," I said.

Iphigenia took it up now, looking teary. "The kitchen is *hamos*, a mess, and we are waiting for it to be fixed. For now, we must stay here with the *paidia*."

I was sorry for the family's distress but I couldn't help but think that there was no possibility of ever renting this house again. Andreas and Marina came home not long after we arrived and seeing them both again, I also remembered vividly the day we had left, when it rained for hours and the car was packed to the roof with our stuff, and Zina was chained up, looking dejected, as we drove out through the big sliding gate. It had been a sad day, leaving the Mani.

"You didn't bring Wallace," said Andreas, pouting. "I wanted to see him."

"I know, but he's old now and he doesn't like to go out much in the heat. Some day we will bring him."

"My mother told you about the fire?" he said, making an exaggerated windmill of his right hand, and grimacing.

Andreas hadn't lost his English at least. It was always better than Marina's but he still had many endearing mix-ups too, as I had in Greek.

"We must stay here for now. The insurance company is taking much time to give the permission for rebuilding the kitchen. They say it should be ready by the autumn, but I have my wonders about it."

I smiled. "Wonders?"

He slapped his knee and looked embarrassed. *"Amfivolies,* Margarita."

"Ah, doubts, you mean."

"Yes, doubts."

But I think I actually preferred his word. It was charming, just as he was.

I had my own wonders that the situation here was as easy as the couple said it was. Like all Greeks, they were incredibly stoical. When we had been living here the couple had spent more and more time at the little *spitaki* in the corner of the property that they were fixing up, and which was still far from finished. They came nearly every day during the week and often stayed over at the weekends, even though the *spitaki* was very small and cramped. It was their refuge, they called it, from the stress of city life in the crisis and from all the typical senior anxieties of the two mothers. But this set-up now, in the big house, was a matter of practicality for all of them.

We spent a nice afternoon with the couple and promised to meet up again while we were in the region.

"Well, it looks like the old house in Koroni is the only option we have," said Jim, as we set out on the long drive back to the Messinian peninsula. But I started to feel slightly panicked about it.

"I just hope it scrubs up the way the family have described it, or we're pretty well sunk," I said.

"Hmm. It does seem as if things are going pear-shaped this time. Nothing has quite gelled for us, has it?"

"No, it hasn't."

That's when I remembered one of the curious sayings of my Scottish grandmother, Euphamia. "Aye, lass, trouble wears five hats." Meaning trouble never comes along in its simplest guise.

This year, trouble would feel like it was wearing five big Carmen Miranda hats festooned with fruits, parrots, critters, and the odd scorpion with giant maracas. We had been lucky with our original odyssey to the Mani. We had met splendid characters, had great adventures and had the three most magnificent years of our lives. But it came at a price, too. They had also been hard years. Most British expats go to Greece and buy or build their dream home so that at least they don't have to rely on renting, as we had done, even though they then spent their lives going backwards and forwards between the two countries like weary shuttlecocks, trying to stay on the right side of the British tax office and the NHS, as most of them are retirees.

At the beginning of the crisis, we couldn't afford a dream house in Greece, or an early retirement and, unlike many expats, we had been dubious about how long the crisis would last and how it would impact, especially on home ownership. As time went by, we knew we were right to be cautious about buying, but our experience of renting houses in Greece was just as tough, taking on old but interesting properties, with strange set-ups that would never pass muster in the UK system.

And here we were in 2014, four years on, still living the nomadic rental life, and still seeking Greek adventures. Yet we reasoned that we would probably never be able to do another long odyssey like this one again, especially with Wallace in tow, who was now older and more prone to health problems. So while we had the opportunity, we would go for it, no matter how crazy it seemed to folks back home. As Zorba, in the classic novel *Zorba the Greek* by Nikos Kazantzakis, said: "Throw off your belt and live." Or words to that effect.

I had all these thoughts as we drove along in the late afternoon, the sun glinting across the Messinian Gulf, the air so hot and smooth that it finally lulled me into a state of peaceful resignation. But now and then in the following days I did hear the busy swish of a Carmen Miranda hat, festooned with its crazy cargo.

※※※※※

A few days after our trip to the Mani, we went down to the old house to see how the renovation work was progressing. It was now taking longer than expected and we were due to move in on the second week of June. There was a mass of junk and old furniture on the front veranda, dragged out of the house. We found Stavroula and her husband Thodoris inside, painting the walls and ceilings, with Yiannis helping, wearing a pair of his signature striped trousers like he was on prison detail. It might have felt that way to him as he angled a very long-handled brush against the high-pitched ceiling in the main room.

While the rest of the house had a loft of sorts built above it, with a low, slatted wooden ceiling, the main room had a pitched ceiling made of wide planks of wood and cross beams below. The planks had previously been a dingy brown colour, probably from decades of the wood-burner belching out oily smoke from olive wood, but it was now a kind of off-white, which made a huge difference. And the marble floor had been scrubbed and gleamed, showing all its detail.

Yiannis saw us staring at everything with a slightly more approving demeanour than previously, and kissed the tips of his fingers again.

"*Teleia*, perfect, yes?"

"It's better, yes, and I can't believe how quickly you've fixed things up."

I could, once I'd stood for a while and watched Stavroula's husband working. Thodoris came originally from a Maniot village. He was tough, handsome and dark-haired, with a tendency to call a spade a road digger. He was a man of few words – and none of them English. But this man was a powerhouse of energy. A real worker. When he had a job to do, he went at it with frenetic determination until it was finished. I don't think I'd ever seen anyone work so hard and in such an uncomplaining fashion. It inspired confidence, at least.

"It's been a lot of hard work, Stavroula," I said.

"I know. And soon my son will be on school holidays and I have many things to do with the business. But you know, this project with the house is so nice for us now, as I told you. It is a very traditional place. Look," she said, pulling us over to the doorway, where a piece of plaster beside the frame was missing.

"Mud bricks. That's how they made the old houses. Can you imagine? And still it stands, after many earthquakes too."

We stared at the hole in the wall and, sure enough, you could clearly see the small light brown bricks packed together, which had kept this house standing for generations. Later we stood on the front balcony, where you could see the olive orchards in the broad valley below and the gulf beyond. The balcony was shaded by a grapefruit tree at one end, already full of miniature green fruits, hard and small like olives, and a sweet orange tree in front. But through the middle, and to one side where the stone steps connected with the balcony, we also had a direct view of Villa Anemos and its side balcony, just a few yards away. This would be a problem, trying to keep Wallace from rushing around the place, terrorising tourists.

I tried to explain the problem to Stavroula without making it seem as if Wallace was a psychopath. She was nothing if not laid-back and I was often in awe of her ability to seem calm in any crisis. And it was a bonus that she too had a dog at her Kalamata apartment.

"You're worrying too much, Margarita. You don't have to. Wallakos will be fine."

That was her funny little name for Wallace that needed some care in pronunciation. If you said it quickly or incorrectly, it sounded like the Greek word for jerk or wanker: '*malakas*'. To this day, I have no idea if she was just being ironic.

Stavroula looked across at Villa Anemos and the little garden in front of us. "I admit it's not very private for you, or the other people, but we will fix it, you will see. We will get some thick *kalamia* (bamboo) and make a nice fence in front and you will have more privacy."

It sounded like a good plan, even though it wouldn't actually keep Wallace from running out around the fence, but we would have to worry about that when we moved in.

A few days before the move, we wandered down again to watch the makeover from ancient folky hovel to bijou cottage with character. Thodoris arrived with the *kalamia*, a huge roll, six-foot high. He had it on one shoulder and looked like

Hercules staggering down the concrete drive, sweating profusely. He dumped it on the ground and set to work building posts so he could attach the long continuous curtain of bamboo, pinning it finally behind the sweet orange tree.

"*Kalitera*, better," he said.

Although privacy is something Greeks never worry about, the couple agreed that the new fence would give everyone their own space. And all we would ever see of tourists would be when they trudged up the concrete driveway to their cars.

When moving day arrived, there wasn't much to take to the house, apart from a few suitcases. The house had been spruced up by the family's cleaner from Russia, a stocky blonde called Svetlana, who always wore a baseball cap and talked a strange, gargling kind of Greek. She had mopped the marble floor until it shone. It wasn't made from perfectly even slabs of marble and some of the grouting was missing here and there, but it was eye-catching and showed that in the old days, good materials were cheap and long-lasting.

The rooms were fresh and white and although the furniture was fairly basic it was enough for us. Stavroula and Yiannis were there to help us move in and to check that everything was to our liking. Thodoris disappeared for a moment and reappeared carrying something in his hands, which he flung over us. They were rose petals from Stavroula's grandmother's old rose bush near the front balcony.

"*Kaloriziko*," they chorused, meaning 'may it (the house) be blessed'.

It made us laugh, as if we'd just got married and this was our honeymoon home. Yiannis was kissing his fingertips again, his big brown eyes gleaming with a slight case of 'I told you so!'

"Good house now, yes? All British are looking for this kind of little white house with blue shutters. You told me this once," he said.

"You're right, Yianni. It's a British fantasy," I said.

"Now your fantasy has come true," said Stavroula.

Steady, I thought, let's not go that far.

It was impossible not to be impressed by how the family had turned this wreck around in such a short time. So why did I have a nagging, uneasy feeling about things?

7

Wallakos goes large

ON a hot June evening we were sitting on the side balcony of the house we had christened *Palio Spiti*, the Old House. Simple. The front balcony was the wider of the two, shielded from the sun by its roof and the *kalamia* fence, and was cooler during the midday heat. The side balcony, which was a corner balcony, was lovely in the early evening as the sun cast a velvety glow as it went down behind the Mavrovouni hills that dominated the lower Messinian peninsula.

The side balcony also caught the late sea breezes blowing up the valley from the gulf. This was where we spent most of our time, eating, reading, or admiring glimpses of the gulf through gaps in the sweet orange tree, a sprawling grapevine and the family's wild rose bushes. We planted some crops in the small piece of garden Yiannis had given us just in front of the *kalamia*. We had tomatoes, aubergines, peppers and chilli peppers. and every evening Jim partook of his happy evening ritual of watering them and standing silently with arms akimbo, which is the default male position for admiring gardening accomplishments.

The farm at the bottom of the hill, with its outdoor seating and fluttering Greek flag, quickly became a source of fascination as we watched the family tend a massive field of grapevines and olive orchards. In the late afternoon, when everyone had woken from their siesta, the place buzzed with activity. There were several dogs tied up near cages filled with baby goats, piglets, turkeys and chickens, guarding them from foxes and other predators. During the night the dogs howled like banshees and one in particular sounded like a baby with colic. It was terrifying at first but gradually we became accustomed to it, even though we occasionally baulked at the idea that the dogs might actually be hungry or lonely. We also thought about Pluto quite often, up in his compound at night, fending off interlopers.

Part of the problem with the farm was the fact that sounds travelled up from the bottom and across the hillside with remarkably clarity. We could hear the grandfather every time he coughed or gave his young grandson a scolding. The son was no more than 10 years old and yet he played a decisive role in the farm after school. We were surprised to pass him one day on the road below while he was driving the farm's pick-up truck. We could hardly see his head over the steering wheel.

We finally said farewell to the twitchers just before we moved, over a bottle of wine. Jed took great delight in saying he'd known all along we'd end up taking one of the houses below.

"What made you think that?" Jim asked.

"Oh, we bird watchers have a lot of down time to cruise the thermals of human destiny," he said, giving me a knowing look with his big robin redbreast eyes.

I laughed. "That's a lot of hot air."

"Bollocks, basically! I know but, hey, there could be a small grain of truth in it, too."

In the end we thought we might even miss the twitchers a bit. They were genial eccentrics.

"Pity you didn't score that new villa. That would have been jammy, instead of the old one. Mind you, it looks a lot better than it did before. I hope you get reasonable guests in the villa, no Austrian yodellers or yoga fanatics up at dawn doing salute-to-the-sun routines," he said.

He was enjoying the wind-up and it was probably his way of getting back at us for setting Wallace on him when we first met him, twitching behind trees in his undies. But he had a point, as the two dwellings still seemed pretty close to each other, despite the *kalamia* barrier. We were sure we'd be driven mad by some of the guests before summer was out.

The first visitors arrived in June, staying for a month. They were an English couple with their daughter, and in the beginning we didn't see much of them, which was fine as we had planned to keep ourselves to ourselves for the summer and we imagined that's what the villa guests would want as well. However, it was a scare over a stray dog that flushed us all out.

The couple tended to walk everywhere and also to the nearby supermarket, taking a shortcut through the olive groves. While we were on the side balcony one afternoon, we heard a mad scampering of feet and a round of deep barking. The next minute a large Rottweiler cross head-butted the 'gate' on the balcony. It was a makeshift piece of hardboard, like a door turned sideways. We'd scrounged it from one of the derelict houses nearby to keep Wallace from escaping, and from darting across the nearby road in pursuit of real or imagined prey.

The Rottweiler knocked the gate down with a mighty crash. We got the fright of our lives. When it saw Wallace, sitting on the back door mat, it looked like it was up for a fight, but we quickly pushed some balcony chairs in its path and Wallace dashed into the house with a lot of screamy barking and mayhem.

After another attempt to invade the balcony, the dog scarpered through the olive groves, circling around Yiannis's small *kotetsi*, chicken coup, which we could just see from the side balcony. That's when we saw the couple from next door, red-faced, carrying bags of food. Had they brought their dog along with them? This would be a challenge. But then we heard a tale that was familiar in Greece. The couple had seen the dog chained up at the restaurant next to the supermarket and felt sorry for it, offering it a snack. When they started the trek back to the villa, the wily beast slipped its collar somehow and followed them.

"We didn't know how to shoo him away. He just kept following us," said the woman, looking embarrassed.

"That's as maybe," said Jim, with a kick-ass expression on his face that I found amusing. "But please don't encourage him back in future. He looks feral and we have a dog too. We don't want Wallace getting mauled by this brute."

The man was tall and very composed. He had seemed disinterested in the fray and probably had us pegged as a couple of busybody expats, out to upset his holiday – until the mention of Wallace.

"Did you say Wallace?" He looked around as if he might see him outside, then gave me a squinty look. "Wait a minute. You haven't written a book about Greece, have you?"

"Em... Yes."

"Things Can Only Get Feta?"

"Yes, that's right."

"I'm just reading it. When you said Wallace, I thought, 'No, there couldn't be another British couple here with a dog called Wallace'."

"What a funny coincidence," I said.

"I know. I'm half way through the book and enjoying it, I must say."

Thoughts of the nasty Rottweiler were suddenly displaced by a warm wave of satisfaction. Jim saw me offering the man my best smiley face.

"Recognition at last, Margarita!"

Well, let's be frank, recognised for having a crazy dog like Wallace. Yet what were the chances of this happening: a couple moving in next door and reading your book? And what were the chances of the man also being a TV journalist, though not one I imagined with any interest in a TV exposé of our crazy little Greek life.

"I'll look forward to seeing Wallace very soon," said the man.

"Ha! You might be sorry you said that," I told him.

"We'll keep him inside at the moment while the Rottie's on the prowl," said Jim.

Wallace, however, had already scheduled a meet-up. The next evening, while we were preparing dinner, we heard a round of screamy barking coming from somewhere outside. I went out to the side balcony and discovered the 'gate' had been overturned – a new manoeuvre learnt from the Rottie perhaps.

"It sounds like the noise is coming from Villa Anemos," said Jim.

We walked on to its side balcony and called Wallace's name, but the barking continued. Light was slanting through half-open venetian blinds. We tiptoed to the side window and glanced in. The family were in the kitchen, the woman in her apron cowering against one wall, the man waving a set of kitchen tongs, the daughter stirring a large pot on the stove, but never taking her eyes off the floor, where Wallace was unfolding his crazy Jack Russell offensive, feet planted firmly, head thrown back, screamy barking to the max. What the hell!

Jim and I looked at each other and couldn't help but smile. It did look funny. I wondered if we should shout "chicken!", the one word that has always brought Wallace under control when no others can and which we used quite a few times on him when we were living in Megali Mantineia.

We didn't have to resort to this because, moments later, we saw Wallace through the window, skittering through the sliding door on the front balcony. He came racing round the corner, flying straight past us, and very pleased with himself. Jim gave chase. The man appeared next, looking red-faced, still holding his kitchen tongs, to what end I couldn't be sure.

"Ah, you've met Wallace finally. Sorry for the disturbance," I said.

"Oh, not at all. Don't worry," he said, wiping a slick of perspiration from his forehead. "We were in the kitchen, cooking dinner, and Wallace came rushing in, stood beside the stove, looked at us all and then barked furiously, as if we had no right to be there at all."

"It's the territorial Jack Russell in him coming out. He thinks this whole hillside is his basically."

The man laughed. At least he saw the funny side of it.

"Well, it's all rather odd. On the one hand I'm reading about Wallace's misadventures in your book and then I'm getting a reality tie-in with a guest appearance. This could be a new kind of reading experience."

"Or a book giveaway where the winner gets to keep Wallace for a week."

"I dare say I could cope with Wallace for a week or so. He's quite a character. I can see that now."

I smiled. "Oh, you don't know the half of it."

Our fears over living so close to the other villa and Wallace being a disturbance were more or less allayed for the time being, as we were lucky to have laid-back Brits next door. But in any case we realised that we would rarely see other guests. They would be out all day doing their own thing, and out most evenings at one of the many tavernas in Koroni, as we often were. But it was early days and Stavroula told us that German and Austrian tourists had booked for the coming months, and we knew they wouldn't be quite so sanguine about Wallace's crazy behaviour.

※※※※※

We quickly settled into the routine of living in *Palio Spiti,* even though we didn't feel enamoured of the place. Maybe it didn't help that we had seen it beforehand and I kept thinking of the members of this family who had lived here in years gone by, in stoical circumstances, and had probably died here as well. Despite the painting and cleaning, it was still mutton dressed as lamb or, more appropriately, mud-bricks dressed as glam. It reminded me of the traditional croft houses in Scotland that carried the weight of a troubling past in their black, peaty walls, which no amount of trendy makeovers could shift. I still lived with the fantasy that another rental property would come along, preferably in the Mani, but for now we were Velcroed to the old place.

What bothered us most were critters, even the small ones that seemed to morph out of the floors and walls during the night and appeared in the morning as if they lived in wall spaces or crept through the cracks under the doors. They were mostly beetles and skinny black worms that in the other peninsula were called Mani worms. The worst critters inside, though harmless, were the dozens of slater bugs that would turn up by morning in piles around the corners or under the bed. While they look like small armadillos, they are actually crustaceans, I discovered, more closely related to crabs or lobsters. As they are attracted to warm, moist environments, I imagined the foundations to the house were rather damp.

Every morning, before we could do anything else, I had to round them up all up and sweep them out the door, along with the constant piles of dust that appeared from nowhere every night. At least nothing worse had turned up. Not yet!

My favourite room in the house was the small bedroom that I had turned into a study. While I didn't have a view of the sea from this room, I loved to gaze at the vibrant almond tree, into which colourful jays flew at certain times of the day, as well as clouds of tiny green finches.

The room was plain, with a blue *kafeneio* table at the window and a typical Greek wooden chair with a rushwork seat. There was a deep inset bookcase on one wall, a feature of most old Greek homes. With a few books on the shelves and some pictures on the walls, it almost looked homely, in a stark monastic way, which kind of appealed to me.

Not for the first time on our Greek odysseys did I enjoy the feeling of not having many possessions with us, apart from what we had brought in the Fiat and the few bits and pieces we picked up in Greece: souvenirs, copies of icons, sea stones, driftwood, talismans of our adventures. It was an existential life, free of clutter and distractions, which was just as well because I had two-thirds of a book to write yet.

It seemed like a grand idea, coming to Greece to write another book. I felt sure that getting into the soul of the place again, absorbing the sights and sounds, hearing the language every day, would prove beneficial and jog the book along nicely. That was true up to a point, yet how I thought it would be easy to write a book for hours on end in a sweltering Greek summer I couldn't imagine.

There were few real distractions during the day, but by mid-afternoon I was often in the grip of SDD, Scribbling Deficit Disorder, with the sheer fug of the heat and the rasping sound of cicadas outside. Then there were the images that constantly came unbidden into my mind of a cool turquoise sea and how it would feel to be swimming through it. Sometimes I just had to find out, and work would be suspended until the evening.

The beach of Ayia Triada (the Holy Trinity) was named after the small church near the beach car park and was our closest and favourite swimming spot. It was long and sandy, enclosed at the back by high russet-coloured cliffs, which in the height of summer created a swathe of shade at the back of the beach. It was a perfect location, with the added charm of the tiny white church of the Panayitsa standing like a sentry on an adjacent cliff-top. This was the beach we often retreated to when it was too hot to work.

Yet the writing days, when they were going well, were something to cherish: quiet, satisfying, and even though I was writing about the Mani while living in the opposite peninsula, at least when I walked on to the front balcony I could see it shimmering in a heat haze across the gulf. On some calm and clear days, I could even see the village of Megali Mantineia, nestled at the top of a hill not far from Trikitsova castle.

While I wrote in the study, Jim worked at a small desk in front of the bedroom window on his book-editing business. He had several large projects to finish while we were in Koroni but when he wasn't working, he pottered about in the garden. One day while I was writing, he came shuffling into the study, wearing old shorts, a baseball cap and gardening gloves. He was glistening with perspiration.

"You'll never guess what I've found, Margarita," he said in a thin voice I didn't like the sound of.

"What?" I said without looking at him.

"Two great big scorpions."

"Oh NO!" Every time I heard the word 'scorpion' now it chilled my blood, especially after the last visitation, on the lemon tree.

"Did you hear me, Margarita?" said Jim, wondering why I was sitting at my desk motionless.

"Scorpions? Yes. But not in the house, surely?"

"No, but come and look."

He took me outside, down some steps, to a lower paved terrace in front of the side balcony that we rarely used, as it caught the full force of the afternoon sun. Mostly, I only saw it from the study window. It seemed like it had once been the heart of this property, with a low stone wall separating it from the olive orchards. Apart from the almond tree, there were eating olive trees and fig trees, which we raided in late summer for their fat, syrupy fruits. There was a *fournos* set to one side where, in past decades, the family would have done most of their baking and cooking in deep metal trays. But it was now an abandoned, cobwebby space, and a wide stone trough nearby was fashioned into the side of the house. It had probably been used to crush grapes for wine making by trampling on them, and the juice flowed down a spout at one end.

In front of the *fournos* was a collection of breeze blocks, left there for no particular reason, and it was these that Jim had brought me to.

"Look at that," he said, pointing to the large mangled body of a beige-coloured scorpion.

"Holy Moses!" I said, figuring that when alive it would have been at least four inches long with its tail extended.

"I was trying to tidy up here and lifted one of the blocks and there they were, two big ones, sleeping. I just dropped the block back on top of them. The other's totally smashed."

"I suppose we can expect more of them. There are plenty of places to hide here."

Jim nodded. "Let's just hope they don't come into the house."

I looked at main bedroom window at the back of the house, not far from the *fournos*, and made a note to myself never to leave the window open without the flyscreen firmly pulled down.

Scorpions weren't the only problem lurking around the house, however.

8

What lies above

IN late June we had resigned ourselves to living in *Palio Spiti*, with all its limitations, and felt lucky to have somewhere to live at all. But one night in bed we heard a strange noise. At first it was no more than a faint skittering on the narrow slats of the ceiling above our bed. The ceiling was an old construction, long strips of wood hammered on to cross beams, creating a loft of sorts. In village houses in the Mani, pieces of *kalamia* were often used, fixed tightly together, making an intricate pattern.

"Sounds like mice," Jim said.

The noise continued for a while and then stopped. We finally fell asleep but were woken several more times during the night by the skittering above us. The next night we heard the same thing, except the critters had called in a few beefier friends.

"They are definitely not mice, unless they're wearing boots," said Jim as we lay on our backs glaring at the ceiling, listening to the tap-dance routine on the wooden slats.

"What's that other noise?" I said, "That thumping noise?"

Jim was silent, listening. There was a peculiar business going on amidst the dance moves. It sounded as if one of the critters had got hold of a stone and was dropping it on to the wood from a good height. "Bang!" it went and "Bang!" again.

"What the hell is it doing?" said Jim.

"It's as if there's an evil gremlin up there deliberately trying to get our attention. It's scary."

"Hmm. I'm thinking it could be a rat," said Jim, rubbing his chin and wincing at the ceiling.

"Or a *kounavi*?" I said hopefully. It was a better option – just.

Kounavia in Greece are small furry animals that look like a cross between a ferret and a pine martin, and are mischievous like Aussie possums. They are adept at swinging from trees on to roofs and finding their way through loose tiles into lofts, where they can be tormentingly hard to get rid of.

In the morning I decided to ring Stavroula and tell her about the interlopers.

"I am sure they are only mouses," she told me, using her endearing plural form. If only the problem were this sweet. "We will come later in the afternoon and Thodoris will go into the loft and check."

They were true to their word and arrived at the house with their four-year-old son, who wanted to play with Wallace but was mortified that Wallace didn't want to play with him, which was to be the start of a mutual strop between them. Jack Russells, I have found, don't mix well with children. It could be something to do with the fact that both terriers and kids are small, hyperactive and noisy, moulded from the same cookie cutter. They tend to wind each other up.

Thodoris climbed up a rickety ladder, clutching a torch and the neck of a paper bag. The outer wooden wall that closed off the loft from the sitting room looked like a triangular pediment with a small door in the middle. He opened it and squeezed through the narrow space and moved along the length of the loft on his hands and knees. I could see dust in his wake, puffing lightly out the small doorway.

"Thodoris will put some mouses traps down and also some *karameles* in case it is a big mouse," said Stavroula.

Big mouse? How big were we talking about? I wandered into the study and checked out my Oxford Learner's Greek Dictionary. It told me the word for 'mouse', *pontikos,* can also mean 'rat' in Greek, which was odd in a language that is normally so annoyingly precise. I couldn't be sure if 'big mouse' therefore meant hideous, mutant, large rat. My palms were sweating.

Stavroula was standing in the kitchen, staring up at the loft.

"Em, why is Thodoris giving the big mouse caramels?" I asked, thinking that's what *karameles,* logically, must be.

"No, Margarita," she said with a laugh. "I don't mean sweets. It is the name we also give for the little tablets we put down to kill the mouses."

"Poison?"

"Yes, but not harmful for others. The mouses will eat it and go away to die somewhere else."

Oh, how thoughtful of them not to croak in the loft above our heads. But I didn't much like the idea of poison up there, not when there were a few gaps in the ceiling slats and we had Wallace in the house, snuffling around the floors, as dogs do.

Karameles, I soon discovered, were a blue-coloured poison pellet regularly used to kill mice and rats in old properties. While it might make us wince, it was part of common practice here and showed the tendency of Greeks to be more accepting of toxic substances than we are – hence the innocuous name for them, and the innocuous name for rats as well. A dumbing down of the inimical factors?

The couple told us to monitor the situation and call them again if the pests came back. Sure enough, we had another restless night listening to the mouses/rats kicking up a ruckus in the loft. Tap-dancing, stone throwing, and finally crashing into cross-beams in their death throes perhaps.

"The *karameles* must be hitting the spot," said Jim, as we lay awake again with the sheet pulled up over our heads for no other reason than it seemed safer. We lay there whispering, like two restless kids on a sleepover.

"Stavroula said they go *away* to die. As if!" I moaned.

We decided to leave it a day or so before calling the couple again, but a few nights later we were sitting on the sofa side by side with dinner plates on our laps watching the TV news when Jim suddenly stopped eating and turned white.

"Did you see that thing up there?" he asked.

"What thing?"

"On the ledge!"

There was a ledge along the front the pediment where the loft door was. There was a small gap at the far end of the ledge that seemed to go straight into the loft.

"Bloody hell! I looked up and there was a face staring at me!" added Jim.

"What kind of face? Like a rat's face?"

"Not sure. Maybe. But it had big eyes and pointy ears, cartoon-like. Perhaps a *kounavi*. Hard to say."

"It must have been attracted by the cooking aromas."

"That's another showstopper routine to look forward to tonight," said Jim, rolling his eyes.

He wasn't far wrong. We had another sleepless night and a Riverdance solo on the ceiling, as well as thumping and banging, as if we had a rookie percussion group above. The next morning, I called Stravroula again and told her about the face on the ledge. She promised another visit in the late afternoon, and it was lucky for us that the couple had now decamped to the parents' house in Koroni for the summer holiday.

When I opened the door to Thodoris, he was on his own this time. He looked weary, poor man, having had a long day fixing up another house somewhere. He was holding the torch and another paper bag.

"*Kanane paniyiri pali*, eh? The mouses had another party?" he asked, laughing.

He was a genial guy, but I couldn't tell if he thought we were perhaps just a couple of nutters with mouse-phobia. Up he went again, and slid about in the loft for a bit, his knees clanging on wood beams. When he climbed back down the ladder he did a lot of shoulder-shrugging.

"I don't know why the traps are all empty. I expected to see some dead *pontikoi*."

We told him about the face on the ledge and our suspicion that it was a *kounavi*.

"Pah, I don't think it's a *kounavi*. You would have a lot more noise." I wondered how much noisier it could possibly get.

"Do not worry. We will come back in a few more days and see how things are going," he said with a tired smile. And off he went.

At the weekend, he was back again with Stavroula. We told her our *kounavi* theory and she grimaced, the way Greeks do, pulling the corners of her mouth down, jutting out her chin and half-shutting her eyes, like a member of the All Blacks about to start the Maori Haka. She and Thodoris had a spirited discussion about it, however, in which she seemed to be convincing him that it was a *kounavi* and not 'mouses' and that the creature must be climbing up into the orange tree and running along the overgrown branches that touched the edge of the roof. We all filed outside and Thodoris stood with arms akimbo, pulling faces at the tree.

"Okay I've got the solution. I will saw the ends off the branches and I will fill every hole on the roof."

While he got his tools together, she wandered off to check the garden. Thodoris set his ladder against the *kalamia* fence and climbed up halfway. He was then a blur of activity, sawing his way vigorously through several fat branches. It was tiring just watching him and in no time he had hacked off one side of the tree completely, leaving the branches with pale-edged amputations that were a good foot from the roof.

I could hear Stavroula walking back and shouting: "Not that much, *agapi mou*, my love, you'll kill the tree. My grandmother planted it. It's old."

"It'll grow back," he said, shrugging philosophically.

He jumped down from the ladder and ran off towards the large *apothiki*, store room, under one of the adjacent old houses, where the family kept all their tools and harvesting equipment. On the driveway he quickly mixed up some cement on an old piece of hardboard and trowelled it into a plastic bucket. He moved the ladder and carried the cement up to the roof and engaged in another routine that was dazzling, like some rooftop sprite in a Marc Chagall painting. Fearless, he leapt across the pantiles, hurling trowel loads of cement at the arched ends of each of them where there were gaps big enough for critters to shimmy through. He left nothing to chance. I was reminded of an ancient Greek saying: "If you throw many darts, you'll hit something some time."

Anyone who ever says that the crisis is the fault of "lazy Greeks" might like to book Thodoris for work detail. He is a force of nature, as are many Greeks, especially in the building trade. He simply does not tire. It was such a rousing performance that it drew our neighbour off his side balcony to get a better look.

"What's happening on the roof?" said the man, looking at Thodoris leaping about with a bucket and trowel.

"Mice," I whispered. "Or rats. In the roof."

"Really? Have you seen them?"

"No, but we've heard them. Hell of a racket up there. Can't sleep for it. Have you had problems, heard anything?"

"I don't think we've got vermin in our villa — not yet," he said, with a tiny lift of his chin, showing his confident nature and that good old British spirit that doesn't buckle under foreign mayhem. But I almost felt sorry for him. A few weeks in Greece and already a stalking Rottweiler, a delusional Jack Russell ... and now rats.

"There are worst thing than rats, actually. There's scorpions. Jim killed two big ones the other day," I said.

He lost his cool at the scorpions and I suddenly warmed to him, even more than when he told me he was reading *Feta*. I liked the fact that someone else shared my scorpion jitters.

"Inside the house?" he asked, pulling a face like a suck on a lemon.

"Outside. This big," I said, holding out my index fingers six inches or so apart. It was cruel to toy with his fears, but I was in that sort of mood. It had been a bugger of a day.

"Well, it will give you something else to write about for the next book, won't it?" he said, recovering his composure.

While he went back to give his family an update on the critter blitzkrieg, I wandered back to *Palio Spiti*. Jim was standing on the edge of the balcony.

"I overheard your chat with the neighbour. You're supposed to cultivate loyal readers, Margarita, not scare them away with scorpion tales. That's no way to sell books."

"I can't be worrying about books right now, not when there's a man dancing around on our roof throwing cement, trying to save us from a plague of rodents, like Moses on a Greek sabbatical. What will it be next, Jimbo: a flood, a plague of locusts?"

Jim shook his head. "Don't say it, Margarita. Don't temp fate."

Yes, that would be right, I thought, especially the locusts, bearing down on us in a dark cloud. But that night it was still very much the big mouses on our minds. We didn't sleep well. Every time we heard the wind sigh outside, or the wood on the ceiling creak, we jumped. We didn't hear the old shenanigans, the dancing or stone hurling, yet we couldn't believe the ordeal was over.

"I read somewhere," said Jim, in a languid voice, "that in some countries, scorpions will eat small mammals, like mice."

"If that were true, Jed would have told us about it. But I just hope that's not why everything's gone quiet up there, with mouses eaten by mutant scorpions."

Now I really wasn't going to sleep.

⦿⦿⦿⦿⦿

The late afternoons in June were among the nicest hours of summer, after the midday heat had died down and especially if cooling winds made a gentle susurrus through the olive orchards from the sea below. It was impossible not to be seduced by the ease of life before the big heatwaves of July and August bore down on us all. We would often go for a late walk, taking the road that continued north past the turn-off for the villa complex. On either side were orchards with ancient olive trees standing in rows, their trunks thick and gnarled with age, but nowhere near past their usefulness. There were small farms, some no more than patches of land with chicken wire enclosures for a few goats, turkeys and chickens, watched over by a few chained hounds.

On the right-hand side, another track ascended to a high plateau of land overlooking the gulf. This had been a village once, called Ayios Dimitrios, which was settled in the 18th century. It was encircled by olive trees growing right to the edge of the cliff-face with the sea below. All that remained of the village now were the skeletal outlines of walls hidden in long grass and herb bushes, and a large grinding stone from the village's olive press.

It was a quiet place, with a peaceful sense of the past, of lives well lived and not quite forgotten. Against one of the olive trees a rickety wooden ladder, used for harvesting, was abandoned and leaning against the trunk, as if offering a stairway to heaven. This place came pretty close already. And on another part of the bluff stood the tiny white church of the Panayitsa, which was never closed and always had fresh flowers inside and an aura of being visited on a regular basis, though we never saw anyone else inside it in the year or so we lived in Koroni. I think it possibly had the best view, looking down on the beaches of Lochanou and Ayia Triada and north towards the top of the peninsula.

It was while wandering around Ayios Dimitrios one afternoon we first met Eleni. We found her deep in concentration, hovering over a vibrant bush, picking tiny green berries and dropping them into a plastic bag.

"What are those?" I asked as we walked by.

"*Kaparia*," she said, wheeling round and looking slightly bemused at the sight of two foreigners and a small dog in this quiet rural backwater. She handed me some berries and I recognised they were capers, which the Greeks pickle at this time of year. She stared at Wallace.

"What kind of dog is it?" she asked in soft but halting English.

"A terrier." I didn't think to explain it was a Jack Russell, as few Greeks have ever seen them.

"A terror," she repeated, and I smiled at her mispronunciation, as 'terror' very accurately describes Wallace sometimes. I explained to her the mistake and she laughed.

"He looks like one of my baby goats. All white body and some black here," she said, pointing to her face. She seemed intrigued by that idea. A breed of dog that resembled a goat. It wasn't the first time Wallace had been mistaken for a farm animal. Foteini had also made that error and it was part of the reason she stopped us on the village road in our first few weeks in the Mani. So, in a way, Wallace had often set our Greek agenda more than we realised.

"I like him," Eleni said, nodding her approval.

"You have goats then?"

"Yes, come and see." She moved away from the *kaparia* and led us into a nearby field, where a group of nanny goats were eating wild herbs and grasses.

They were all tied by one of their back legs to various trees, on long pieces of rope, to keep them from wandering off. They were fine-looking animals, well cared for, and Eleni had rather fetching names for most of them: Mavroula, Asproula, black one, white one. One of them she called Manekin, or mannequin. Eleni had named her this because the goat was thin, young and a bit mincy. Foteini had always claimed her goats were shy. I asked Eleni about hers.

She switched to Greek to tell me about her goats and their funny ways. It's a favourite subject in rural Greece.

"It's not only people who are odd, you know. It's animals as well. Goats especially."

We followed her about as she filled water pots from a nearby tap for the goats. She reminded me a lot of the good-hearted Greeks we had first met in Megali Mantineia. But in no way did she resemble Foteini, as I didn't think there was anyone else like Foteini on the planet.

Eleni was in her fifties and was worldly wise. She had an easy manner infused with good humour. She lived with her husband Tasos in Koroni, where they worked, but every day they came to check the animals and in the summer they decamped to their nearby farmhouse because it was cooler than living in the town, and they liked to swim in the afternoon at the nearby beaches.

The farm was a typical southern rural property, with old cars, piles of wood, and an endearing assemblage of junk, as well as animal enclosures, and a 'guard' dog called Carmen, which was an incongruous name given the dog's swarthy build and a tendency to bark like a pneumatic drill. At least there was no evidence of a minxy Carmen Miranda hat.

It was one of the curiosities of rural life that everyone had guard dogs and yet it seemed to us that, superficially, there was little worth guarding. But Eleni told me once that they had suffered a few thefts of their animals and scrap metal and wood, even an old car had once been stolen by passing gypsies. Mostly, the dogs deterred foxes.

"Have you seen any foxes yet?" she asked.

"Not yet, but I'm sure we will," I told her. Then we could add them to our tally of critter visitations.

"When my *kaparia* are ready, I will give you a jar of them, okay?" she said.

"*Poli* okay," I told her. I looked forward to fresh pickled capers and, more than that, I looked forward to getting to know this lovely rural woman. We had been blessed with the friendship of many gregarious Greeks and I was glad that despite our doubts about living in Koroni, the people at least never disappointed us.

Some days in June, when the winds were cooler or the writing muse was having a strop, we would walk from the house to Koroni Castle, taking shortcuts through the narrow alleyways along the north of the town. While there isn't much left of the castle itself, its main draw now is the unique monastery of Timios Prodromos, dedicated to the 'forerunner' or 'messenger', which refers to John the Baptist, who baptised Jesus in the River Jordan.

The monastery is sheltered within the remaining walls of the castle and is something of a leafy Tardis beyond the high front gates. Once it must have been a glorious space with high battlements, overlooking Zaga and Memi beaches on one side and Koroni harbour on the other. The orchard here still contains glorious sweet oranges, lemon trees and fragrant flower gardens.

The monastery dates from the end of the 18th century. It has two churches and dozens of monastic cells in the grounds, now mostly unused. There are many stone steps leading upwards to the battlements, with tiny chapels built along them at various intervals.

One long staircase leads to a crumbling segment of the original castle, a kind of watch tower with a sign warning visitors they enter the building at their own risk. That's the kind of notice that makes me smile in Greece, having a vague stab at health and safety, but never actually forbidding something. It's something you experience in every strata of Greek life.

Elsewhere, because of the monastery's encircling walls, it offers a feeling of sublime peace and refuge, but also one of uncompromising surrender to the faith, encapsulated in a tiny stone doorway, seemingly built for the Seven Dwarfs, which leads to a narrow graveyard. Etched into the lintel of the doorway are the words *'Orthodoxia H Thanatos'*, meaning Orthodoxy or Death. It points to the belief that there is no spiritual life without Orthodox belief, and certainly no real life beyond this religious Xanadu.

From its inception, the monastery supported a healthy number of nuns, though now there are just six left. On one of our visits here, on a somewhat hotter day, we sat in the front garden under the shady trees, where we found one of the younger nuns, Sister Dimitra (though in her sixties), sitting at a table painting sea stones with Greek images to sell in the nearby monastery shop.

She got up when we arrived and brought us some cool water and pieces of *loukoumi* (Turkish delight). Wallace was given a watering can filled to the brim. Sister Dimitra was an easy-going soul, who seemed to like dogs and company as well. While she painted her stones she told us a little about life in the monastery.

She had been in the monastery since she was a young woman under the care of the founder, the Archimandritis (Abbot) Theodoulos Anagnostopoulos, which would have to be the longest title I've ever encountered. She was also there when this much-revered leader died. His tomb is to be found in the narrow graveyard under a vibrant bougainvillea and his 'cave' cell is nearby, kept as it had been in his life. The memorabilia on display is a curious, somewhat lonely, snapshot of the life of an Orthodox aesthete.

I asked her if the crisis had affected their lives here, as it had in other monasteries I had visited in southern Greece.

"We lead very simple lives here, so the crisis has not affected us greatly, but there is the monastery to look after and less money for that now," she said. The fact that so few women would choose any more to live this kind of life, and the numbers are not being replaced, would probably add a degree of difficulty too. Yet Dimitra radiated a warmth and a palpable contentedness that was rare.

Even if the crisis had impacted on life here, Greek monasteries are used to challenges, especially historic ones. This one, she told me, had been drawn into the vortex of violence during the Nazi occupation of the town in the Second World War. When the Germans arrived in 1941 they quickly made their presence felt by taking over the police station in the town, removing the Greek flag and hoisting the swastika. They also commandeered some of the best homes in the town and took over the castle, though curiously they didn't touch the monastery. She told me a story that has become legendary of how, when the Germans had a brutal hold over the town, starving the townsfolk into submission by taking all available food stocks, the nuns carried out acts of bravery to help others.

They grew enough food in the monastery plots to share with the people of Koroni. They would slip out late at night, with food hidden in their long black habits to take down to those families who needed it most. People came to rely on these regular hand-outs, which was a risky undertaking, as the Germans would have exacted harsh punishment on all concerned if they'd been caught. Partly because of this, the town has a great affection for the monastery. Yet it's not the only 'religious' story to have touched the hearts of Koroni residents.

The church of the Eleistria, where we had gone on Easter Thursday, that sits below the monastery on the south-western side of the castle, was at the centre of one of the most curious happenings the town has ever witnessed in recent history, and it is still honoured in an important religious feast day every March.

In the late 19th century, a local woman claimed to have had a series of communications with the *Panayia*, Virgin Mary. The 50-year-old Koroni woman, Maria Stathakis, started to have regular dreams about the Panayia, who each time indicated a place where three holy icons were to be found buried underground. Greece abounds with such stories of visitations and instructions on finding holy icons, and many of these icons grace churches all over the country. But while many are vague in their details, the Stathakis story has been well documented and was very exact in where the icons were to be found, which is the current site of the Eleistria church.

Stathakis claimed the vision told her: "Go and gather together your townsfolk and come and dig in this place, and you will find in the crevice of the rocks three small icons. There, where the icons are found, you will build a church."

However, it took Stathakis a long time to pluck up the courage to explain her visions to the townsfolk for fear they would think she was crazy. But she finally persuaded a group of Koroni citizens to start the dig and, after several attempts, the crevice was discovered. In 1897, the icons were also found: an icon of Christ, the Panayia and Luke the Evangelist. Building work quickly began on a church, and when finished the icons were incorporated into one large icon. There are claims that it is a miraculous icon, and the church has documented many healings.

It's a charming story, and whether or not you believe in miracles and visions, there is something strangely uplifting about this particular church and its magnificent view of the western bay of Koroni.

9
There's a grasshopper in my underpants

ONE scorching afternoon, after I had collected the washing off the line that we had strung up across the front balcony, I heard a manly kind of scream coming from the bedroom. I hoped it wasn't another scorpion. I was all stocked up with scorpion encounters. I raced inside to find Jim standing naked in the bedroom after taking a shower, dancing about on the marble floor, furiously shaking his underpants.

"What the hell are you doing, Jimbo?"

"There's a bloody grasshopper in my underpants. It's leaping about. Just as well I looked before I put them on."

"It's a while since anything jumped that high in your undies, Jimbo!"

"Oh yes, very funny, Margarita. At least I didn't scream like a fire alarm, which you did when you found a big spider in your knickers."

I remembered it very well. "The spider wasn't funny, Jimbo. It could have been a 'recluse spider'. Remember one of the expats in Megali Mantineia telling us they were flesh-eating spiders. Imagine getting bitten down there by a recluse."

Jim laughed – and I didn't like where his mind was going.

One of the worst critter stories I had ever heard came from a newspaper story in Queensland, Australia, after a woman sat down on her toilet one night, without bothering to switch on the light. She felt a large snake slithering out from behind the toilet, between her legs, while she had a pee. Petrified, she didn't move an inch. Luckily, the snake slid away through the open bathroom door, and she managed to creep out and raise the alarm. A snake expert was scrambled and the deadly Taipan was finally caught.

Critters were always on our mind in the summer, but as far as the 'mouses' were concerned, whatever Thodoris had done up on the roof, it seemed to have worked. For now...

One afternoon, while I was working in the study, Jim came shuffling in.

"You'll never guess what I've found, Margarita!"

I whipped around and stared at him. "Not more scorpions, please God!"

He shook his head. "Nope. A snake this time, sleeping under a metal tray. Come and look."

We hadn't seen that many snakes and we were always on the lookout for the infamous *ochia,* the poisonous, horn-nosed viper. Jim took me to the grape-crushing trough. On a cement shelf on one side, a battered metal tray, used long ago in the nearby *fournos,* had been left lying about until Jim had the sudden urge for a garden clean-up, yet again.

"It's under there. I lifted the tray and saw the snake coiled underneath, sleeping. It's small but it has markings."

"How small?"

"Oh, I don't know, about a foot long, I think, but skinny. You can't concentrate on length when you're in a panic."

"I've never known a man to lose concentration on length, Jimbo."

"Very droll, but let's concentrate on this particular snake, shall we? It has markings. The *ochia* has markings, I think. We don't want this bugger to slink away."

"Let's call Yiannis. He'll know what to do."

I don't know why we didn't think to just leave it. It was going to wake up sometime and slide away into the long grass, where there would be dozens more. But we seemed to think it called for an instant identification and removal. I called Yiannis's mobile. It was close to 5pm and a respectable time to call anyone during the siesta period. But Yiannis had often told us to call him any time there was a problem and that he never took siestas — or is that what 'real Greek' men are supposed to say?

A few weeks earlier, I had called him at the less respectable 3pm when we found a goat loose in the olive groves, charging about with a length of rope trailing from its back leg. It seemed distressed. When he answered the phone, Yiannis sounded like a man talking through treacle.

"I hope I didn't wake you up."

"No, I told you, I don't sleep in the afternoon," he slurred.

"You sound tired."

"Is there a problem, Margarita?" he asked, sighing.

I told him about the goat and asked if he knew who it belonged to, as I felt sure the owner would want it back. Yiannis didn't seem very interested. He was keen to hang up, until I told him the goat was heading towards his beloved *kipos*, garden, which was nearby. Yiannis was passionate about his *kipos*, which was surrounded on all sides by lush trees: orange, lemon, pomegranate, persimmon. It had old CDs hanging from the branches by strings to deter birds, particularly over a fecund patch of courgettes, thick and ready to be picked. The goat would make short work of those. Under an olive tree was a battered plastic chair.

"*To grafeio mou*," my office, he would say. I knew he liked coming to the garden whenever he could. It was his escape from the outside world, the pressures of running a business in the midst of a crisis, and from thoughts of his health problems that required many regular trips to Athens. When I reminded him of the courgettes, he was over in 15 minutes and rounded up the stray goat.

Now here I was, yet again, telling him about another problem. But Greek summer is full of things going wrong, from overheated air-conditioners to burst pipes or water shortages and so forth. I told him about the snake.

"I will come over and look at it for you. I have to come over to the villas anyway."

Half-an-hour later, he drove up to the villa, followed by Stavroula, Thodoris and their little boy. Perhaps they wanted to see the snake or just enjoy another segment of *xenoi* neurosis over critters, which I'm sure entertained them hugely. Yiannis came over first, carrying an 8ft-long pole of *kalami,* and the others followed behind him.

"Now, Jim, I give you a lesson in dealing with the snakes," he said, as we all gathered in front of the grape crusher.

"You get a long pole, like this one. And first you will lift the tray, like this." He approached it carefully, holding his pole in front.

"This better be a big snake, Jimbo, after all this faffing about," I whispered.

"It's not really that big ... I think," he replied in a thin voice.

Yiannis expertly wedged the stick under the edge of the tray and pushed it up, revealing a small, curled-up snake underneath. We all shuffled quietly forward to get a better look. It was skinny, green and asleep. It was also ridiculously small.

"*Ach, teras einai, re Dimitri!*" said Thodoris, grinning vibrantly, showing all his teeth. "That's a monster!"

"*Kai tha mas skotosei olous.* It's going to kill us all for sure," said Yiannis, with a giggle.

Stavroula translated for Jim. His cheeks flushed.

"Okay, it looked big when I first saw it," he said.

"It's not an *ochia*," Yiannis told Jim. "I don't know what it is, but probably harmless."

Just in case, he whacked it round the head with his pole and tossed it over the low wall into the olive orchard, where the cats would feast on it later. We all sloped away to our various afternoon chores, Yiannis holding the pole over his shoulder.

At that point, I was reminded of a story shared by an expat when we first went to the Mani in 2010. We met an English couple, Nigel and Ruth, who had come to the area to live permanently and were among the pluckiest expats we'd met: learning Greek, and working at various jobs, renting a house in a small hillside village. Early on, Nigel had been doing some building work on a local house with a gang of burly Albanian stonemasons. While he was clearing up some pieces of stone, Nigel uncovered an *ochia*, though he didn't realise it at the time. He bent down, picked it up just behind its head and took it over to the Albanians and waved it at them.

"I've never seen a group of men get up and move so fast. In five seconds they'd all scattered, shouting '*ochia, ochia!*'. It was only later that I found out it's a venomous snake," he said, laughing heartily.

@@@@@

On the beach in summer, we finally let Wallace have a paddle in the sea, even if this wasn't up to his usual water-borne antics. But his charming Kalamatan vet Angelos at least would approve.

While we had been in the Mani in 2012, Wallace had become ill after a long swim in the sea, though it wasn't clear if the water had caused his problem or just exacerbated an existing one. Either way, it meant we had to go to a special animal hospital in Athens for tests in August, which was tormenting and expensive. At the hospital, Wallace was diagnosed with a stomach ulcer and, after treatment, Angelos told us only to let Wallace paddle about in the sea because if he accidentally drank some water, it might stir up his problem again.

There's A Grasshopper In My Underpants

"He must not swim. He's a dog, not a fish! Riiight?" he would say, showing his amusing tendency to elongate the word 'right' to make a point.

Wallace has loved the water from his early days swimming in the peaty streams near our Scottish village. He is an athletic, confident swimmer and it was hard to deny him this little pleasure in life and keep him in the shallows. On that particular day, at Ayia Triada, we had let him come as a treat and settled at the far end of the beach, where there were fewer people, so we wouldn't disturb anyone. We managed to keep him busy at the water's edge, chasing sticks around in circles, while we swam nearby.

So far so good. Wallace hadn't reached the point yet that I knew so well, where boredom finally tips into craziness. I'm convinced that most dogs are somewhere on the crazy spectrum — and people too for that matter — but Jack Russells are way up at the top end. When Wallace goes mad in the water he wants to break dog-paddle records or chase swimmers half way out to sea.

At Ayia Triada, however, everything was well under control but then we got distracted by two swarthy, Greek-looking guys walking down the beach, who stopped by the shoreline and stared hard at us the way Greeks often do when you let your dog play in the sea because many of them think it's a dirty habit.

I was expecting a gabble of angry Greek but what came out was a broad London accent: "You wrote that book, didn't you? *Things Can Only Get Feta*? I just read it before I left London. And now here you are. Amazing!"

Jim and I looked at each other and laughed. I was waiting for him to trot out his line again: "Recognition at last, Margarita!" I was about to luxuriate in the comment. My second 'Feta moment' in a month, but I didn't get a chance.

"And that's the famous Wallace, isn't it? He's just like you described him in the book, isn't he Darren?" he said to his friend. Then he pulled a mobile phone out of his pocket and took a photo of Wallace in the water, ignoring the two of us. Jim arched his brow at me in commiseration.

"How did you know it was us?" I asked him, though I knew the answer already.

"How many people have a crazy Jack Russell in Greece?"

If he thought Wallace, roaring about, chasing sticks in the sea, was crazy, he had seen nothing yet.

But it bothered me that Wallace could be 'famous' just for being recognisably crazy, in or out of the water. Or did Wallace perhaps play up to attention in a way I just didn't see?

We got home later in the afternoon and congratulated ourselves on keeping Wallace under control without him swimming all the way to Crete, but the following day he started shaking his head and sticking his paw in his ear. It was a sure sign he had an ear problem.

"Did you see Wallace stick his head in the water yesterday?" I asked Jim.

"I don't know. We were too busy talking with those lads from London…. you know something, you worry too much about Wallace. He's a dog, not a Ming vase."

"Ach, you know what his ears are like when they get wet."

I rang Angelos and explained the situation and told him I'd just run out of eardrops. I asked if it would be all right to come to his surgery in a few days and pick up another bottle. Or did he want us to come to his surgery immediately, which was no trifling matter as the drive to Kalamata took around an hour-and-a-half and it was especially tormenting in summer with so much more traffic on the 'Coronary Road'.

"Do not worry, Margarita, I will put a bottle of the eardrops on the Kalamata to Koroni bus this afternoon. The one that leaves at six o'clock."

"Is that possible?"

"Sure! We do it here all the time. When the bus gets to Koroni you will find the package in the baggage compartment. You ask the driver. Everyone does it."

That's what I loved about Greece, that things still operated on a human scale, pretty much as they had always done, which is why during the crisis there were so many ways around problems that were old and workable, like the fact that people without much money started bartering anything they had, whether it was food, olive oil or spare car parts, for other essential things.

That night we decided to go down to Koroni and wait for the bus, then have dinner afterwards. The bus was a bit late and many people were milling on the pavement. When it finally arrived next to the main *plateia*, the excitement level was palpable. The bus here was such a lifeline to people, especially those who no longer had cars because they had to mothball them during the crisis.

There was a great rush of people coming off. When the driver opened the baggage compartment at the side of the bus, passengers formed the usual rugby scrum, as queuing in an orderly fashion isn't written into Greek genes. We stood back a while and when there was a small window of calm between passengers leaving and those trying to load in their bags, I searched a slew of boxes and packages left on the compartment floor. There were other items as well with labels attached to them: a car tyre, a new kid's bike and, oddly, a toilet bowl. I riffled among the packages and finally spied a large padded envelope with *Kiria* (Madam) *Margarita McGinn* written in large letters. I was filled with excitement. My first bus package. The system worked.

People think that Greeks are disorganised, as well as impatient, and blame that for the economic situation getting out of control. Yet they are not the least bit disorganised – they only seem to be that way. No similar system could exist in Britain. If packages arrived on a bus somewhere in the

UK, more than likely they'd all be stolen. In Koroni, packages that are not collected for whatever reason are left at a local barber's shop. It's a system that everyone knows like the back of their hand.

We had dinner at one of our other favourite tavernas, Bogris, in a side street opposite the secondary school. It had a charming courtyard and was owned by a man called Dimitris, who had a small farmholding not far from our house. He had good English and we often chatted to him while he took our order. We were surprised to discover he owned the bolshy Rottweiler we'd encountered a few weeks earlier.

"He looks fierce," said Dimitris, "but Rex is not very brave really. The problem is he's always trying to escape and breaking from his chain." The family had another taverna near the supermarket and the dog was often tied up there or down on the farm, guarding a great big sow in a pen and a scattering of other farm animals. Many times after that we saw Dimitris on his motor scooter buzzing through the olive groves, calling for the dog.

We had developed a habit when we went to Koroni of having dinner and walking along the harbour front, filled with tavernas and bars, a couple of ouzeries, *kafeneia,* and we often stopped to talk to the same people each time. We had our favourite places and favourite characters and there was always an opportunity to practise Greek as well. One of our most entertaining stops was at an old tourist emporium, the likes of which you rarely see now outside of the flea markets of large cities, but this was so like shops I had visited in Athens in the 1970s, when I first lived in Greece.

Artemios, the owner, spoke good English and had a certain cynicism and mock chagrin about him that would have been irksome had he not had a good sense of humour and a candidness that was entertaining. I loved wandering around his shop, where every flat surface was heaving with souvenirs. They seemed to have changed little over the decades, or perhaps Artemios had them a long time. There was a collection of striped cheesecloth shirts that were popular back in the 1960s and 70s and kitsch T-shirts emblazoned with Greek gods and pithy sayings from Socrates.

"Haven't you got a T-shirt with Koroni on it?" I asked him.

"Sure," he said, rummaging about at the back of the shop, where T-shirts were squeezed in between snorkelling equipment, bikinis, racks of sunglasses and flip-flops. He pulled a T-shirt out of a plastic bag.

"You have to have this one," he said. It was black with Greek writing on the front. '*Eho barba stin Koroni*.'

"I have an uncle in Koroni," he said.

I pulled a face. "That's a strange saying. Something lost in translation perhaps?"

"No, no, it's famous in Greece. It means I have someone in Koroni who will help me. *Barbas* can mean uncle or a well-respected older man, like a godfather. You see, there is a famous story that during the Turkish occupation of Greece, the pasha in Tripoli was very grateful to someone in Koroni who had supported him during an upheaval and he made him a Bey (chieftain) of Koroni. When anyone here needed a favour, the Bey, or *barbas*, would write straight away to the pasha on their behalf and the problem would be solved."

I had never heard the expression before, but sometimes in Greece we are all desperately in need of a *barbas* – any *barbas* at all – who can instantly sweep away the latest disaster.

10

I should be souvlaki

GREEKS from ancient times have had a zest for life and feasting. The Athenian poet Eupolis once wrote:
"Nor fire, nor bronze, nor steel
Debars me from a meal."

They also have a passion for good local wine served in chilled metal containers that bead with condensation. Greeks probably invented wine, as archaeologists have found earthenware jars in 5,000-year-old palaces for storing oil and wine. But the Greeks have had nothing to do with the teetotal philosophy.

The poet and playwright Cratinus once said: *"A water-drinker can produce nothing clever."*

Add some music and dancing to this mix and a great helping of *parea*, company, and you have the thread that connects the ancients to the modern Greeks – and most of it revolves around the summer season.

There is something bewitching about high summer in Greece, when everyone is on holiday at the same time and children have an epic three-month break from school.

The summer zealot is an essential Greek who, no matter what life has thrown at him during the rest of the year, will embrace the joys of summer with an intensity that could light up the whole of downtown Athens.

It's infectious hedonism at its very best. It's also something that during the years of economic crisis brought condemnation from some foreign onlookers who don't understand the Greek psyche.

"How can they party in the summer when the country is on its knees?" Or they would chide the Greeks with a sarcastic "Crisis, what crisis?" as Jed the twitcher had once done.

Greeks answer this by saying that summer is their time, a chance to forget all the troubles that beset them: to swim, to camp out on the beach all day with their family and at night to gather together in large groups to enjoy company, simple food and wine. It's probably the healthiest attitude to life. It irks other people simply because they don't have the Greek ability to live properly in the moment and forget whatever else is going on around them.

I have always relished the sight of Greeks on a summer beach. It's something of a revelation. On Ayia Triada beach in August, we saw a family from one of the summer houses on the cliff top erect a marquee on the beach below, running a power cable from their house down the jagged cliff-face so they could have music and maybe run a few appliances as well, just inches away from the water's edge. It was a breathless two fingers up to health and safety. They stayed all day and put up a little brazier on the beach at night to barbecue their dinner.

Much of the exuberance of summer in Greece also takes place at the *paniyiria,* the feasts/fairs that are hosted by village groups all over the country and advertised on posters a few weeks ahead. These *paniyiria* are popular and cheap, featuring local or city musicians. If you want to see Greeks at their elemental and eccentric best, the *paniyiri* is the go-to event.

In August we decided to try one of the bigger *paniyiria* in the village of Chrisokeleria, on the eastern flank of the Mavrovouni hills near Koroni. It is a large working village, somewhat raw in parts, but free of the flanks of whitewashed holiday villas you see elsewhere in the region. This was a large *paniyiri,* which would attract people from all over the peninsula, and as far away as Kalamata, because Greeks love to spend summer going from one event to the next.

The local school was hosting the event, and its vast playground was lit up like a sports pitch. A band was warming up and the air was pinging with the sound of bouzoukis being tuned and singers testing the microphones. There was the usual crowd of swaggering gypsies you always see at these events, selling a slew of cheap Chinese-made toys, light sabres, and junk basically.

The school yard had rows and rows of trestle tables already heaving with punters, many huddled over white paper parcels filled with steaming roast meat, along with plastic containers of salad and bread and plastic cups of wine and beer. At the back of the yard, in one corner, a table had been set up to sell the *gourounopoulo*, which Greeks go mad for at this time of year. If you want to appreciate a *paniyiri*, you have to come to terms with *gourounopoulo*, a long word for what is basically spit-roasted piglet, the preparation of which is often done by any number of companies, who bring the cooked meat to the venue and arrange it on a special serving table you see everywhere in southern Greece, which comes with a plastic surround and a plastic hood.

I had always been intrigued by the plastic hood, which I imagined was there to keep the food warm and safe from flies after it had been cut. Never having been to a large *paniyiri* like this with catered roast pork, I was none the wiser until this particular event. There was nothing much else to eat here apart from the pork, so we decided try this 'speciality' for once.

Gourounopoulo is hugely popular in Messinia and the rest of southern Greece. Greeks here will tell you it goes back to the years of Turkish occupation in the region, when Greeks started to keep pigs in great numbers as the Turks were forbidden by their religion to eat it. But the animals had to be kept well out of sight. At one time it is said there were as many pigs in Messinia as people. A slight exaggeration perhaps, but whatever its history, the Messinians go mad for *gourounopoulo*. Perhaps it is also a nod to a nourishing food that in tougher times had saved their bacon.

We queued behind some Greek guys, who seemed not to be moving very quickly, although there wasn't that much meat left and the big plastic hood had been pushed back. I had no idea what the protocol was and the longer we stood around, the less appetising the whole thing seemed. After five minutes of waiting, I asked the man in front of me why no-one was moving forward to buy the remaining meat. He gave me a quizzical look and then tapped his nose. Meaning what? The meat was off? Several others in the queue turned to look, to see what the *xeni* woman was asking.

"We are waiting," said the man finally.

"Waiting for what?"

"There's freshly cooked *gourounopoulo* arriving shortly. You will see."

We didn't have to wait long because soon we heard the sound of a van rattling up the incline into the schoolyard and it parked beside the queue. The driver opened up the back of the van and lying on a sheet of plastic was a newly spit-roasted piglet, complete with head and legs. It was lifted out and laid out on the serving table, with the hood pulled over the top.

I could see the others in front of me licking their lips at the smell of the hot, greasy meat. We were not far from the van and couldn't help but peek inside. It looked like an ordinarily tradesman's van, with tools and various other bits and pieces further inside. It certainly wouldn't pass muster in the UK, but right at that moment we didn't care. The man in front whom I'd spoken to turned and gave me a meaningful look.

"This is what we were waiting for, not the old stuff."

The guy cutting the pig picked up a meat cleaver and hacked it into large pieces after chopping off its head first. Bits of meat and pork fat began to spray everywhere. I suddenly understood the role of the plastic sides and hood. Jim and I winced at each other. The idea of pork had lost its final shred of allure but we were hungry, as we hadn't had any dinner. Worse, I had no idea what to ask for, or how much. My Greek vocabulary didn't extend to butcher's cuts of meat. I started to feel panicky as others joined the queue behind us. The helpful man in front had picked up his substantial piece of pork and wandered off. When it was our turn, the guy serving asked how much I wanted. I looked at Jim and pulled a face. He shrugged back.

"*Ena mikro kommati*," I told the guy. A small piece.

"How small?" he said, shaking his meat cleaver. It glistened with fat.

I turned and looked at Jim again. He shrugged. An old man standing behind him offered a sympathetic smile.

"*Kiria*, ask for half a kilo. That should do."

So that's what I did and the server hacked the piece off and slapped it on some white greaseproof paper. It looked massive, with a thick wedge of fat and shiny skin covering it. I looked at the old man. He nodded his approval. Success. It reminded me how the simplest things in Greece can seem tormenting when you're not sure about the procedures or the language.

We picked up some bread and salad on the way and a couple of beers and wandered aimlessly, looking for a place to sit, until we found half a long table near the front with another couple seated at one end. They seemed to be Greek and had more or less finished their meal and were drinking beers. We made short work of our pork in its nest of paper, discarding the muffler of fat and skin. Even without it, I reckoned we'd eaten our whole day's ration of mortal lipids. The salad and bread were very welcome, and the cold beers. We binned the food wrappers and settled back to enjoy the *laiki*, popular music, and *rembetika*, Greek blues, with its iconic songs that everyone knew.

During a break in the music, the couple at the other end of the table became chatty, wanting to know where we were from, what we were doing in Greece, what we thought of the crisis and so forth. The woman spoke only Greek but the man spoke passable English, which he occasionally mangled but since he seemed intent on improving it, I let him rumble on. They were a genial pair, on holiday from Athens and staying at their beachside villa. The man was in business, but what kind I wasn't absolutely sure, as his explanation was lost on me. I had no doubt from their general demeanour and dress that the crisis had not affected them at all. The man, Adonis, had a confident, buoyant personality and gave the impression he was not fazed by very much.

At one point in the night, a young gypsy girl in a flamboyant red dress was skirting about the tables, selling single roses. She stopped beside Jim and me and implored us to buy one.

"No thanks," I told her, which was her cue to pull a face and unwind the polemics of misery that most gypsies in Greece have down to a fine art. I realised from her accent she wasn't Greek, however, but an Eastern European gypsy/migrant – not that it made any difference to me. In the end, I gave her a euro just to get rid of her, which seemed generous. Instead of leaving, however, she stood her ground, moaning more loudly about how I was ripping her off. She wanted more money. It was awkward and I was aware that people were turning around to watch this piece of impromptu entertainment. Adonis had been talking to his wife but suddenly lugged into the conversation.

"*Fiye!* Go away!" he bellowed at the girl. "You've got some money. This is a foreign woman here. Don't pester foreigners with your poxy roses." Or something to that effect. She scurried away. People kept staring and muttering, but no-one did so with a trace of disapproval at Adonis's outburst. Greeks are kind to a fault but they don't buy into the philosophy of political correctness. Rather, they say exactly what they think, and it's something that a Brit can take guilty pleasure in now and again because we no longer dare to be so bold in modern-day Britain. No matter how you feel about gypsies, there were times like this one when you were glad to have Greeks on your side to save you from an awkward situation. I thanked Adonis for helping out.

He shook his head sadly and told me in Greek, more for the benefit of the other listeners I thought: "I apologise for the rude behaviour of the gypsy girl. It is another aggravation we must deal with in Greece today, I am afraid." The others muttered in agreement.

But Adonis wasn't about to let the incident dampen his evening and decided to haul us up to dance.

"The Kalamatianos, my friends, you have to do this."

He ushered us over to the dance floor in front of the stage, where a large group of people were forming a circle. His wife stayed at the table to mind it. We had no choice but to join in. Adonis knew the dance well, as his family, he told us, originally came from Kalamata. He bounced along very nimbly, despite being a curious shape for a middle-aged Greek man, with a pot belly and spindly arms and legs. He looked like a set of bagpipes infused with Levantine spirit.

For years I had wanted to learn the Kalamatianos properly. During our time in the Mani, the dance had been shown to me by villagers in Megali Mantineia and once by Andreas and Marina's children, when we formed a chain and danced through the olive trees at an Easter Sunday lunch. But I still hadn't grasped all the steps.

It's quite a simple dance of the type called a Syrtos, which is always performed in a circle, but the Kalamatianos is slightly more lively and was named after the city of Kalamata it is said to have originated in, sometime in the 19th century. It is a dance with 12 steps moving anti-clockwise, and the sequence of steps is simple enough, with the left leg sometimes going behind the leading leg and sometimes in front. Just remembering when this happens can snarl you up. Jim and I were a blur of tangled legs and kept running into each other.

We stayed at the *paniyiri* until midnight, when the dancing became more intense and male-oriented, with some of the men getting up to perform the Zeibekiko, a solo dance originating in Turkey but now iconically Greek. It's a macho performance, with only one man allowed to dance at a time, and the steps are as wild and innovative as you like, with spectators crouching on the ground to clap and offer encouragement, or to throw rose petals or ripped-up serviettes. Once it was de rigueur to throw plates.

When I first went to Greece in the 1970s, I remember spirited dance sessions when plates were hurled around with terrifying abandon. I was once urged to throw a pile of plates in a Cretan taverna, and although I loathed the practice, I did it to please the people I was with. Fragments ricocheted around the dance floor and one small piece of shrapnel flew into the face of the man I was dancing with and gashed the bridge of his nose. It bled profusely and despite my fussing, he acted like a true Cretan *palikari* and didn't miss a beat with the dance.

Adonis also crept on to the dance floor to perform his Zeibekiko. We crouched on the ground, clapping our encouragement. His was a strange mournful creation – just one man and his dance floor, giving vent to his frustrations and hopes. But it later involved some curious manoeuvres: a slow corkscrew motion down to the ground and a wiggle of the bottom, like a pelican laying an egg. I don't think I'd seen anything quite like it and his wife scurried to the floor to clap her support as well, or perhaps wait for the arrival of warm eggs, I couldn't be sure.

We saw a few different men getting up in turn to strut their stuff: some danced with great gusto and athleticism, some just trailed over the floor with their arms out wide, like weary poltergeists lost in their own world. I thought, for the umpteenth time in my life, what an amazing place Greece was. If men danced like that on a British dance floor they'd probably end up being featured on TV's *Crimewatch*, victims of a fatal stabbing. But most of all, Greek men, when they dance, challenge the notion of what it means to be macho. In Greece, it doesn't mean being aggressive or vain, it means being free to express yourself in a manly way, however you like, without attracting ridicule.

As the dancing began to wind down, we bade the couple farewell and while there was talk of meeting up for a meal in Koroni one night, I didn't imagine we would. Even though we liked them, there was a feeling that this was a thing of the moment and it wouldn't translate into a lasting friendship. It had been fun though and we all hugged and wished each other well. Jim and I wandered back down to the car park as the pork men were packing up their trucks and gypsies were still flogging red roses and wind-up toys. It had been a great night but I couldn't help but wonder how much more vibrant and easy these *paniyiria* had been in years gone by, when life was more simple and less traumatic than it was these days.

11

A man needs a little madness

ONE September day we found ourselves in the shady garden of a white house overlooking the popular beach at Stoupa, in the Mani. Sitting at a large round table under the trees, we were being offered a unique window into the life of one of Greece's most famous writers, who had spent some of his early life in this region.

We were peering at a spread of newspaper clippings and memorabilia about Nikos Kazantzakis, who wrote the seminal book *The Life and Times of Alexis Zorbas*, translated into English as *Zorba the Greek*. The material belonged to a charming local woman, Maria Georgilea, whose family have lived in the area for many generations. It was an earlier member of her family who had helped Kazantzakis with accommodation when he came to the region in 1917 to run a lignite mine.

While Cretan-born Kazantzakis set his book on that island, it was his stay in the Mani and his escapades there that provided the storyline for the book. It charts the adventures of a rather effete intellectual who, nevertheless, goes to Crete to run a lignite mine with the larger-than-life character Zorba. It was the writer's real-life friendship with a man called Yiorgis Zorbas, who went to the Mani with Kazantzakis to be his mining foreman, that lit the creative spark for the book. Zorbas was the inspiration for the fictional character but he was no less charismatic and maverick than the original. Most of the locations in the book are also recognisably Maniot, not Cretan.

As a great admirer of the Zorba philosophy of living vibrantly in the moment, I jumped at the chance to meet up with Maria, a young woman we had briefly come across during our first years in the Mani through her villa rental company in Stoupa. Maria's family became quite close to Kazantzakis and Zorbas during their time in the Mani, and Zorbas had even become godfather to her grandfather, Georgis Exarchouleas. She has collected memorabilia about both men over the years and has many family stories to share about their friendship and escapades.

Kazantzakis came to Stoupa to oversee the running of the Prastova lignite mine, in the cliffs behind the village, parts of which are still in evidence. In the war years, the Greek government was offering incentives to mine lignite, a precious commodity. As a little-known writer at the time, Kazantzakis took up the job as a money-making exercise. It was a risky venture and back-breaking work that was doomed to failure for many reasons, all of which was spun into literary gold later on in Kazantzakis's 1946 novel, which similarly features a doomed mining operation. In reality, Yiorgis Zorbas oversaw most of the work and built the cable railway that took the lignite to a beach jetty in Stoupa, where it was transferred to Kalamata by boat.

After we perused Maria's collection of media cuttings, many of which spanned several decades, we set off for the beach at Kalogria to find the house, built in the late 19th century by Maria's great grandfather Andreas Exarchouleas, that was rented out to Zorbas, whereas Kazantzakis had chosen to be more bohemian, with a simple hut on the beach.

Kalogria, just north of Stoupa, is a small, sheltered cove with pale, sparkling water, enhanced by underwater springs that filter down from the Taygetos mountains. On the north side of the cove, on a rocky promontory, is a set of small white houses with red pitched roofs, one of which was rented by Zorbas.

Just below the front terrace of the house is a bank of rocks at the edge of the cove and a small but deep 'pool', with the spring water bubbling up from below. Called the Prinkipa, it is like a cold plunge pool and was a favourite bathing spot of both Zorbas and Kazantzakis in the summer. The writer's beach hut, or *'paranga'* as it was called, was built by the pair out of bamboo and bits of flotsam, though it is no longer in evidence.

Maria told us her grandfather Georgis, who remembered the shack as a young man, described it as being a very simple kind of structure, whitewashed on the inside, with nothing much apart from a table, chair and a straw-filled mattress. Among Maria's newspaper stories there is a great wealth of information about the writer's links with the Mani and many colourful quotes from locals. Kazantzakis was described as being rather disinterested in the lignite operation and left it up to Zorbas.

"Kazantzakis never worked (at the mine)," one local said in a story dating from 1987. "He stayed in his hut, reading, writing and researching." One other local said he could be tetchy and no-one dared to antagonise him, especially when he was writing. It is not clear if this complete delegation of duty to Zorbas was one of the reasons the mining operation eventually failed. But for Kazantzakis, the beach hut was at least the perfect place for creativity – and for studying the local women, according to one of the newspaper stories. It was said that Kazantzakis like to talk to the women who came to Prinkipa to collect water. They were often startled by the curiosity of this *'xenos'*, stranger, from Crete, and it prompted some of the local men to hide at the back of the cove and 'spy' on him, though in fact he only ever wanted to talk to the women about their lives and record their stories.

While a great deal is now known of Kazantzakis, particularly through his autobiographical book *Report to Greco*, very little is known about the real man behind Zorba, the character who has fired up generations of Greeks and has been one of the country's greatest role models, a kind of uncompromising *mangas*, the almost untranslatable word for a smart, swaggering but lovable rogue.

Born in northern Greece in 1867, Yiorgis Zorbas had worked in various countries as a miner before he took the job with Kazantzakis and went to the Mani, taking his wife and some of their eight children with him, though the family preferred to live in Kalamata.

After he finished at the mine each day, Zorbas, then in his fifties, and Kazantzakis, in his thirties, regularly decamped to the shoreline of Kalogria with their supper, often cooked for them by a member of the Exarchouleas family or by Zorbas himself. Over a few carafes of wine, Zorbas would play his bouzouki and sing. When Kazantzakis created the fictional Zorba he replaced the bouzouki with a santouri instead, which gave him a slightly more exotic edge.

It is reported that the pair were often fond of dancing along the shoreline and it is this habit that inspired the scene in *Zorba the Greek* where the protagonist, who Zorba only ever calls 'boss', is taught to dance the syrtaki.

When the film of the book was made in 1964, with a memorable score by Mikis Theodorakis, the dance scene became an iconic image, not only for the film but for the country as well. Zorba's dance is an eternal symbol of self-expression and defiance against conformity. Zorba's repeated message is that a man needs a little madness. In the book, Zorba tells the 'boss':

"You're on a long piece of string boss; you come and go, and think you're free, but you never cut the string in two...You need a touch of folly to do that..."

Yet few people until very recently have known about the link between the Mani and *Zorba the Greek* and its inspirational role. The reporter of the 1987 story made the point that no-one outside the Mani even knew that Kazantzakis had been there until 1955, when a local reporter arrived to do a travel piece and discovered the link. After the film was

A Man Needs A Little Madness

released, other journalists began to visit the area. In recent years, however, the link has once again faded.

Maria is one of the few locals who has retained an interest in this piece of literary history. She told us she was brought up hearing many of the outlandish stories, about Zorbas in particular, from her grandfather. She said Zorbas was a unique character and had been faithfully captured in Kazantzakis's book and that her family had for many years kept in touch with Zorbas's children, who remained in Kalamata even after he moved away and went to live near Skopje, in the former Yugoslav Republic of Macedonia, where he took another 'wife' and later died.

Maria says there was no doubt that Kazantzakis must have found the real Zorbas a liberating force. When he first arrived in the Mani, Kazantzakis was seen as a reclusive, complex character, while Zorbas was the complete opposite. In the book, Zorba was described as "a living heart ... a great brute soul", which would equally fit the real Zorbas. Yet Zorbas was clearly not all rough edges, as it was at a Mount Athos monastery in 1915, where Zorbas was once considering the priesthood, that he first came across Kazantzakis, who was visiting. They became friends and the rest is history.

In the Mani, the locals instantly took to Zorbas's antics, his bouzouki playing, his songs, his *kefi* (high spirits). Emboldened perhaps by Zorbas, the pair regularly visited nearby Stoupa, where their bohemian behaviour delighted and sometimes scandalised the locals and became the stuff of legend, much of which was recorded in Maria's newspaper cuttings. Locals were particularly enthralled by Kazantzakis's penchant for wearing Cretan-style baggy trousers. One local recalled that the children in Stoupa would follow the writer about, shouting after him: "*Vraka, vraka!*" Breeches, breeches!

Stoupa in those days was a small fishing village, with just a few tavernas and *kafeneia* on the seashore. The villagers had seen nothing like this pair of outsiders, or their visiting friends – a cast of international characters who descended on Kalogria beach for lively soirees and included famous Greek actors and intellectuals.

Kazantzakis and Zorbas left the Mani about a year-and-a-half after they arrived, and they rarely, if ever, met again. It was on hearing of Zorbas's death in 1941 that Kazantzakis was inspired to write *Zorba the Greek*. Yet it was in his autobiographical masterpiece *Report to Greco* that Kazantzakis confessed what Yiorgis Zorbas had meant to him. He says if he had only been able to choose just one spiritual guide or "guru" to inform his life, it would have been Zorbas.

At the end of our fascinating tour it was hard to look at Kalogria beach, even with a few dozen tourists in evidence, and visualise how this strip of sand and sparkling sea must once have been filled with song and raucous laughter. The beach hut is no longer there. It was dismantled in 1928 for firewood. Where it once stood, at the southern edge of the cove, is now overhung with trees.

Some of the locals I spoke to in Stoupa said they lamented the disappearance of great characters like Zorbas and that the Greek crisis and an overly oppressive EU had cut the Greek hero down to size. That may be so, but I believe the Zorba philosophy at least is very much alive in Greece and still has something to teach the rest of Europe. If nothing else, it reminds us that the Greek character is unique and cannot be shoehorned into a northern European template. It simply won't go. It was a ham-fisted strategy from the start. Greece has a different history, a different story. It is the least European country in Europe, still leaning gently towards its old Levantine influences, which makes it the exotic, appealing, often chaotic place it is. That's why the rest of the world loves it.

The need for the EU to dominate Greece's national character as well as its fiscal policies is a sign that it doesn't actually understand this essential difference between Greece and the rest of Europe – and probably never has. It would be more helpful to everyone if the head honchos of the EU gave up trying to change Greeks, became more Greek themselves and got in touch with their inner Zorba – kicking off their shoes, finding a beach and dancing on it!

These thoughts came to me forcibly while standing on the soft sand of Kalogria beach. Had there been no tourists there that day, I'm convinced I could have talked Jim into linking arms and giving the spirited syrtaki dance our best shot – up and down the shoreline. It would have to remain one of the things I had to do before I left the planet. Even better, I could even try the Kalamatianos as well.

@@@@@

We stayed the night near Kalogria beach in a studio apartment, where the owner was happy to accept Wallace, and drove back to Kalamata the next morning after what had been a fascinating return to the Mani. The route took us past the beach of Santova. From here it's a 10-minute drive up to the village of Megali Mantineia. We had been back to the village a couple of times during our stay in Koroni, for reunions with some of the villagers we had grown fond of in our first year, most especially Foteini. As we had some spare time that morning, we thought we could make a quick visit and perhaps see a few other people.

The Chrisanthi taverna, where we had spent so many evenings in our first few years, was shut. I imagined that the owners were in Kalamata at the huge *laiki* market, buying their week's fruit and vegetables. We drove further through the village and, oddly, there seemed to be almost no-one about. We could hear sonorous chanting coming from the main church and I guessed that a funeral or *mnimosino*, memorial service, was in progress. We drove right through the village and out the other side to Foteini's *ktima*. Her gates were padlocked and Riko the donkey was not in evidence, a sure sign she wasn't there either. We were disappointed but decided to head back to Koroni, which was a long drive via Kalamata, taking the infamous Calamitous Coronary Road.

The next day, I called Foteini and was lucky to get a reply first time. She told me most of the villagers had been in the church the previous day. It was a *mnimosino* for one of the old men, who had died a month earlier, aged 90.

"Come for coffee one day," she shouted down the phone. I told her as always it was a long way to go for a coffee when we'd just done a Mani trip.

"Why don't we meet one day in Kalamata?" I asked her.

Foteini went to Kalamata at least once every few weeks, sometimes on the bus, or sometimes dropped off there by one of the villagers. There was always someone going to Kalamata and villagers offered a ride to anyone who needed it.

"*Nai, endaksi koritsara mou*. Let's meet on Wednesday morning. I have to do some shopping and then we'll have a *kafedaki*."

"What kind of shopping?" I had visions of Foteini in shops, especially food stores, picking up loaves of bread and squeezing them, or sniffing cakes extravagantly, as was her habit. I was smiling at the very thought of it.

"*Kaltses*, socks, for the autumn."

Socks? I don't think I'd ever seen Foteini in socks, and rarely even in proper shoes, apart from in church. Most of the time she wore wellies.

"Is that all you want?"

"No, *koritsara mou*. What do you say we go and look for those soft harvesting gloves you once bought me? I can never find gloves like them." There was a slightly playful, wheedling edge to her voice that I knew very well.

Ah, the gloves! Foteini had a thing about harvesting gloves. Once we had picked up a pair for her in a hardware shop in Kalamata and she proclaimed them the best she'd ever had. Not rubbery all over, like so many harvesting gloves. These were made of strong cotton on their uppers, with rubbery grips only on the palms for gripping olive branches and stripping the cut branches of olives later. Foteini had around 200 trees to harvest every year and she went through a lot of gloves, doing the harvest the old-fashioned way, with a *katsoni* stick to smack the olives down on to a ground sheet.

We agreed to meet her on Wednesday morning by the Church of the Apostles in March 23rd Square, which took its name from the liberation of the city during the Greek War of Independence. This was a favourite meeting place in the historic centre of Kalamata. I had only ever been shopping with her properly, in the Mani once, at a small supermarket and the results were hilarious enough. But Kalamata!

I remembered one of our friends, Yiorgos from Megali Mantineia, warning me when I offered to take Foteini shopping in Kalamata. He told me in his engaging English, learnt from watching too many cowboy movies on TV: "You go craaaazy taking Foteini to shops. She takes you all over city. No buy. Complain, complain, complain! No buy. More complain. Drives man crazy!"

How crazy could it really be? I was about to find out.

12

Socks and the city

WE saw her from a distance at the doorway to the Church of the Apostles, waving an arm about and talking loudly and vibrantly with an old woman dressed in black, wearing a headscarf, which you rarely see in modern Kalamata any more. Foteini was also wearing black: a stout cardigan, despite a hot day, a patterned skirt ending at the knee and black ankle boots that seemed almost risqué on Foteini, who was more at home in wellies and mannish layers at her farm. She had a black handbag hooked over one arm and a tortoiseshell headband smoothing back her hair. She looked a vision of normality – almost.

Foteini's shopping had begun an hour before our meet-up apparently and she held open a canvas bag filled with disparate items to show us what had been on her wish list: freshly ground Greek coffee, a couple of goat bells, nails and headache tablets. While we peered inside, an old man in a battered linen jacket stopped beside us and stuck his head over the open bag for a good look inside, greatly amused by the contents, going "Hmmm" every now and then.

"Did you know him?" I asked her when he finally trundled off.

She shook her head emphatically. I laughed. Only in Greece can someone invade your space with such familiarity and make it seem perfectly ordinary.

Foteini hadn't had time for the socks yet, so our first task was to accompany her to a nearby shop. Like many stores in this historic sector, it was old and atmospheric and wouldn't have looked out of place in a Dickens novel. I found these kind of shops rather intriguing, as we no longer have them in most of Britain. They specialise in one thing only – shoes or hats, or buttons – and they have that one thing in every colour and style.

There used to be a shop a few streets away that sold worry beads and they were hung on narrow ledges down the windows, creating a kaleidoscope of colours and patterns. Despite its popularity, it was one of the shops that closed during the crisis, when people didn't even have enough money for a good worry.

This particular shop was crammed with socks of every kind, from plain to plain crazy, everything except the type Foteini wanted, which seemed unimaginable, as all she desired was a plain black wool, knee-high number. However, she wasn't going to budge on that choice.

The salesman was a short, middle-aged guy, with slightly bulbous brown eyes and a bald head. She called him Kostas and appeared to know him somewhat, as I expected she would because these shops in the old sector had been a part of its commercial life forever and she would have been going there all her life.

The shop had floor-to-ceiling shelves stacked with rows and rows of socks in all colours and sizes. Kostas had a stool near the ancient cash machine, and on the glass-topped counter was an empty *briki* on a brass tray with a small white cup, its rim crusted with cold coffee, and beside it a plate with the flaky remains of a sweet pastry.

Along the front of the counter he had assembled serried rows of dark socks in navies and browns, trying to persuade Foteini that despite not having her size in black, the others were just as attractive. I thought he'd be used to her by now but it transpired that she had previously dealt with his very old father, who had passed away, and the son was now at the helm. After 10 minutes of showing Foteini every dark sock he had, his head was beading with sweat.

"*Kiria*, if you don't want another colour, I am certain that black, in the next size up, 38, would be fine. Or you can wait until we have new stock in your size."

"Ach, I can't keep coming to Kalamata to look at socks. I need them today," she grizzled.

He held up a pair in size 38. She took them from him and held one up in each hand, twisting them this way and that in mid-air. She even sniffed their toes. This urge she had, to smell everything, always made me smile. Usually, it was confined to food. Now it was socks. I saw the man's left eyebrow twitch with curiosity as he watched her.

"Too big," she said at last.

The shopkeeper sighed and I tried to persuade Foteini to try them on at least, but she stubbornly refused. He darted a look in my direction and spoke for the first time in English, with a heavy accent, about the advantages of a bigger size, thinking perhaps I could still convince Foteini.

"*Kiria*, the sock, it shrinks after many washes in the machine. Please tell your dear friend it is better to have a bigger size," he told me.

"*Kiria* Foteini doesn't have a washing machine. She has a *kazani* (cauldron) at her *ktima*," I replied, knowing this would wind him up.

"I can well imagine it," he said, his eyes flickering shut for a moment and opening with a red tinge of fatigue.

"You don't have to talk in *xeni glossa* (a foreign language). Margarita speaks Greek, doesn't she," Foteini said with a proprietorial air, like a doting mother.

"*Liga*, some," I told him.

"And what's that you're saying, Margarita, about my *kazani*?"

The man shot me another look. "It's nothing, *Kiria*, don't worry yourself. Let's concentrate on the socks."

Jim had been standing on the other side of the shop, trying to listen and occasionally fiddling with his mobile phone. I could tell he was becoming very bored. He suddenly had that skewed look in his eyes that a cat gets when it's about to run up the length of an expensive sitting room curtain for no other reason than having something to do.

"I think I might go and search out those harvesting gloves Foteini wants. It will save time. The shop's not far from here, I seem to recall," Jim said, and bolted out of the door.

"Where's Dimitris going?" Foteini asked.

"Off to get the harvesting gloves."

"Ah," she said with a beatific smile.

"Can we return to the feet now," pleaded Kostas. "Let me see yours, *Kiria*. I am sure you are not a 36."

He came round to our side of the counter and peered long and hard at her ankle boots, probably thinking, much as I had, that they seemed incongruous with her rural matron persona, as she appeared that day. He asked if she could take one of the boots off. She seemed to be mouthing oaths silently as she huffed and puffed, bending over to undo a side zip and then handing over the boot, her face flushed with effort. He examined it, trying to find the size, but it must have been scuffed off long ago. He placed the boot on a metal measuring scale attached to one end of the counter.

"Yes, a 36, I am afraid," he sighed, returning it.

Foteini dropped it on the floor and a struggle recommenced to get it back on. As she did, I spied a diverting piece of repair work, a stitched hole on the big toe of her beige stocking done in white jagged stitches. It seemed not to worry her one bit but the shopkeeper looked slightly bemused.

"Why not try a patterned sock, *Kiria*, just for a change?"

"Like what?" she said, her eyes wide with disbelief, as if the very idea of patterned socks was almost delusional.

He turned back to the shelves, plucking specimens. Soon there would be nothing left. He laid them out before her on top of the others: diamond shapes, stripes in diverting colours, spots, one pair purple and black. She picked them up and snorted. He looked at me and winked. Was he having a laugh now?

"Do you expect me to wear these?" she said, waving the purple polka dots at him.

"Well, not to church, *Kiria*, but around the *ktima*, under another kind of boot perhaps? Who's to know?"

He turned around again and repeated the process, plucking specimens more forcefully. While his back was turned, Foteini gave me a squinty look and made a claw of her hand and twisted it back and forth beside her head, the Greek sign for 'bonkers', and spluttered with laughter. I also felt the faint twitch of a giggling fit start in my chest and fought it down with a cough.

The man turned and wiped his head with a handkerchief. "So, what have you decided?"

She stood for a moment, scraping her top teeth over her lower lip, making a small sucking noise. She was deep in thought, as if she were about to commit to some outrageously expensive purchase. Kostas sat down, his elbows on the top of the counter, observing Foteini over steepled hands, like a psychotherapist trying to get the measure of a patient's new and unaccountable vein of madness. I knew just how he felt.

Foteini's eyes paced the pile of socks in front of her, back and forth, until they finally alighted on something hovering on the edge. She grabbed them.

"Are these my size?" she said.

He checked them with a dubious look. "Yes, *Kiria*."

"I'll take them," she said, triumphantly.

"That will be five euros," he told her.

"Five euros for these?"

"All right, four for you, *Kiria*," he said quickly, keen no doubt to draw a line under this encounter.

"Hmmm," she said, as she turned her back on him and rummaged around in her handbag for her purse. It was a small leather square with a twisted metal fastener. Inside I could just glimpse small notes folded up like origami experiments – and probably bedded down in there with moths.

With her back still turned, he shook out the socks she'd chosen and held them up for me to see before dropping them on the counter. They were knee-length and patterned with small hairy sheep, like you might see in a woollen mill in the Scottish Highlands.

He made an extravagant gesture: drawing the corners of his mouth into a grimace while holding his arms out either side of his body, rigidly, with the palms facing outwards. It's the amusing Greek gesture that shows total surprise or disdain. In this case it seemed to say: "What the fuck! I never saw this coming. Did you?"

This time I started to laugh. I couldn't keep it in any longer. He smiled mischievously. Finally, Foteini handed him a folded five euro note and he gave her change along with the socks in a small bag.

"*Kaloforeto*," he said. "Wear them in happiness", which is commonly said in Greece when you buy an article of clothing. As she turned to leave, her canvas shopping bag collided with the glass-fronted counter and there was a jangle of goat bells from within it that seemed amusingly well-timed.

He winked at me and smiled, and with an exaggerated sigh he gathered up all the socks and started to put them away again.

When we got outside I was curious and asked her why she had picked those socks when she had been so set on black, but I knew the answer, of course. The sheep. Would this be the start of a new and dangerous dalliance with patterned socks?

The morning shopping was a success, especially when Jim caught up with us on the street, carrying another small package with the soft harvesting gloves she always craved.

"Last pair in your size, Foteini."

He'd remembered the size from the last time we bought her gloves. She clutched the package to her chest a moment and rammed it in her shopping bag, along with the socks.

"Is there anything else you need to buy now, Foteini?" I asked her.

She thought for a moment and glanced briefly in Jim's direction.

"I do need underwear. You know …" she whispered to me, tapping her chest.

I used the word for 'bra'. "Yes, exactly," she said blushing, as much as an olive tree can blush, or a combine harvester for that matter. Foteini generally didn't blush.

I had a panicky moment, wondering what it would be like helping her to buy a bra in a Kalamata underwear/lingerie shop, such as I had visited myself, where the assistants have none of the legal hang-ups we have in the UK and will barge into your cubicle when you're topless and tether you into a bra with force, as if you were being suited up for a parachute jump. But buying a bra for Foteini would be like crossing the old TV shows *Are You Being Served?* with *Worzel Gummidge*. *Sex and the City* it would never be.

And then I had a funny image of the manic fashionista character Carrie Bradshaw morphing into Foteini, dressed in a bra and tutu, fluttering down the road, pulling a tethered goat behind her. My head felt light. You get like that after being with Foteini for a while, but in the end I just laughed at the craziness of it all.

Foteini was one of the most intriguing people I had ever met. While she had a toughness, a resilience about her, it was overlaid with innocence and, of course, a liberal dousing of craziness. When you were with her, you felt it sprinkle you like olive pollen in the wind.

"We don't have time for bras, I think. Another day, what do you say, Foteini?" I said briskly, pulling her down the road towards the square. "Let's have lunch. I'm starving!" I steered her towards a favourite lunch spot and suddenly bras were forgotten.

I suspected Foteini would be ravenous as well, having been up since about 6am. The minute we got near our favourite *yiros* shop in the square I could see her nose quivering. This was a tiny place beside the landmark Church of the Apostles and Archaeological Museum. It was no more than a kitchen with two serving hatches, run by a guy called Jimmy, who had spent some time in America. It was a favourite, lively meet-up place, with a couple of chairs and tables at the front, and the food was always delicious. We were lucky to get the last table.

We ordered three *yiros* with everything on it: meat slices, cucumber dip, tomato, onions and a couple of chips all wrapped up in warm pitta bread and encased in greaseproof paper. Street food at its best.

We sat for a while enjoying the stream of life passing in the square: Greeks hurrying home for lunch; priests from the nearby cathedral walking in groups, their black robes flapping like crows' wings; hawkers with their cheap cloned designer wear.

We had just finished our lunch when a man ambled past us, turned back and approached our table with a bemused look. He was one of the Greeks who lived in Megali Mantineia, part-time.

"What is this?" he said in English, with great emphasis. "The Three Musketeers."

We had met Neophitos a few times when we lived in the village and I had always considered him to be rather brusque for a Greek and not very popular. It was hard to say why. Perhaps the other Greeks viewed this 'interloper', originally from Athens, as another 'foreign' eccentric, as he left his wife and children each year in Germany, where he now lived, and spent part of the year alone in Greece, building a summer house on a hillside.

A Scorpion In The Lemon Tree

He had seen us with Foteini at her *ktima* a few times and had always seemed bemused by our friendship, perhaps even a little condescending.

"Why do you spend so much time with Foteini? What could you possibly have to talk about?" he once asked.

Yet he had never taken much time to talk to her, or relate to many of the village farmers for that matter. Despite that, he always seemed to know everything that was going on there, unless it was by some severe form of osmosis.

He drew up a chair and asked if he could sit for a moment, and it was hard to refuse when he ordered Greek coffee for all of us. Foteini bristled. I could tell she didn't much care for him, and neither did I. Although he had good English, he spoke in Greek for Foteini's benefit, and slowly, for mine.

"Have you heard the news from the village?" he asked, directing the question to me. "The body of an old woman was discovered under her house a few days ago."

Foteini looked away and frowned. All hilarity had just gone out of the day. He assumed that Foteini knew what he was talking about and concentrated on us.

"This is a very strange case, my friends. Just a few days before the body was found, the woman's daughter, who also lived in the house, had tried to kill herself. She was taken to Kalamata Hospital, treated, and then sent home again. But why did she try to kill herself? Guilt. Did she perhaps cause the death of the mother?"

Foteini gasped. Unusually, she was a villager who didn't much care for gossip, especially this kind.

"The villagers had been saying for weeks that things were very strange in that family. Perhaps you've heard all this before, *Kiria* Foteini?"

She shook her head.

"The neighbours said they hadn't seen the old mother for many weeks. There were suspicions. And then the attempted suicide of the daughter. When the police came to investigate, sure enough they found the body of the mother wrapped in an eiderdown in a space under the house that had recently been covered over. It looks like a murder, doesn't it?"

"Pah!" said Foteini finally, giving him an angry look. Like many villagers, she didn't like to talk about death – anyone's death.

"Do you think that's why the place was so quiet when we were there on Saturday?" I said to Jim.

"Perhaps. Obviously a lot of people knew something was amiss."

"It's quite a terrible thing for the village," Neophitos said, looking at Foteini under his slightly crinkled brow.

She sipped at her Greek coffee, a little moustache of froth playing over her top lip.

"I know who these people are you speak of and they are not from the village. They come from somewhere near Athens – your city," she said, waving her hand dismissively towards him. Now it was his turn to bristle.

"They may not be villagers, but it is still a frightful circumstance. Don't you agree, my friends? There seems no other plausible explanation, apart from the daughter murdering the poor old woman, when you put all the villagers' suspicions together."

"Why would the daughter do that? It doesn't seem very Greek, does it?" I said.

He shrugged. "We Greeks are capable of the same barbarities as anyone else."

One thing that seemed clear about Neophitos was that his life abroad had made him less tolerant of his countrymen, especially during the crisis, which was probably why he was a loner in the village. He often railed against the 'Greek way' of doing everything, about the crisis, bureaucracy and the time it was taking him to complete his house. Some of this was true, but the villagers didn't appreciate hearing it from this *xenos*, outsider.

"The daughter has now been taken away for psychiatric evaluation and I imagine the police will easily charge her with murder."

After having brought down our mood entirely, he finished his coffee and announced he was leaving. When he was well out of sight, Foteini made a windmill of her arm and swung it around several times, in the Greek manner.

"*Paraksenos anthropos*," she said. Strange man.

We paid and left, walking to the Apostles Church nearby. Foteini had arranged to meet one of her farming friends from the village for a lift back and I marvelled at how organised she really was, and how the rural network could be relied on for help on a daily basis. I was relieved that we didn't have to drive her back to the village, as it would have added at least another hour to our journey home.

In the church, Foteini lit some candles in front of one of the icons, as if she needed to purge herself of the previous discussion. Before we left I gave her a hug.

"Did you enjoy your shopping?"

"Oh yes, *Margarita mou*. We'll do it again, shall we? I still have to buy some…" She touched her chest. I knew what that meant, but I was in no hurry to bring chaos to the lingerie shops of Kalamata.

⦿⦿⦿⦿⦿

A few weeks later, we discovered what the body under the house was all about from a story in one of Kalamata's oldest newspapers, the *Tharros*. It was indeed a tragic story, but not at all what Neophitos had suspected, and the culprit turned out to be the economic crisis.

There had been no suspicious circumstances, no matricide at least. It transpired that the mother had been very ill in the summer and was taken to Kalamata Hospital by the daughter who, the story claimed, had been devoted to her mother.

After the hospital visit, the pair returned home in a taxi. Some days later, the poor woman died naturally and the daughter panicked, realising that her mother's public sector pension would now be stopped, which was all the pair had been living on for years. The unmarried, unemployed daughter now had no income at all, so in desperation she decided to 'bury' her mother and keep drawing on her pension. She wrapped her mother up tightly in the eiderdown, squeezed her through a space under the house and later covered the opening. The body had lain there for some weeks, undetected.

In this close-knit community, questions had been asked about the sudden disappearance of the mother, and it emerged during the investigation that the daughter had made up elaborate stories to keep the neighbours quiet. She told them finally the mother had gone to Athens for specialist treatment and had died there. But it was the daughter's erratic behaviour and her attempted suicide that prompted them to call the police.

The story was macabre and disturbing in such a remote and traditional setting and caused some distress among the locals for months, not to mention embarrassment. They wanted to distance themselves from the incident and the daughter, who was never charged with any offence but sent to a psychiatric hospital.

One day I saw one of the elders of the village in Kalamata and we spoke about the incident.

"The two women were not villagers. We would not behave in such a way," he said, his amber worry beads trickling anxiously through his fingers.

"But the daughter was desperate, with nothing to live on," I said, hoping not to offend him.

"Yes, that is true. So we should blame the crisis. This is what people are driven to now in Greece."

13

Pear group pressure

WE were sitting in the outside 'cabin' of the Parthenon restaurant one late September morning, drinking coffee and enjoying some of Oreanthi's homemade cake. The sides of the cabin were rolled up on this warm autumn day and ripples of water were fizzing gently against the harbour wall below. Schools of fish were feeding on the bread that diners were throwing into the water. People were buzzing past on motor scooters.

We had been in Koroni for six months and had discussed whether we should stay for the winter or not, as the place had really grown on us. We hadn't ruled out the possibility of checking out some bargain houses, with a view to buying something. The cooler, less frenetic days of winter would be good for this undertaking. For the moment we were content to stretch out our existence from day to day without making too many plans, which was precisely what we had done in the Mani, and why one year had easily stretched to three.

While we sat by the water, enjoying the morning sun, a pick-up truck clattered past with a set of scales in the back, swinging from a wooden post. It pulled up in the car park in front of the high school. There were a few regular hawkers who came here on different days. This one had boxes of fruit and vegetables in the back and it took the *manavis* a minute to set up his operation.

Jim decided to stroll across and buy some fruit, while I finished my coffee. I watched as he engaged the *manavis* in some diverting conversation and I guessed he was trying out his Greek. Jim had put a Herculean effort into his Greek but he struggles with languages. His French is slightly better, having done an exchange programme through his English school as a teenager. He was sent to a school near Paris for eight weeks, where he learnt to swear like a wharf worker and smoke Gauloise cigarettes and drink Pernod with reckless abandon. Jim was never destined to be a polyglot, a word deriving from the Greek, of course: *polyglottos*, many tongues/languages. To Jim's way of thinking, a polyglot is a kind of DIY wood filler.

As I watched Jim toying with fruits, I saw the *manavis* break into a hearty gust of laughter with a sandpaper edge from a 40-a-day habit. He was laughing so much he seemed to have grabbed himself around the crotch, which seemed rather peculiar. I was intrigued, as were several other passers-by, who stopped to stare at the unusual hysterics over fruit and veg. When Jim finally ambled back again, carrying a brown paper bag, I noticed he was looking flushed.

"What was all the laughing about?"

"Margarita, why do I bother trying to speak Greek?" he said, sitting down with his bag of fruit perched on the table. "I've just asked the guy over there for a bag of testicles. Talk about a language balls-up!"

I stared at him in confusion – and burst into laughter.

"Okay, okay, I get the point," said Jim with a grimace.

"So that's what that little scene was all about," I said, smirking and opening his brown paper bag to check out the fruit for good measure. "I've got it now. You got your testicles, *archidia,* somehow muddled up with pears, *achladia*. Easy to do, I guess. Too many vowels as usual."

"Well ... that's what the guy was explaining as best he could about pears and testicles, grabbing himself by the balls. I suppose you saw that."

"Oh yes, we all saw that! That would really have made his day."

When I looked over at the *manavis* he was still laughing.

"That little joke will go all round Messinia now," said Jim, with a long face.

Oreanthi came over to bring us the bill and asked what the *manavis* was laughing about. She spoke very good English and I explained about Jim's language mix-up. She laughed as well, tapping him sympathetically on the back.

"Don't worry, Jim. We make mistakes with our Greek as well."

"You're just trying to make me feel better."

"We do! It is a hard language. Too many words. Too much grammar. Ach!"

She stood with her hands on her hips a moment, deep in thought.

"You know, I remember now there may be some free classes starting soon in Koroni for beginners' Greek."

She told us about a Dutchman called John, who lived near the castle. She was sure he knew more about the classes. We had met John earlier in the summer – a gentle guy who had come to Greece to retire, to get away from the cold and the overcrowding of Holland. He was brave, I thought, coming alone and renting a house. He had dived into Greek life by trying out olive harvesting and had signed up for the language classes. We had his email address and decided to contact him.

There was a certain Grecian irony in all of this because during the summer we had heard from other sources some vague news about classes organised by the *dimos*, council, in Koroni. We had gone to the council building near the harbour to check it out. It was one of those local government set-ups, where employees seem to sit around doing not very much but looking sour and resentful. Not hard to understand when there had been so many cuts to jobs and wages during the crisis.

When we asked about the classes there was lots of shoulder shrugging and dark looks. We were told there was no local money for language classes for *xenoi*, as there had been in the past. The mere idea of spending money to help foreigners probably seemed an alien one to them. Yet when we contacted John he told us there were indeed classes due to start at Koroni primary school, near the castle, in the autumn. They weren't *dimos* classes but the fact the local office knew nothing about them showed the kind of bureaucratic sink holes that are common in Greece. As it happened, the classes were to be run by the Ministry of Education, with funding from the EU. It proved that nothing is ever a sure thing in Greece until you see it with your own eyes.

After our coffee at the Parthenon, we took our regular tour of the town, which had become something of a habit, walking up the *paralia* road first and visiting our friend Artemios in his tourist shop. He always had something to say about the state of the nation, though increasingly over the summer he had become petulant about the pressures on small businesses due to new EU rules, taxes and austerity. He said he was tired of working 12 hours a day, seven days a week, and having to deal with the whims of tourists.

In late August, with the town full of tourists and the temperatures at night still unbearably hot, Artemios had a spectacular strop when a Jeep on the *paralia* knocked one of his tall newspaper stands into the road. The driver, probably a foreigner, didn't stop. Artemios went to retrieve the stand but in a fit of temper started to kick it all over the street. We had been driving two or three cars behind the Jeep and saw the whole scene unfold: the stand splayed across the road and poor Artemios kicking newspapers. There have been times in my life when I've wanted to do the same. It was clear, however, that Artemios was at the end of his tether and a few other shopkeepers eventually ran over to help him. It had all been unnerving, but not surprising under the circumstances.

We found him that particular day perched on a stool in front of his glass-top display of jewellery. He never seemed to have recovered from his summer strop and remarked at regular intervals that this would be his last season.

"I am tired of working this hard and for what, to give most of my money to the government in taxes? And tourists now, even wealthy ones, want to haggle over silly little prices. I suppose they think in a crisis we will take anything they offer. You can't imagine how anyone can see an object for just a euro and want to cut it down to 50 lepta (half a euro). How can I make a living if I cut everything by half?" he said, slapping a palm on his forehead with exasperation.

While we were talking, a few tourists ambled into the shop, lingering over one table with its myriad small keepsakes: miniature Greek churches, caiques, mythological figures. There must have been a hundred objects there. I could see Artemios's eyes darting to the table to make sure nothing was lifted.

"Oh, yes," he said, lowering his voice to a whisper, "that's a problem too."

"You have too much stuff in the shop," I told him. "Why not cut it down a bit and make more of certain things, like all your wonderful old Greek jewellery, or your T-shirt collection." But it fell on deaf ears. He liked the shop cluttered.

We made some small talk and he asked if we were staying for the winter.

"We'd like to. We haven't absolutely decided yet," I told him.

He seemed puzzled. "Why not? You like it here. What is there to think about? Just stay."

It was something that people said a lot. As if life were that simple. Maybe life is. And I wished it were, too.

"You have to learn more Greek if you want to stay. I know Margarita has some, but Jim must learn too."

That was my cue to tell him about Jim's testicles gaffe. He laughed heartily. But I was reminded too that English pronunciation is also open to serious pitfalls when we started a conversation about Koroni and how it had changed over the years.

"Everything is different now," he said. "We no longer have droggies in the town."

Jim and I looked at each other. "Droggies?" I asked him. "You mean people who take drugs?" That seemed like a change for the better at least.

"Drugs? What are you saying, Margarita? I mean droggies, don't you know. Things that go 'heee haw!'"

"Ah, you mean donkeys," said Jim.

"Of course that's what I mean," he said, giving us a very odd look.

We said farewell and dipped in and out of other stores, ending up at the family shop of Stavroula's family, run by her charming father, Anastasios. It had once been an *oinopoleio*, selling wine and other groceries. It was like a snapshot of the past, with hessian bags of beans and rice on the floor and old wine kegs fixed to the back wall, now purely decorative.

There was a friend there that day, sitting opposite at the wooden table at the back of the shop. The friend was a middle-aged Greek. The pair had been talking about the Second World War, as Greeks often do, and the Battle of Kalamata in 1941, when retreating British, New Zealand and Australian troops launched a last-ditch rearguard bid to save the city from German invasion. They were finally overpowered by the Nazis and many surviving allies were taken to prisoner of war camps, although thousands were evacuated by British ships waiting offshore. Anastasios told his friend we were British.

The man suddenly looked rather emotional. "So many of you died in the battle, trying to help the Greeks. That means a lot to us, you know. You all made sacrifices to help us."

Then he did something unexpected. Tears started to trickle down his cheeks and he could no longer speak, his lower lip trembling. We stood beside the two men, saying nothing. Anastasios later told us that many people in this part of Greece still became emotional about the war, even though they were never in it themselves.

There are many stories of bravery on the part of local Greeks, who made sacrifices to help the allies to escape from the Germans. The story of the famous human rights lawyer George Bizos, who became an anti-apartheid campaigner in South Africa, is prominent. Now aged 90, Bizos was born in the village of Vasilitsi, a few miles from Koroni. His father, Antonios, was a well-respected mayor in the village and like many Greeks at that time rallied to assist the allies, no matter what the cost. When he heard about seven New Zealand soldiers hiding in the fields south of the village after retreating from Kalamata, he decided to meet up with them.

In Bizos's memoir *Odyssey to Freedom*, he describes how his father had heroically decided to help these men to escape to Crete, even though by doing so he had been warned there would be German reprisals against him and the family. Bizos's father decided it would be safer for everyone if he left with the soldiers. His son George, then 13, persuaded the family to let him go as well. A friend managed to secure a permit for a boat from Koroni and they left with the New Zealanders. After three days, drifting off-course, their boat was discovered by a British destroyer on the way to the Battle of Crete. The men were all transferred to Egypt, as Crete was about to fall to the Germans.

Later, as refugees, George and his father settled in South Africa, where the rest of the family joined them in the 1950s. It was here that Bizos pursued his distinguished legal career, famously defending Nelson Mandela at the Rivonia Trial in 1963, where he received his life sentence, though it is claimed that Bizos's brilliant defence saved Mandela from the death penalty.

14

Things get worse before they get Feta

BY the end of October, we started to think seriously about staying the winter, as we had no urge to pack up and leave. However, we accepted that it would be in Koroni and that the plan for the Mani would finally have to be forgotten. Yet the longer we stayed in Koroni, the more we liked it, especially the location of the villas overlooking the gulf. It was a dreamy spot, a haven of tranquillity, but no less appealing in autumn, with its changeable weather and big dramatic skies.

We had the same conversations here that we'd had in the Mani, while bobbing around in the clear and still-warm waters of the gulf. "What if we could stay a bit longer. Another winter. Another summer. Another year, perhaps."

"Ach, let's just stay forever," I said to Jim, while we were having the 'should we stay or go' conversation.

It was a fantasy with a shard of possibility glistening within because we had sold up in Scotland and had put all our possessions in storage. For two nomads who had criss-crossed the globe together for 20 years, mostly between the UK and Australia, this was the most untethered we were ever likely to be, without a home, with jobs we could now do anywhere, as long as we had an internet connection. In terms of staying in Greece, it was tempting, even though the economic crisis continued to make the future perilously uncertain, with unknown taxes ahead that would impact on buying property. Then there was the constant threat of the country defaulting on its loans at some point in the future, with the ensuing chaos that would cause.

Many Greeks also told us, though, that this was a good time to find a modest, bargain property. We had enough contacts and friends who had houses to sell or knew others who did as well. Many people struggled to offload homes they had no money to renovate, properties often left by deceased family members or friends, but which came with a considerable tax bill for those who inherited them. Buying a house was something that for now we kept in the back of our minds as a possibility.

Once we finally decided to stay the winter, we knew we couldn't remain in *Palio Spiti*. We may have grown used to its tiny, grumpy space, its small windows and critter visitations, but we had no desire to spend winter in it. It would be cold and dark and probably the 'mouses' would return. We told Stavroula of our plan to stay another six months or so. Naturally, she was pleased, but not so much when we told her we didn't want the old house. We suggested Villa Anemos, as we imagined there would be few bookings from now on. Stavroula had always been easy-going about the villa rentals and agreed the old house was an unknown quantity for the winter. No-one had stayed a winter for several years.

So it was decided we would move over to Villa Anemos in late November. We were inwardly jubilant that finally we were getting the place we had coveted from the beginning. But we had to get through two weeks of a German couple staying at the villa with their daughters, one of whom was loud and angsty and prone to strops, especially in our vegetable garden, stomping around the newly planted baby cabbages and broccoli. It was almost rather funny. I didn't imagine when we came for another Greek odyssey that we would be obsessing over baby veg.

It had been a curious experience living beside Villa Anemos, with its endless troop of tourists from all over

Europe, with their incomprehensible gabbling on balconies, shouting down mobiles to Stockholm or Berlin. We'd had one couple with a guitar-playing teenager who sang and played naff Eurovision ditties at the open window at night.

At least there was one Greek couple, rather colourful and extrovert, the man a TV director who always wore a black beret and appeared from behind bushes with a small video camera always turned on, in the hope of catching people, any people really, doing interesting, daft things. You feared where his video grabs might turn up. No doubt there was secret footage of Wallace acting like the maddest dog he'd ever seen. There was one couple from Ireland, who arrived in high summer with skin the colour of snow. They spent every spare minute on the front balcony in sun loungers, soaking up the sun, and left two weeks later resembling smoked mackerels.

There were visitors who were annoying, who would bang on the front door, imagining perhaps that we were dotty caretakers with a 'guard' dog, wanting to know why the water wasn't on, or why the washing machine didn't work, or the wi-fi, especially, or where Yiannis was. Even though most tourists were out most of the time, it was curious living your life beside this stream of humanity, with their foibles and their whims, speaking languages we didn't understand. We wouldn't miss it much.

While we waited to move in November we spent a lot of our spare time swimming at Ayia Triada, or other nearby beaches, with almost no-one else around but with the weather still gloriously warm. It was during these moments that we relished our good fortune in being able to have this second, long odyssey in Greece at all. We had become more adept at living in the moment and our enthusiasm for the country would always override the negatives.

When we finally moved into Villa Anemos, it felt like we had been spirited back into the modern world, to luxury living, which was daft because in essence it was just a very nice but simple kind of holiday villa. Yet the clean kitchen and American-style fridge were especially welcome. And it seemed near critter-proof, with huge double-glazed sliding glass doors opening on to the front balcony, with a thick roll-up metal shutter in front.

Compared to the old house, it was perfect, and whatever the villa lacked, its forté was the view, with the uninterrupted aspect of the gulf and the Taygetos Mountains ahead of us, which changed colour all day long, depending on the weather. And in front of all this were the olive groves, where small brown owls perched at night and every morning a flock of white doves would fly around in formation.

I quickly established a new study right in front of the glass doors. I set up my *kafeneio* table from the old house for my laptop. It was the perfect spot to finish off the second book, which covered our last two years in the Mani peninsula in 2011 and 2012. Although I wasn't writing it in the Mani, ironically I had the best view of it from a distance and never more so than at daybreak, when the sun rose over the mountains and ascended the sky in a blaze of colour.

Jim had taken over the kitchen table to work on his editing projects, so we could both share the view, and the oil heater, which was the best source of reliable heating in the house. We spent our days and nights, when we were at home, working and talking, discussing our respective endeavours. We had never felt happier with so little. Life was pared down to a minimum, without the distractions of the outside world. It felt slightly monastic, apart from the Greek music we often played, or the TV, which we watched mainly for the news, to keep up our Greek language practice.

Often I would write while the TV was on, when Jim was watching a certain programme. I'm one of those writers who can operate almost anywhere after years of working in noisy newspaper offices, especially on Sydney papers, where Jim and I had first met. Journalists would regularly have hysterical slanging matches as the deadline drew near, swearing and sometimes threatening to kill each other, as Aussies are lively and given to expressing themselves wherever they are, and work places were much less rule-bound than Britain.

I had seen all manner of human foibles played out on Sydney newspapers, including one memorable day in the 1980s when a hot-headed feature writer was asked to rewrite his copy and went into meltdown, picking up his typewriter and hurling it through an open window on to the pavement below, where it smashed into bits, narrowly avoiding a few pedestrians. Unsurprisingly, he was sacked and spent a few weeks in therapy.

But while I can shut out noise most of the time, I had discovered, especially in Greece, that inspirational thing: 'the room with a view'. The view I'd had in the summer in *Palio Spiti* was soothing – olive groves and an almond tree, home to colourful birds – but not enough to dampen the pain of writing a book in temperatures soaring to the high 30s and beyond. But this view was like no other.

On the odd occasions, writing the second memoir, when words and ideas seemed to be shunted up a siding somewhere and irretrievable, I would sit and stare at the ever-changing view. Apart from the height of summer in Greece, when the sky is indelibly blue for months on end, there is normally such drama in the Greek sky and the landscape; big movements and shifts of colour, winds changing direction all day long.

Here on this far-flung peninsula there was always something to watch and admire: caiques chugging in and out of Koroni harbour, or flocks of birds wheeling over the water, and fighter planes in practice manoeuvres over the small uninhabited islands at this southern tip. There were also big, luscious storm clouds rolling in from the Ionian Sea and sometimes multiple forks of lightning.

The scenes were always enervating and inspirational, and if my mind hit the buffers sometimes, it didn't last long. I had some of my most contented writing moments at Villa Anemos. But if there's one thing in life I have learnt it's this: just when you think you have cleared the top of a peak, you realise there are more in the distance that have hitherto been out of sight. Whenever you say 'life is sweet' some Olympian ne'er-do-well above drops an anvil on your head. A month or so after we moved into the new villa, I encountered a problem that I didn't see coming, though there were intimations of it earlier in the year. It was the kind of problem that wouldn't be easy to deal with from Greece either. It was all to do with my first memoir, *Things Can Only Get Feta*.

It had really started in October when I noticed that the paperback version of the book, which had been selling well, was slowly running out of stock on Amazon, still an international indicator of a book's general success, or not. It wasn't completely unexpected, as my publisher Sir Ambrose had told me months earlier the book would soon be sold out and was due for a reprint. Good news, ordinarily, even though my queries about when the reprint would happen were never answered. And now here was the book, its numbers dwindling, with increasingly alarming messages on the book's Amazon page as to the status of the stock, and the number of weeks that customers would have to wait becoming longer and longer. Finally, there was a note on the page saying the book was 'temporarily unavailable', and with Christmas on the horizon that was bad news for sales.

I sent several emails to Sir Ambrose about this issue and was finally assured the book was on the verge of being reprinted. Yet a few weeks later, the status on Amazon remained the same. The other alarming fact was that my April royalties were now long overdue. Several emails on that score had brought promises to address the oversight, but no statement or money was forthcoming. I had now reached the second royalty period of the year as well. By late November, I found myself in the troubling position of having no paperback and no money. Eventually, I was forced to call Sir Ambrose at his London office. The mobile reception was poor but I could certainly pick up the discernable flapping at the other end when he realised it was me.

"Ah! You're wanting your *royalty* payments," he said, rather majestically, as if the notion of a writer wanting to be paid for their creative work was an alien concept, and bothersome to boot.

Sadly, this wasn't the first time we were having this problem. When he had failed to pay my first royalties on time in December 2013, six months after the book was published, there had been promises to rectify matters, and then broken promises, until a final stern threat to take some legal action finally brought a payment, but only at the last moment before Jim and I were due to leave Scotland for Greece, in 2014. It had soured the relationship for me, and so early in my book publishing career. Yet here I was in the same position again, dreading more useless communications and feuding for something that was my contractual right.

This particular (expensive) phone call to London, however, was even more vexatious, as I no longer trusted the man. Worse, there were rather ridiculous attempts to sound contrite.

"It's all *my* fault!" he whined in histrionic fashion, at least admitting that he had been hugely inefficient. If it hadn't been so frustrating, it would have been laughable.

Before I hung up, I was assured the royalty statement and payment would be organised as soon as possible and that paperbacks would be in the distribution warehouse in a week or so. It put a new spin on the old expression "the cheque's in the mail". However, two weeks after the phone call, and despite a written demand for him to fulfil his obligations, there was still neither money in the bank nor books in the warehouse. The books, under his imprint, would never eventuate.

Despite having some august scribblers in his list, and a couple who were reasonably well-known, it seemed he had a serious cash-flow problem. Indeed, one of his authors told me that this was not the first time Sir Ambrose had "got into a pickle" with his finances.

However, it was a problem I didn't need in Greece, where phoning on a mobile to the UK from a Greek hillside was as difficult as it was costly, with calls frequently breaking up mid-sentence. All the same, after weeks of prevarication from Sir Ambrose, I decided to seek advice from the Society of Authors in London, which I had earlier joined, and was advised on the procedure for getting the rights of the book back under the terms of my contract. It meant that, with several mandatory steps, if payment wasn't finally received by a certain date, the rights would automatically revert to me.

I could see no other way of proceeding, despite the fact that I didn't know exactly what I would do with the book once I had the rights back. But that was another matter. I had no choice but to push on and stop the book from freefalling. As every writer knows, a book takes up a huge chunk of your life and your thoughts while you're writing it, and for years afterwards. It's an infant that you've nourished against all odds and there's absolutely no point in writing one just to let it perish. Such were my thoughts at that time when, with a heavy heart, I faced Christmas in Greece writing letters to Sir Ambrose that I knew he wouldn't respond to. It would prove to be one of the most disappointing and vexatious experiences of my life, and so ironic that it was playing out in Greece, the place that had inspired *Things Can Only Get Feta*.

In December, I made contact with a delightful Spanish author, who also had a book published with Sir Ambrose and was one of several people who were now owed money. As fate would have it, she had just bought a house in southern Greece and had contacted me with the suggestion we meet one day in Kalamata to discuss the situation.

Jim and I met her in one of our favourite tavernas, the Argo, near Kalamata marina, where we had been going for years and where the chief waiter Adonis was a real character, and almost an institution in this part of the city. He was a very welcome sight that day and his usual comic self. He had his own inimitable way of reciting the menu in Greek. He even acted out certain dishes on the menu, for what reason, other than sheer entertainment, I couldn't imagine, so that *mavromatika* (black-eyed peas with spinach in a tomato sauce) were explained by him suddenly pointing to his eyes with two fingers of one hand. It never ceased to make me smile. It cracked the Greeks up as well.

The afternoon was such a pleasant interlude in those frustrating times and over a lunch of seafood and salad, the Spanish writer confessed to a similar problem with Sir Ambrose, although her book at least was not sliding out of print – yet. We discussed strategies and together resolved to offer each other moral support in the quest to retrieve our rights, no matter how frustrating the process was. All going well, I would have mine back first, by the end of January.

The only redeeming factor in the whole sorry business was the fact that while Sir Ambrose in late summer had read my submission for the sequel, and while he had finally agreed to publish it, he had never bothered to send out a contract in the stipulated time, which was not a surprise, so the publication of the second book by him would not go ahead. Luckily, I had not signed its future away as well.

Meanwhile, I had to put my disappointment over the publishing debacle to one side to concentrate on doing the final rewrites on the second book, *Homer's Where The Heart Is*, which would be my continuing story of life in the Mani region during the intensifying crisis. It would also set out to examine my long love affair with Greece. This started during my earliest visit to Athens in the 1970s, when the country was ruled by the military dictatorship that overthrew the country in the mid-sixties. It had made life dangerous for Greeks and foreigners alike, although it had not dimmed my love for Greece on the first big odyssey of my life. I had woven this back story into the main narrative. There had been plenty of research to do for the book, but many of my anecdotes and impressions had come from a diary I had kept in Athens, without which the task of replicating these times would have been more difficult.

At least the writing was a great joy to me and in the midst of feuding with the publisher, I fully appreciated that the creative endeavour of writing was the one thing in my life that I had complete control over and gave back exactly what I put into it. It became both a refuge and a consolation.

@@@@@

One sunny day I was outside hanging out some washing when I saw a figure in the garden of the old house clipping herbs and collecting grapefruit from the abundant tree that grew between the old house and Villa Anemos. The fruit was huge and hanging heavily on the boughs of the tree like small footballs. It was Anastasios, the father of Stavroula. We invited him for a coffee and sat outside at the balcony table.

"I understand why you wanted to move here," he said, "but the old house would be much warmer. It has thick walls."

I feared we had offended him with our move to the newer villa and I didn't want to say too much other than "I am sure you're right…" and "we just felt like a change". He shrugged stoically. I could sense that for a man in his eighties, who had survived the German occupation of Koroni as a teenager and later some serious health issues, a 'change' should be something more drastic than just moving from one house to another.

I imagined that in the old days, when life was simpler, *Palio Spiti,* with the rustic fire stoked up and plenty of company around, might have been cosy. It must also have been idyllic, living on a hillside surrounded by olive trees and goats. All the family had lived in this collection of houses at one time or another, but I guessed that as the family dwindled and people passed away, or moved away for work, there was less attraction for those left. Anastasios also left the hillside, worked in some colourful occupations in Athens for a while and finally settled back in Koroni. The old houses here became no more than weekend homes, or occasional retreats. However, he couldn't quite let go of the place and was often to be seen drifting about the gardens, collecting his herbs and *horta,* or overseeing renovation work for his children.

While we sat chatting on the balcony, dusk was drawing in and just the right time for great clouds of birds, possibly starlings, to appear at the edge of the gulf. We had seen them for a few days in a row. It was mesmerising the way they formed and reformed into pixilated shapes with lightning speed. I pointed them out, but the old man shook his head.

"That means the winter will be long and bitter," he said.

I admired these old Greeks for being able to read the topography, the skies, the stars, the sea, like books, with predictions of everything to come. How wonderful to be so melded with your environment.

"The soroccos is blowing today. We shall all be mad by bedtime," I had once heard an old sailor complain of the hot African wind that Greeks fear.

Yiannis would often tell us in the morning: "There are waves on this side of Koroni today, so the sea on the other side will be calm for swimming." Yet when we tried to chase down the calm sea, driving quickly to the other side of the Koroni promontory to the sandy beaches of Zaga and Memi, facing the Ionian Sea, we would still find waves. I often wondered if it wasn't just a cheeky wind-up.

However, Anastasios wasn't far wrong about the birds. Storms were on their way, but it wasn't just the storms that caused high drama. Just when we thought we were safe from critters in the cooler weather, they came calling.

One morning I opened the front door to hang some washing on the balcony line, and I saw it, on the front door mat, as if it had been trying to reach the door bell. Another scorpion! Unbelievable! Big and beige, it was startled by my appearance and aimed its long tail at me, in a jabbing motion. I froze, but Wallace had sensed the door was open and came roaring up to escape into the garden. He froze as well but, true to his crazy genes, he started up a vibrant barking session, as if this could beat the interloper into submission, like you might a pesky Jehovah's Witness brandishing a clutch of pamphlets and a pitchfork.

"Scorpion!" was all I had to shout and Jim came running with a sweepy brush. It was part of our well-practised 'critter emergency' drill. In just moments, the scorpion had gone the way of all the others, poleaxed by the brush and sent over the edge of the balcony. This house proved to be a scorpion magnet, like all the others we had rented in southern Greece, because of the mess of rubble and rocks underneath the building. I expected there would be more of them in the spring when they came out of hibernation. But what did I ever really know about scorpions, the little blighters that seemed to turn up with painful regularity, with their crab hands and angsty pitchforks? The forerunners of disaster.

So many sightings in half a year couldn't be normal, surely? To me, they were fast becoming a kind of metaphor for all the uncomfortable dimensions of Greek life, fearful things that usually lie hidden but would come out eventually, even if you never poked around with sticks. They were there in a parallel world, going about their business, because not

Things Get Worse Before They Get Feta

everything in Greece is bright and sunny and shot through with summer hilarity all the time. Mostly it is, but it's the dark side, when it emerges, that always comes as a surprise, especially to foreigners, whether it's a critter, a cowboy with a hunting rifle, or an economic meltdown. Greece can hurt you, too. Sometimes. And it's good to know at least where the enemies are sleeping.

However, at that point in my life, I had enemies beyond the battlements of Greece, and despite my phobia about scorpions I realised there were bigger, nippier things to worry about – and many of them were lurking in the world of publishing. As my grandmother Euphamia might have said if she'd been in Greece: "Lass, it's the things that don't look like scorpions on the outside that will banjo you in the end."

Perhaps the scorpion had just been looking for a cosy place to hide ahead of the winter storms because, just as Anastasios had predicted, these arrived soon enough. We had already lived through several cold winters in the Mani and many storms. The worst of them hit at different times. In Koroni, it happened one December day, late in the afternoon, with sheets of rain slicing horizontally at the peninsula like a karate chop from the direction of the Ionian Sea.

The wind was powerful, whipping the heads of the olive trees into a frenzy. The heavy ripe grapefruits began to fall off and bed down in long grass. Then hailstones arrived, ice-cube sized, crashing on to the roof and tinkling off windows, a sweet percussive interlude before the thunder rolled in. In this part of the world, thunder is war-like. You feel it in your whole body like a terrifying explosion. The lightning too is extreme, though mesmerising, zig-zagging down over the gulf for hours until you feel you've over-dozed on sensation and long for a quiet dark room. If you like a wild storm, though, Greece in winter is the go-to place for tempests.

During the December storm there was nothing else to do but sit at our respective 'desks' and watch the sound and light show through the closed windows. It was mostly thrilling, apart from the old worry that Wallace would go spare, running around the house, over furniture, barking at the thunder as he always did, bunching up rugs. He has done this since he was a puppy.

Shortly after the storm began, Jim suddenly said: "Where's Wallace?"

I looked around and saw his empty dog bed. "I don't know."

"That's odd," said Jim, getting up and walking into the bedroom. I followed him and there was Wallace, lying at the foot of our bed, fast asleep.

"He isn't barking at the thunder," I said. We looked at each other, puzzled.

Wallace, with a laconic sigh, opened an eye and observed us. Just then, a great blast of thunder boomed in the sky overhead. The house vibrated, but Wallace didn't budge.

"What's wrong with him?" I said.

"I don't know but perhaps …," Jim said, thoughtfully rubbing his stubbly chin, "the wee man has gone deaf, Margarita."

I looked at Wallace curled up on the bed. He had either cracked the issue of thunder anxiety or indeed he had gone very deaf, as he was now 13½. I thought then of his ear infection in the summer, one of many in his lifetime, and wondered if it had been the final straw or just a coincidence. It wasn't as if we hadn't noticed he was slightly deaf at times and didn't always respond to commands, but then he rarely did anyway, apart from acknowledging the "chicken" word. He was slowing down. He couldn't roar about the place like he did when he was a puppy, to the extent that I once described him as a pinball with fur. And he couldn't leap unimaginable heights any more without the aid of a trampoline.

Poor Wallace, growing old before our eyes, fast tracked into senility in just a few short years, it seemed to us. I twiddled his ears and he just grunted in appreciation. If we looked on the bright side, however, it was possible that for an old and high-wired Jack Russell like Wallace, deafness could almost be a blessing. So many things wouldn't wind him up any longer, like thunder, cars backfiring, crockery rattling, front door bells chiming on TV sitcoms. There were so many things. I had, in my freelance years, done several stories on canine mental health and I remembered a vet telling me that in a domestic, especially urban, setting, dogs' superior sense of hearing was almost an anxiety for them because they could hear everything they didn't need to hear for their survival, and for nervous, bonkers dogs like Wallace, it could be torment.

Wallace was also calming down, finally. Not at five years, as one Jack Russell owner had assured me, but at 13. There was a part of me, however, that missed the hypermanic Wallace, even if others didn't. Some of the people in our Scottish village had been unnerved by Wallace's energy and his screamy barking habits that we had never managed to train out of him. In fact, we had hardly been able to train Wallace at all. And in my most frazzled moments I would instantly recall his wonderful Scottish breeder, Brigit, saying: "Ach, he's a Jackie dear, not a poodle."

I like to think that Wallace is a dog who has celebrated his own inimitable life to its limits. Yet he has not always been easy, especially on our travels, particularly to Greece, where we constantly had to make choices about routes, hotels, rental accommodation, based on how Wallace would fit it, otherwise it wouldn't have worked. It prompted one Kalamatan real estate agent at the start of our odyssey in the Mani to ask if we were renting a house for the dog rather than ourselves. In a way we were, because if we hadn't, it would have been stressful for all concerned.

Some of our friends who love Wallace have nevertheless asked us how we can deal with a dog that requires so many compromises in our lives. Yet all relationships, whether with humans or animals, involve compromises of some kind. One day in Koroni, I was thinking about that issue and I ran through every difficult choice we had ever made to accommodate Wallace, particularly in Greece, and I realised that each one had turned out to be a huge gift to us.

We would never have considered the remote hillside village of Megali Mantinea (and perhaps I would never have written my first book about our time there), had it not been for the fact that the expat landlord of the house we rented was happy to accept a dog. There were countless other examples of times when we made a decision to fit Wallace in and it turned out to be the right one and wonderful new opportunities presented themselves. Can a Jack Russell possibly chart your course through life? You bet, as long as you have a high tolerance for mental behaviour, and you're well stocked with chicken.

I thought of Brigit's words again, and here was Wallace curled up on the bed like a sleepy … well … poodle. Or at least a bowling ball, rather than a pinball. It was hard to know whether to laugh or cry.

15

What's it all about, Alfa?

IT was a Spartan classroom. The wooden desks were scored with names and other small etchings of torment. The desks were built on a small scale for kids in this *dimotiko skoleio* (primary school), with hard, bum-numbing chairs. We sat in three long rows, like multiple bears from the Goldilocks story, trying to squeeze ourselves into miniature furniture. It was more like the school rooms I remembered from my own childhood and bereft of anything techie or modern. There was an icon of a saint beside the blackboard and a map of Greece. Across the top of the blackboard the verb *diavazo*, I read, was fully conjugated in all tenses and took up the width of the wall, as only a Greek verb can.

At the back of the room was a worn bookcase, a few posters on the wall, drawn by the pupils, with one of them stating: "*Ochi sti via*". No to violence. Which I took to mean 'No to bullying', and served to remind us that this was an issue in Greek schools as much as it was everywhere in the world.

Sitting in a school room to learn the language wasn't what I ever envisaged for our latest odyssey in Greece, but it seemed as good a place to be as anywhere on a winter's afternoon. The Greek classes held here were organised by the Greek Ministry of Education, with funding from the EU, and the programme was aimed mainly at new migrants to Greece. The classes were taught mostly in English, as it was the language common to everyone. Christos, the teacher, was a genial young guy from Kalamata, with short, dark hair, who looked more like a musician and was always dressed in jeans and a western-style T-shirt.

Jim had enrolled in the class, starting at beginners' level. It was a fast-tracked system running twice a week in three-hour sessions, and I had asked if I could come along a few times out of interest, with the aim of joining it properly when it became a bit harder. I had no urge to go through all the rudiments of Greek again, learning the αλφάβητο (alphabet) and the basic grammar, as I had struggled with it myself for years. Besides, I had a book to finish.

It was a mixed group of around 14 people: Germans, Swiss, Dutch mainly, who had various levels of Greek, as some of them had already done the beginners' class a few times. The room was cold, with high windows overlooking the playground. Christos told us the central heating was switched off early in the afternoon to save the school some money. During the height of the crisis in 2012, I remembered reading reports in Greece about how some schools couldn't afford heating at all and many students sat all day in freezing rooms in winter wrapped in overcoats, some of them sent off to school without breakfast because their parents couldn't even afford that. They were dark days. I now got a feel for what it must have been like for those kids.

Part of the aim of this syllabus was to promote Greek history and culture, but inevitably the 'culture' discussions veered towards politics, especially as Christos had strong feelings about the austerity that Greece was still in the grip of. His discussions were quite animated and everyone relished the idea of hearing about the crisis from his perspective. One night, while we were discussing the cuts to wages during the crisis, he confessed that his own wages hadn't been paid for nearly a year. And for the past two years he had also been forced to use his own money to pay for petrol for the trips to Koroni and some Messinian villages where he also taught the course, five days a week. This was a total of 400 miles' worth of petrol a week, putting an extra burden on his family budget.

His wife was also a teacher but on maternity leave on a risible amount of money by UK standards. With a toddler as well to support, we asked Christos how he coped without a wage. He shrugged and gave the answer that most young Greeks would give: "Our parents help us with money when they can, but they have also been hit by the crisis. We live very simply and most of the money we have goes to the children."

It was clear from many of his thoughts on politics that he was quietly left-wing, without ever becoming polemical about it. Once he was wearing a colourful T-shirt with the Greek letters EPT and underneath the words: "*Anikei sto lao*" "EPT belongs to the people". This referred to the closure in 2013 of the Greek broadcasting service (ERT in English), which had been one of the most controversial and hated 'reforms' carried out by the Samaras government to appease the Troika, the international lenders.

ERT was the Greek equivalent of the BBC and a much-loved institution that had been running since 1938. It had not even been blacked out during the rule of the military junta from 1967. ERT had four main radio stations, five TV stations and a number of regional radio stations. The government closed it, saying that its operations were corrupt and journalists were overpaid, a fact denied by most of the low-paid 2,656 employees who lost their jobs. It seemed that Prime Minister Antonis Samaras had carried out this action in a frenzy of cost-cutting in the public sector, including the dismissal of 15,000 other government workers, with the aim of impressing the Troika.

The government, however, hadn't anticipated the huge groundswell of protest over the closure of ERT, or the pirate operations that would follow, with former staff and volunteers in Athens and other cities borrowing equipment from the European Broadcasting Union to continue transmitting live news coverage and political discussions. This would become one of the most defining protest movements of the crisis.

The ERT station in Kalamata had also been shut down but continued to operate with a couple of former journalists and volunteers, using borrowed equipment. Christos had been one of those volunteers and still did some work on a regular basis at the station. It was hard to imagine a more industrious professional.

Despite sometimes looking exhausted during the classes, he had a nice sense of humour. One night he was explaining how to form the plural of certain types of nouns. He wrote a sentence on the blackboard *'to panteloni mas'* (our pair of trousers). One of the German students was quick to point out: "Surely it should be *'ta pantelonia'* (trousers, plural)?"

Christos covered his mistake by offering a cheeky response: "No, this is Greece in crisis. We all have to share one pair of trousers now." The class erupted in laughter – but there was a dark grain of truth in it.

The lessons ran from 4pm to 7pm and there was a break at 5.30. There was nowhere else to go in the school, as it was mostly shut in the evening, so Christos would wander away to use his mobile and the students adopted the habit of standing outside the building, smoking or chatting. It was hard to imagine a more inspiring location for a school. This was an area of Koroni situated on a high cliff, a short walk from the castle.

The area is called Asine, which has narrow streets of old houses, hunched together, and a few shops. The name alludes to the area's ancient history, as it was once a colony of the city state of Asine, in Tolon, in the northern Peloponnese. The city state was mentioned in Homer's *Iliad* as it contributed a garrison of men to the Trojan War. However, in 700BC it was destroyed by warring Argos (the town, not the ancient headquarters of the UK shopping chain) and its inhabitants moved down to Messinia.

This slightly charmless village sprawl is all that is left of the noble heritage of Asine in this peninsula. Yet the original founders of this colony, that later became Koroni, would have seen a strong resemblance to the layout of the Tolon original as both had high fortifications and a long beach below. George Seferis, in his famous poem *The King of Asini* (in the translation by Edmund Keeley and Philip Sherrard), was referring to a search for remnants of the king's rule in Tolon in ancient times, and yet it reverberates with Koroni too.

"On the sunny side a long open beach,
And the light striking diamonds on the huge walls.
No living thing, the wild doves gone
and the King of Asini ...
Unknown, forgotten by all, even by Homer."

The primary school is an unremarkable whitewashed building, but the back of it overlooks the "long open beach" of Zaga and Memi, with a panoramic view of the Messinian Gulf and the Mani peninsula opposite, none of which, from this vantage point, has changed all that much in centuries.

The students in the Greek class were a fairly genial bunch, most owning holiday homes in the area, but some living here more or less permanently. I was struck by their determination to live in a country still racked by crisis. The only thing that really bothered them was health care in Greece, or lack of it, as the health sector had been one of the hardest hit by austerity. In 2009, health care had been good, with some £12 million allocated yearly. By 2012 that figure had fallen to £8 million – and even less in the following years. Most of these people admitted to going back to their own countries when they were worried about health.

One afternoon in break time, I asked one of the more outspoken and amusing of the group, a German called Jorgen, what the doctors and dentists were like in Koroni. Dentists were always of particular interest to me, as I had something of a dental phobia. He twiddled his thick moustache, and his eyes watered with the promise of mischief. He told me never to go to a certain dentist in an outlying village. I asked why.

"He has an old foot pump for the drill. You remember them?"

He demonstrated by pumping his right foot up and down, like an Appalachian musician marking time for his banjo buddies.

"It's so slow. And he has bottles of booze lined up in his surgery, to give you a shot of something when you need some local anaesthetic."

He laughed uproariously. Some of the others who spoke English joined in and I gathered that Jorgen liked a good wheeze.

"You're kidding, right?"

"No, I am serious. Never go there. And if you need an eye doctor don't go to the one here. He is very good but he has no equipment. It is all in his Kalamata surgery."

"How can he examine you without equipment?"

Jorgen took a step forward and put his face close to mine. He stared into my eyes.

"That's how!"

Everybody laughed again, except for his long-suffering wife.

"Stop it, Jorgen. You'll frighten everyone," she said.

Christos returned to start up the lesson. He asked what we were all laughing about.

"Oh, nothing," said Jorgen, winking in my direction.

I decided that even if I didn't learn very much Greek this semester, at least I'd have a bit of a laugh.

@@@@@

One morning, there was a knock at the door of Villa Anemos. I opened it to find a muscly blonde woman in a baseball cap.

"Can you move car," she said in Greek with a thick guttural accent that had an East European edge to it.

"Sure, what's the problem?"

"We are here to harvest the olives and the car is under one of the trees."

This was Svetlana, the Russian, who also cleaned the villas. Now she had a sidekick whom I assumed was from Bulgaria because he left his clapped-out banger nearby with Bulgarian number plates. Jim was out walking with Wallace, so I got the keys and moved the car. On the way back to the house we got chatting.

"You've lost weight," Svetlana said to me, grabbing my arm and surveying me from head to toe. "You look different, more beautiful. Not the same woman who came here in spring."

In fact, I didn't feel like the same woman, for all kinds of reasons, but more beautiful was a stretch. I quite liked her robust, if eccentric, style though.

"I turn 50 tomorrow. Pah!" she said. "You get old and everything goes to hell. *Gamoto*! Fuck it! All the bits falling down. No, it's not for me."

Then she started to pat her pockets vigorously, as if they were alive with critters, then gave up. I was intrigued.

"You have *spirta*, matches? I am desperate for a cigarette before we start work." She rolled out a few sentences in Russian that sounded like someone gargling with treacle.

I took her back to the villa and found some matches and we sat out on the balcony in the sun while she smoked a quick one. We chatted and I thought how bizarre it was the pair of us speaking our imperfect Greek together, though hers was more fluent than mine at least. There were eastern Europeans everywhere in Greece in the crisis, trying to scratch out a better living for themselves, which meant that life back home must have been pretty hard indeed.

Most of the Russians in Greece, however, were wealthy part-time residents. On the road west out of Koroni was a massive villa with stone towers built on the edge of a hillside overlooking the sea. It was owned by a Russian oligarch with, it was said, Greek roots. The estate was rimmed with a heavy duty fence and huge metal gates and bollards, CCTV cameras and armed security guards on patrol.

While the oligarch was said to have donated money to various local charities, that was as cuddly as he was ever going to get. No-one was permitted near the front of his property or in the sea near his house. One day, while a group of young Greek students were swimming there, they were approached by one of the armed guards, telling them to scram because the beach was private. There was an altercation over this point, but in the end, the kids had to leave the scene.

Greeks don't take kindly to being pushed around by *xenoi,* especially Russians, so the group rallied their friends as far away as Kalamata and the next day a convoy of day-trippers arrived and settled on the beach again, right in front of the mansion, and swam in the sea. Guards were scrambled again and the kids were threatened, until one of them called the local police. Soon after, a squad car arrived from Koroni and the argument was settled when the policemen told the guards they were out of order and that no-one owns the beaches in Greece.

Svetlana had lived in Koroni for about 10 years. I asked her if she preferred crisis-ridden Greece to Russia.

"I like Greece. Good climate. Work is here for now but one day I want to go back to my own country."

"Really? To all that cold weather?"

"Yes, but home is home."

I watched her at various times during the afternoon and in the days to come as she and her workmate did the olive harvest in the orchard around the villas, even when the weather turned bad and it rained for days on end. She worked like a Trojan; they both did, with the usual petrol-driven, hand-held harvesting wands that shook the olives down to the ground sheets. At this rate they could do around 15 to 20 trees in a day.

The next morning after our chat, I saw the pair trudge past our side balcony on the way to work again. I wished her *'chronia polla'*, many years, and gave her a bottle of wine I had in the fridge.

"I guess you won't be celebrating tonight then, since you've still got work tomorrow."

"Don't be crazy. I celebrate. Greeks are tough. We Russians – tougher," she said, slapping her chest with a powerful hand. Who could doubt it?

16

The Hand of God Tree

IT was Wallace who discovered the curious tree with the shape of a hand on its trunk at the 12th century monastery of Ayioi Theodoroi, in the hills north of Koroni.

The monastery is a half-hour walk past olive groves near the village of Homatero. Like most of the old monasteries we have seen in southern Greece, it was slightly isolated and almost chilly in its solitude as it hadn't been properly occupied in recent history, but there were other more macabre reasons for that forbidding atmosphere, as we were to discover. Without the narrow track leading to it, it would be hard to find, nestling on the side of a small wooded ravine with the sounds of a natural spring trickling over river stones nearby.

Despite its lonely position, the church within the monastery grounds was a beautiful example of Byzantine architecture with a pantiled roof and dome. The building was bathed in winter sun when we got there, though the side garden under the bluff of the hill lay in shadow. We were in a hurry to get inside to see its reputedly interesting frescos and didn't want to hang around the gardens just yet. But Wallace had other ideas. He pulled us up a small path into the side garden and there we found the strange shape on one side of a tall carob tree.

It was an old tree, the trunk thick and gnarled, and on the lower section, where much of the outer bark had disappeared, was the unmistakable shape of a closed hand showing the knuckles and an outstretched thumb. It was over a foot high and two feet wide and too smooth for a human carving, we thought, but with all the signs of being something curiously natural: fashioned by the wind and the rain perhaps over many decades. We called it the Hand of God Tree, given its surroundings, and found it curiously appealing.

"Wallace must have sensed something there," I said to Jim, remembering so many occasions on what we often called our Tomb Raider tours of the monasteries and churches in the Mani, when Wallace generally didn't want to go inside them because they were cold and damp. Sometimes there were more sinister reasons for his hesitancy. I remembered seeing a TV programme once about dogs' almost otherworldly sense of smell and that they could detect the remnants of food or biological traces in houses years, even decades, after the substances had been left. Could their noses sense the deeds of centuries past?

The church in this monastery was locked and arranging to find the key holder in the preceding weeks was the usual quest we had become accustomed to. With a bit of sleuthing among the older folk in Koroni, we discovered the key was held by Papa Theodoros, a priest who lived in Homatero, and we arranged to meet up with him at his house after the next Sunday service. It was a small village dwelling with an external staircase and a small courtyard in front. He made a modest living, no doubt, as priests do since the start of the crisis. But Papa Theodoros was also the priest to three different village churches, as only a proportion of retiring priests are replaced.

He was dressed in a plain black *raso*, cassock, and a long black cardigan, his hair tied back near the nape of his neck. He was in his sixties, with a kindly face. He gave me the keys to the monastery and one for the 'priest's office', which he said had some books about the monastery.

"There are paintings inside the office too. Take a look. When you get back here, stay a while and drink a coffee. It's good to have *parea*. But if I'm not here, leave the keys under the pumpkin," he said with a glimmer of fun in his pale brown eyes. He pointed to a plastic chair in the courtyard, on which sat an enormous pumpkin. In this remote, old-fashioned village, it seemed quite normal to leave keys under pumpkins.

When we had found the strange tree, it also seemed perfectly in keeping with the atmosphere of this secluded place, but we were in a hurry to see the frescos. When we opened the small metal door leading into the narthex of the church, we were glad we'd remembered to bring a torch. It was dark inside, with only a small window behind the altar. On the wooden table in the narthex, there were no candles in evidence. We left the main door open to let in some light and air. We tied Wallace up here, as he wasn't keen to come inside, as usual.

The church is a typical Byzantine design of a cross in a square, with one main sanctuary and two smaller apses either side. On every wall surface there were frescos, some bleached out to mere outlines due to water leakage and also destruction caused by the monastery's more turbulent history.

The frescos are said to date from the 16th or 17th centuries and while the artist is unknown, it is likely he came from Crete. There were fine examples everywhere of the lives of the saints and the stories of the birth and crucifixion of Christ. One of the more curious frescos was a painting of the ocean, a lovely old boat with a strange fish/eagle creature on the mast, and in the water a macabre-looking fish with a human foot in its mouth. One depicted a rather bizarre octopus with the face of an old man. Ghoulish images abound in Byzantine churches, often indicating the grisly fate of unbelievers.

The monastery was built in the 12th century and was originally called the monastery of the *Panayia* (Virgin Mary) Grivitsiani. It had a stout wall about it and a gate and would have been a secure refuge in its day. Little is known of its history up until the 16th century, when the Turks occupied

The Hand Of God Tree

Greece, including Koroni and its surrounding villages, which were subjected to Ottoman brutalities. The monastery, however, came under its fiercest attack during the Orlofika revolution in 1744, during which prominent Greeks had sought the help of Russia to rid the country of the Ottoman Turks. It became one of the most violent periods in the country's history, with the Turks enlisting the help of Albanians to rout out Greek insurgents.

The monastery was singled out at this time, when local Turkish leaders thought the place was a sanctuary for insurgents and attacked it, setting fire to the monks' cells, killing more than 40 monks and destroying many of the monastery buildings.

The name of the monastery changed in the 19th century, when shepherds from Arcadia settled in this area and renamed it for several saints called Theodoros, to seek their protection. It has been closed since the 1930s, for rather unsettling reasons, we would discover later.

It was easy to feel the weight of its history here in the ruins of the monks' cells, where a crisp morning wind funneled through crumbling stone archways and around empty rooms heaped with the rubble of burnt and fallen roofs. If the place seemed timeless in its abandonment, the very old well near the main gate, with its deep, slightly greasy interior and perpetual echoing drip, reminded us that the past is not that far away after all.

After an hour in the church, it was pleasant to be outside again and we sat on the sun-warmed steps leading up to the priest's office, which Papa Theodoros had given me the key to. We ate lunch before entering this small dusty room, with a wooden desk against one wall. Around the room were mementoes of orthodox life, books and pamphlets about the lives of the saints. A priest's stovepipe hat stood on a bookshelf, a curious touch, and on the wall there were indeed paintings, depicting a lone priest in repose in front of the monastery and some rather whimsical pictures of goats and donkeys.

They were painted in the 'naïve' style but had a liveliness about them and seemed to instantly lighten the mood of this beautiful but neglected monastery. We had heard that Papa Theodoros was an amateur painter and guessed these were his works. In one corner we found copies of a book about the history of the monastery, written by a local woman, Panayiota Katsiva-Markaki. Instead of leaving the money in the office for one of the books, we decided to pay the *papas* when we saw him later.

It certainly wasn't the strangest monastery we'd seen in southern Greece, as most of them are infused with a similar eerie or violent history. Some monasteries had been hidden in the mountains, some built down the sides of deep ravines, the monastic cells like limpets on the rock face, defying gravity. Their design had one thing in common: to repel violent interlopers. Many have served their communities well in times of invasion and many have sheltered the heroes of historic skirmishes, particularly the iconic 19th century revolutionary Theodoros Kolokotronis. Just about every monastery claims a link to this local hero. In Greece, he rivals Elvis for the number of reported sightings.

Many of the monasteries and churches we had seen in this southern region were also reputed to have been sired in miraculous circumstances, often with a healing icon or two, and other inexplicable phenomena, like the Hand of God Tree, or even stranger, not just one curious tree but a whole clutch of them, growing out of the church roof.

This was the case in one of the most unique churches we had come across further north in the Peloponnese, in Arcadia, the classical home of Pan, nymphs and rural peculiarity. The church of Ayia Theodora is a tiny stone construction over a natural spring feeding into a cool stream, in a forest near the village of Vasta.

The Hand Of God Tree

This 10th century church's fame rests solely on its mini roof forest, which attracts scores of pilgrims every year. They come to look at the 17 tall trees, mostly holly and maple, sprouting from the roof tiles like a stiff-brushed hairdo of eccentric proportions. And rather than buckling under the weight of it all, the stone structure underneath seems unhampered. Neither is there much evidence of the tree roots growing down through the walls to reach the spring below. How did this phenomenon come about?

Locals believe this is a sacred site and the structure of the church is the miraculous form of Saint Theodora, who prayed before her untimely death for her body to be turned into a church, her hair to become a forest of trees above. It looks like her prayers were answered. Saint Theodora was a pious woman who lived in the 9th century. Her life, like that of many of the Orthodox saints, was turbulent and complex, with many details lost over time.

While she wished to join a women's monastery, inexplicably, she ended up in a male establishment, changing her name to Theodoros and dressing like a monk. The story began to develop all the hallmarks of disaster, or a Byzantine soap opera, when this innocent rural woman was dragged into a scandal involving claims of sexual relations with a young local woman and an ensuing pregnancy, which obviously would have been a bit of a miracle in itself. But Theodora decided to take the rap for the deed, and she was sentenced to death. She was duly decapitated in Vasta.

Once she was dead and the executioners discovered her real gender and unscrambled the whole sorry tale, they decided to honour this martyr and erect a church nearby. It had been while awaiting execution that she uttered the prayer to her fellow monks, and the wish to be turned into a church. As far as locals can ascertain, trees have been growing on the church since the 10th century.

A Scorpion In The Lemon Tree

Many Greek structural engineers and academics have investigated the church over the years. One engineer noted that the weight of the trees on the roof would be around nine tons, which is four times greater than what would normally be tolerated by a structure of this size. None of experts have been able to explain why the church hasn't crumbled or how the trees continue to grow without evidence of much of a root system in the walls of the church. The trees appear to be growing straight out of the roof itself, as if floating on air. Indeed, the whole area has a rather floaty and unreal feel about it and defies logic.

After our monastery visit that day we got back to Homatero at about 3pm and all was quiet around the house of the *papas*. We knocked lightly on the closed door downstairs but there wasn't a sound. Even though it was winter, many Greeks still have a siesta and as the *papas* had been up since dawn it seemed inconsiderate to disturb him. I was somewhat disappointed as I wanted to show him the pictures of the Hand of God Tree on our camera and find out more about it.

We left the keys under the pumpkin, together with an envelope with money for the monastery book. There was nowhere else to leave it and unless Greeks are routinely in the habit of finding money under pumpkins, we thought the envelope would be safe. All the same, that evening I called the *papas* to make sure he had found everything. I told him we liked his paintings.

"I have many more inside the house. Come back another day and see them. But you should have knocked harder on the door."

"I thought you were having a siesta. I didn't want to disturb you."

"Pah! A good priest never sleeps," he said, with a chuckle.

It sounded like one of those quaint *parimies*, sayings, that you hear from villagers.

The Hand Of God Tree

I mentioned the Hand of Good Tree, though I didn't exactly tell him that was what we'd named it. He didn't know what I was talking about, which seemed odd, or maybe he just didn't understand my Greek explanation, rudimentary though it was.

"Show me the photos when you come here next time. I am most intrigued," he said.

Much later on, I read some of Panayiota's fascinating book, which was in Greek and took me a while, but sadly it confirmed that the monastery was even more ill-fated and violent than we had first thought, and I was glad we hadn't known all the details while we were there. In the early 20th century, there were no permanent monks at the monastery, yet now and then itinerant monks from different parts of Greece would arrive and set up home in one of the remaining habitable cells, including what is now the priest's office.

The last monk to live there in the late 1920s was something of a mystery. He had a white horse, which he stabled at the monastery and rode about the district, collecting donations of food and other necessities. One day, however, a local man working nearby in the fields heard the horse whinnying loudly in the monastery yard and went to see what it was about. He found the monk dead in his cell, having been violently murdered.

The news shocked this peaceful rural area, but a suspect was never found. Local stories pointed to the possibility that the murderer was an itinerant farm worker employed in the surrounding fields, who was lured by fantastic stories of money hidden at the monastery. No-one will ever know. And no-one after that dared to live in the monastery again. It was no surprise, therefore, that the monastery had a chill atmosphere.

The strange Hand of God Tree, however, was a curious touch in this macabre story – and we were keen to find out what it was all about when we next saw the *papas*.

17

Knowing your arse from your omega

IN the last beginners' Greek class of the year, no-one had much interest in grammar and conjugating strings of verbs. Instead we had some conversation practice about what we would all do for Christmas in our respective countries, as most of the students were returning home for the festivities, apart from three or four of us. We asked Christos what he would be doing and inevitably he told us it would be a quiet time for him and his family and we assumed rightly there would be no money for the excesses of gift buying and Christmas feasting that most of us took for granted in northern Europe. In Greece, it is a low-key season anyway, a time of religious reflection, with most of the gifts offered to children on January 1.

Once we had dispensed with talk of Christmas inevitably the conversation turned to the state of Greece, everyone's favourite topic, especially with ongoing political upheavals and austerity jitters. During these discussions, Christos was usually careful not to be rude about Chancellor Angela Merkel's role in pursuing harsh austerity measures, as many of the students were German, with a mix of others, and one rather quiet Jewish man with a dazzling head of fair curls, like Harpo Marx, who had been brought up in Israel. He usually kept to himself and did not sit beside the Germans.

Christos was more laid-back on this last lesson of the year and seemed to have lost a grip on his usual diplomacy. He began to lay into Merkel with a certain gusto that took us all by surprise, and delighted the non-Germans in the group at least.

"I think Merkel and Schauble (the German Finance Minister) are driving all the hard decisions about Greece," he said. "They are in control of Europe. Merkel is a tyrant. It is a bit like having Adolf Hitler in power all over again."

The room turned chilly. A few people coughed. The Germans stuck their heads in their books. The Jewish guy at least found it illuminating. Finally, Christos realised what he'd just said and quickly steered the conversation back to Christmas. However, despite the slight embarrassment his strop had caused, everyone rallied at break time and one of the Swiss students, playing the neutrality hand, suggested we have a whip-round and give Christos some money for Christmas. We collected 50 euros.

Before the end of the class, John the Dutchman handed Christos an envelope with a Christmas card inside, and the money, saying it was a gift from all of us. When he opened it and saw the money, he flushed with embarrassment, which we imagined was due to his anti-German comments.

"*Efcharisto para poli, paidia,*" he said, thanking us and touching his heart. "But I really can't take it. It wouldn't be right."

The class went quiet.

"I am not allowed to accept money from my students," he said, almost holding the envelope at arm's length. And the envelope itself was also a worry. In Greece the *fakelaki* is the infamous word for a bribe and for a system that has always operated in Greece, where professionals are given money by clients, stuffed into an envelope, to make sure they do the jobs they're supposed to do, quickly and easily. Corruption was one of the things that had brought Greece to its state of crisis.

Or perhaps it was just the case that his pride was dented; a Greek teacher having to take money from his foreign students – Germans as well! What had happened to Greece!

Christos stubbornly refused the money until Jim had a brainwave and said to him: "It's for your children – our Christmas gift to them." Christos's face lit up and everyone muttered in agreement.

"Oh, that is very kind then. Thank you all," he said, looking touched by the gesture. Given the current economic situation, 50 euros was no mean offering.

The students decided to have a festive dinner together before Christmas and while we were deliberating over where to go, Jim and I suggested a taverna that was outside Koroni and a bit remote. We had come across it on the road to Homatero when we visited the monastery, although it was shut at the time. It only opened in the evenings and we were keen to try it. Called the Ayia Playia, which is a contraction of the name Ayia Pelagia, Saint Pelagia, it was named after the small chapel beside it.

The taverna was in the village of Falanthi, which is part of a collection of villages, including Homatero, and Mistraki up in the hills, with its own distinctive history and story. The area was once self-sufficient and prosperous because of the lignite mine that operated here from the early 20th century, a combustible material valued in the war years. The mine tunnels were given the names of ancient gods and heroes like Persephone and Iraklis. The Germans, however, stopped the operation during the Second World War and put a tight control over the area, as Homatero had become the local hangout for the *andartes*, the left-wing rebels who fought to overthrow the Nazis.

The taverna has its own stream and the original stone bridge nearby, as well as a fountain in the front terrace, with spring water, which curiously emanates from under the altar of the church next door, which is why the feast day of Ayia Pelagia in May is popular with locals. The Ayia Playia taverna was a bewitching kind of place, like a cross between Brigadoon and the Twilight Zone. From the minute you walked into it you had the feeling you had slipped into a time warp to a more gracious era in Greek history.

It reminded me so much of tavernas I had visited in my early years in Greece, particularly in hillside villages miles from anywhere. It was only after you sat down at one of the substantial wooden tables you realised there was nothing modern about it. The décor was quaintly old, with a collection of strange puppets and masks on the wall and shelves filled with bottles of local wine and olives, which is not to say it was ramshackle or untidy, quite the opposite. It also had the strangest hearth on one wall with an ingenious set of metal tubes, like organ pipes, drawing warm air from just below the fire and pumping it out into the restaurant.

The owner Yiorgos added to the taverna's atmosphere: a genial, slightly mischievous soul who also seemed to be straight from another era of Greek life. He had an easy manner and there was always a smile playing round the edges of his eyes, as if he were privy to a delicious kind of joke, the meaning of which we would grasp in time. He spoke little English but was very patient with Greek learners. Only a few other tables were occupied, as this was the time of year when Greeks were harvesting their olives and many of the foreigners had returned home for winter.

We were the usual eclectic mix of Europeans, John the Dutchman, and the Jewish man with his Dutch wife, who were now based in Holland. We talked a lot about the Greek class and Christos. We discussed the language as well and how hard we found it. Jim told them the story of how he had asked for a bag of *archidia*, testicles, instead of pears and reduced everyone to helpless laughter. Yiorgos, who had been sitting nearby at a table smoking, overheard the conversation and came over to slap Jim on the back and congratulate him on his *berdema*, language muddle.

The Jewish man, who had not said much at all, told us his language error, which was a unique case of trying to make Greek words even longer, instead of shorter. Years ago in Crete he had seen *astakos* on a menu (lobster) but instead of ordering a half lobster, he asked for half a policeman (*astinomikos*), with a Greek salad on the side. It caused much hilarity among the serving staff on an island where traditionally there has been an uneasy bond with authority figures.

I told them a story about how our landlady had named Wallace 'Wallakos', which is cute in English but not necessarily in Greek. Once, on a trip to the Arcadian mountain village of Stemnitsa, we stopped for a coffee in the *plateia,* which was full of old men drinking coffee or ouzo and flipping their worry beads with weary stoicism.

The woman serving us was chatty and asked me what Wallace was called. I told her Wallakos, but either I got it wrong or she misunderstood. She laughed heartily and told the assembled Greeks that our dog was called "*Malakas*", the popular word for jerk, or more harshly, wanker.

The old guys suddenly came to life like dusty marionettes and laughed so hard they were close to popping their strings. I tried to explain that while Wallace behaved like a *malakas*, sometimes, his name was Wallakos, but I had lost them with this. It's a name that doesn't figure at all in Greece. From now on, they would only ever remember the wanker foreign dog hiding under the table.

Greek has words that are identical but with the accent on a different letter, which can cause grief. I once went into a crowded Kalamata post office and asked a woman: "Is this the urine for collecting parcels?" *Oúra* is the word for urine, and *ourá* for queue. I had mispronounced it, but at least it made a few crisis-weary customers chuckle.

We spent a long time laughing over Greek mistakes and it might have gone on much longer, except that the *loukoumades* arrived: plates of deep-fried, honey-dipped spheres of dough, sizzling hot, which Yiorgos always served after a meal, and we all suddenly went quiet, enjoying their warm sticky taste.

It had been a lovely, rather serendipitous evening, and just one of many that Jim and I would have at this unusual taverna, and the start of a connection with the area that we had never anticipated.

@@@@@

December brought more rain and storms. Wallace, however, slept through much of it, with his recently discovered hearing problem, as did Jim, hiding under the duvet for two days with a bad cold and his Greek textbook to bone up on over the Christmas break, when he was feeling perky enough.

"Did you know that Greek has some of the longest words in any language? I mean, for example, I wouldn't bother to take poor Wallace to a hearing doctor because I wouldn't be able to say 'ear, nose and throat specialist', *otorinolaryngologos*."

"I don't think he'd be very interested in looking at Wallace's ears, do you, Jimbo?" I said.

"What? Oh, maybe. You know something, whenever I pick up a Greek grammar book I start to feel drowsy. Someone should market these books as an aid to sound sleep."

"What you need, Jimbo, is something racier in the Greek genre. Maybe a sex manual translated into Greek. Would that do it?"

"Oh, very funny, Margarita. But if you'll pardon me, I'm going to finish this lesson now and give myself over to some shut-eye."

He tossed the book on to the floor, yawning loudly.

"Shame on you, Jimbo! That's a clear case of premature capitulation!"

He managed a snigger and fell asleep. Men and illness are not good bed buddies.

Amid the storms of December, there were other storms of a political nature, as the Parliament prepared to vote on a new Greek president, and the only candidate put forward by the government was Stavros Dimas, a former EU environment commissioner.

There were to be three rounds of voting in Parliament, in which Dimas would need to secure 200 votes to win in each of the first two rounds and 180 votes in the last round, or else under the terms of the Greek constitution, Parliament would be dissolved and there would be a snap election. It was one of the peculiarities of the Greek political system that elections could be held for the strangest of reasons. Dimas failed the first two rounds and there were typically vibrant late-night commentaries on TV and a sense that yet again Greece was on a knife-edge, as it had been for five years.

The final voting round was on December 29 and we had gone to Koroni to do some banking and other chores and took the opportunity to schmooze about and get some idea of the mood of the voting.

The seafront was deserted as Greeks crammed into *kafeneia* and bars to watch the voting on TV, not because they didn't have TVs at home, but because Greeks like to watch political upheavals together, to discuss and argue usually over an ouzo, or *tsipouro*, the old guys flicking their worry beads at each other.

Jim had set aside time to have a haircut at one of the barbers in the town, which were like small rooms plucked from another century when male perfection reigned supreme. They also had amusing names like *Chriso Psalidi*, Golden Scissors. The one Jim picked was tiny, with a long bench seat where I waited so I could also watch the final vote on TV, which was nearing an end. The young barber with his jet black hair snipped away at Jim's hair with one gimlet eye on the TV.

"There will be another election for sure," he said, half to us, half to the TV. His worked like Edward Scissorhands in a blur of activity, and Jim grimaced in my direction.

"Will that be good then, another election?" I asked the guy, to see if he was a Syriza supporter or not, as the left-wing party, led by Alexis Tsipras, was tipped to win it.

"I'm not sure," he said, eyeing me up suspiciously, which meant he wouldn't be voting for Syriza then, and he was damned if he was going to share that with a *xeni* woman, his terse look seemed to say. Before the haircut was over, Dimas's push for presidency had been snipped, as he had fallen short of the required 180 votes. The barber rolled his eyes as he swept a soft-headed brush over Jim's neck.

Afterwards we stopped for a coffee in one of the small places off the square, where only one corner table was left. Tasos, Eleni's husband, was there and came over to buy us some ouzos and sit for a while. He was having a break from the olive harvest on some of his hundreds of trees and had been watching the vote. I asked him what he thought would happen now.

"Tsipras will win the election, I'm sure. That's who I'll be voting for."

Tasos was a good, solid working man, somewhat conservative, whom you would not pick as a supporter of left-wing governments and radical solutions, but here he was endorsing Syriza. I asked him why he'd vote for Syriza.

He offered a weary shrug. "What else can we do? We are fed up with austerity. Most people can't take any more. We are all suffering, losing money, and Greek kids are living without hope. My daughter has a good job in Athens, but for how long? She is talking about going overseas to work unless there is a big change in Greece. Tsipras has told the Greek people if he wins the election he will rip up the bailout agreement and do away with austerity," said Tasos, with a sigh of relief.

Tsipras's categorical promise that he would renegotiate the terms of the bailout and ditch the austerity programmes had roused the Greek people and turned him into something of a freedom fighter. The fact that he later reneged on his plan to ditch austerity when he finally won the election became one of the most bitterly debated, and hated, political U-turns in Greek history, sparking protests and a highly publicised referendum in 2015.

But in late 2014, confidence was riding high. To most people, it made good political sense to scrap austerity and find another blueprint, as it had failed to deliver any kind of lasting economic recovery. Greeks believed they had been suffering for nothing for five long years, without the country lowering its debts. Since 2010, the national debt had soared from 120% to 175% of GDP.

Despite all the sounds of euphoria around us, there were people who seemed less than pleased. Koroni was not a Syriza heartland and there were many people here, as elsewhere, who worried about this untried, maverick guy at the helm and the fact he could bring about a default on the loan and tip the country into chaos, a good Greek word of course, along with *katastrofi*.

While New Year's Eve promised some respite from the uncertainties of the current situation, we had planned a night at a taverna with live music in the village of Harakopio, where some of the students from the Greek class had also planned to meet up.

A bad storm had been predicted, however, so in the morning I rang the taverna to make sure it would be open. Many tavernas, especially along Koroni seafront, were closed for the winter, with the owners choosing to do their olive harvest instead. Restaurants that chose to stay open would still shut on nights when there weren't enough customers. The owner of the Harakopio taverna told me it wouldn't open.

"I hear the storm will be bad, *Kiria*. No-one will turn up."

New Year was officially shut. It seemed to indicate another turbulent 12 months ahead for Greece.

18

The Lotus Eaters

THE Greek election was at the end of January, on a Sunday, and we went down to Koroni for the early church service and coffee in one of the *kafeneia*, to get a feel for the outcome and whether Syriza could possibly win the prefecture of Messinia, which had traditionally been a stronghold of the conservative New Democracy party.

The polling station was in Koroni High School and it was a fairly dour event, possibly because Greeks were now becoming sick of elections and the constant upheaval in political life, with still no solution to the crisis. We later swung by the campaign office of Syriza, which was curiously housed in an old *ichthiopoleio*, fishmonger's shop, that was no longer in use. But it still had the aroma of fish about it, which the anti-Syriza lobby would perhaps have found ironic.

The place had a harsh appeal, with its flickering fluorescent lights, white tiles decorated with fish motifs and Syriza posters on the walls, with the election slogan Ελπίδα Έρχεται, Hope is Coming. The slogan at least resonated with most Greeks at a time when there seemed no hope from the dismal toll of austerity. But it would be painfully ironic later that year, when hope would be sent packing by Alexis Tsipras, like a skunk gone wild in a perfumery.

Two big guys were manning a small wooden table at the back of the 'shop'. One looked like Groucho Marx, with a thick black moustache, the other like a detective, in a dark suit and smart sunglasses. We asked them how their campaign was going.

"Syriza will win," said Groucho. "The Greeks don't want to be told what to do any more by other nations. This country has been crushed under the boot."

This is a popular saying in Greece and harks back to the Second World War and the German occupation. It was famously resurrected in 2012, during the height of the crisis, when Yiorgos Karatzaferis, leader of the right-wing LAOS party, said: "Greece can live outside the EU, but it cannot live under the German boot."

We asked if we could have one of their Syriza posters as a souvenir of the day.

"Have you voted?" Groucho asked, unpinning a poster from the tiles and rolling it up.

"We're *xenoi*, we can't vote. We don't live here."

The man looked crestfallen. We told them we were journalists from Britain, living for a while in Greece.

"Good," said Groucho. "You've got plenty to write about now. You're here at the crossroads of Greek history, my friends. You'll see. Things will be different now." They certainly would – but for all the wrong reasons.

We left with our poster, which had a slightly oily, salty feel about it, like a fish supper takeaway. The street outside was deserted, with discarded election pamphlets piling up in its unswept corners. There were no other Syriza punters about. We walked back down to the school, where voters were trailing in and out, looking dazed. In the narrow street beside the school, where the Sunday market was usually held, there were only a few stalls because of polling day. One or two people had brought some fruit and vegetables to sell. We strolled about and recognised one of the men who always sold just a few things but they were always good: sweet tomatoes, oranges, strawberries that had a lovely jammy flavour.

"Don't go looking for testicles," I told Jim.

"Oh, Margarita, don't disgrace me now."

We stopped by the young hawker, who had thick sticky-out hair and a toothy smile. He had a wooden box on the ground with a few cabbages and late-season fruits. Some shiny orange fruits I took to be persimmons, though it wasn't a fruit I had ever eaten before. I picked one up and rolled it around in my hands. It felt smooth and warm.

"*Lotos*, we call it in Greek," he said in good English. "It was the fruit that Odysseus found in the land of the Lotus Eaters. It makes man forget everything."

I vaguely remembered the story from Homer. When Odysseus was sailing around the tip of the Mani, near Cape Tainaron, on his way home to Ithaka after the Trojan War, his ship was blown off-course and ended up dropping anchor at an island inhabited by the Lotus Eaters. They lived on this sweet fruit that induced forgetfulness and oblivion.

"It's a good day for the *lotos*. A day to forget the past," I offered.

He laughed. "We mustn't forget anything here in Greece. Now we must keep our heads clear."

"And have any Greeks bought these today?"

"Not so much," he said with a cheeky grin. "But it's better for you, the *xenoi*."

"Why so?"

"When Odysseus's men ate the *lotos* they forgot their friends, their family, and they did not care about going home."

"Ah, that's us." I said, flapping my hand between Jim and me. "We are forgetting to go home."

"Where is home?"

"Scotland."

He smiled. "Ah, the people who fought the English. Mil Geebson; blue face."

"Yes, that's it."

"He fight the English, like we fight the Troika."

"Something like that."

The Lotus Eaters

Since first coming to the Peloponnese in 2010, every time I said I was Scottish, a Greek would claim kinship because of our historic freedom fights. Back then, the Greeks would say the Scots had the English to contend with, while they had the Turks, but now it had evolved from Turks to Troika, or more especially the Germans, because of their role in pursuing swingeing austerity measures.

I bought four of the *lotos* fruit from the hawker. "Now I'll never go home."

He laughed and gave me a small cabbage as well. "*Doro apo 'mena.*" A gift, he said, touching his heart.

"What do you do for a living?" I asked him, thinking he must be a student, an artist or a writer with a hobby farm. He seemed rather sensitive.

"I am a carpenter," he said, with a shrewd grin, pointing to the arm of his fleece, where I could see tiny shards of wood embedded in the fabric. He shrugged philosophically. "And I have a little farm... but the *lotos* fruit come from my cousin in Crete. It's still warm enough down there for them."

We shook hands and not long afterwards I saw him packing up to go. How wonderful Greece was when a carpenter hawking fruit on a winter's day could talk to you about Homer's *Odyssey* and discuss the lotus eaters with such affection. How fitting that he had sold us this fruit, two strangers on their own long Greek odyssey, still feeling their way, still not ready to go home yet. Did we somehow have that emblazoned on our foreheads?

"If we eat these, Jimbo, and then come back for more some time, it will take us another 10 years or so to get home again."

"Good. Held hostage by a fruit. Perfect —and not even pears, Margarita."

"No, especially not pears, Jimbo. Or even testicles."

On the way back to the car we passed Tasos, heading for the small *kafeneio* where we often saw him. It made me think how lovely it might have been to be brought up in small town like this, where you know everyone, where there are favourite places you have gone to all your life which are so convivial, and well-placed, within a minute's walk to the water's edge. Crisis or no crisis, I thought if there was really such a thing as reincarnation, I wanted to come back as a Greek villager – one who was independently wealthy at least.

"Did you vote for Syriza after all?" I asked Tasos, remembering we had seen him on the day of the presidential vote in December.

"Of course. Who else would I vote for? Not that *vlakas*, idiot, Samaras, who's in bed with the Troika."

He laughed and added. "We'll call around one day when the harvest is over. We'll bring you some oil and a few other things, so you can try our Messinian produce, eh?"

"Oh, that's very kind of you. We'll look forward to it."

I was touched by this offer of a gift. He and Eleni were two of the most self-effacing and generous people we had met.

"Okay," he said with a smile and sprinted to the *kafeneio*.

By Monday it was confirmed that Syriza had won the election, with 149 seats, but not enough for an outright majority, and they would form a coalition government with one of the smaller parties. We watched all the TV coverage that night and the huge rally in Athens for Syriza supporters. Many of them were young people, their eyes glistening with hope, but even the older folks were ecstatic, treating Alexis Tsipras as a minor deity and someone who could deliver them from crisis. Although we didn't know it then, perhaps Tsipras's stirring victory speech would be the finest moment of his political career before Greece once again teetered over loans, Troika interference, bank catastrophes, with the edge looming later in 2015 – for the umpteenth time in six years.

But that Monday night, Tsipras was so jubilant he seemed to scintillate under the TV lights as he fed the crowd his youthful, but inflated, hopes: "Greece leaves behind catastrophic austerity. It leaves behind fear and authoritarianism. It leaves behind five years of humiliation and anguish... Our priority is for our country and our people to regain their lost dignity. The verdict is that the Troika is finished." If only that had been true.

That month, I was beginning to understand a little more about the frustration of promises going downhill. Despite my call to Sir Ambrose before Christmas and a few more emails, I heard nothing more from him about the overdue royalty payments or an acknowledgement of the formal 'letter of notice' I had sent him. No apology either. He had simply ceased to communicate, and when I contacted my Spanish friend in Greece, she reported a similar experience. It all seemed like a strange and slightly dishonourable way to conduct a publishing business, but soon I had heard of other people having similar experiences in Sir Ambrose's corral of disgruntled authors.

He had until the end of January to respond to my formal letter and pay the amount owing, or the rights of *Things Can Only Get Feta* would return to me. I think it was at that point I saw the amusing irony of having given the book that title. Things could certainly not get any worse on the book front, but as the end of January approached what I dreaded most was that Sir Ambrose would somehow pull a rabbit out of his top hat and pay up – and then I would be stuck with him forever and the possibility of the haggling recommencing when every set of royalties was due. And the paperback may well have stayed out of print forever.

When the final day came for him to settle matters, my bank account still lacked a payment, the paperback was still out of print and there was no word at all from him, still no proper note of apology, or farewell. Despite having spent an inordinate amount of time promoting the book right from the start, as most authors are expected to do these days, the business relationship had ended with less ceremony than any British worker would expect after being made redundant. But in my case, there was no redundancy payment.

Such is the publishing industry today that legal contracts can be broken with impunity, and most especially by 'aristocrats' out of step with ordinary aspirations. The word 'aristocrat' is, of course, from the Greek, *aristocratis*, a person of excellence. It was hard to see this quality in many British toffs of today.

There are points in life, however, when it doesn't do any good to waste energy on the poor behaviour of others. You may detest them but you can't change them, so I got on with my books, my life and just thanked God that I had been set free. Although he did eventually pay some of the royalties owing, it was not the whole amount and, to date, this situation remains unchanged.

In early February, with my faith in publishing eroded, I took the logical option and decided to republish the book myself. Jim offered to put his other work aside for a few weeks to help format the book for both an ebook version and paperback for Amazon, which would at least put the latter back in circulation quickly, especially after the disaster of it going out of print just before Christmas, with a loss of revenue.

Thankfully, with the winter months being particularly cold and wet, as Anastasios had predicted, it was ideal weather to hunker down in the 'study' and read through the book again and do a bit more polishing and finish the edits on the sequel as well, as I planned to publish it soon after *Feta*. The artist who had drawn the original book cover fortunately had the copyright and gave me permission to reuse it, with some slight tinkering, but when it was finished, I felt it looked even better than the original, with a few extra elements in the illustration.

Although it was a relief to take control of my writing career fully, there were nevertheless times when I felt nervous about the whole endeavour of republishing and promoting the books myself in such a competitive market. It would be a steep learning curve, especially for the second book.

Some mornings I was awake before sunrise. It was easier to get up and work rather than toss and turn in bed. I would make coffee, roll up the balcony shutter and sit at my *kafeneio* table in front of the windows in the dark, with just the computer's backlight, waiting for the sun to come up over the Taygetos mountains opposite. One morning, the sky over the mountains was so spectacularly clear that I knew the sunrise would be something special, and it was.

In a cleft between two mountain peaks a spec of rosy light appeared like a small eye, the sky around it glowing. Every moment the eye grew, the sky around it brightening in bands of orange and purple. The gulf water was turning deep red and I thought, appropriately, of Homer's 'wine dark sea'. As the eye enlarged it took on the aspect of a sentient being, waking, coming alive, peeping over the mountains.

The notion of God came easily into the equation at that time in the morning, and whether or not you believe in divine creators, there was something majestic and other-worldly about this glowing orb that mesmerised me. Also, if ever I needed a beneficent and all-seeing deity to guide my way, it was at that particular moment.

The apparition fascinated me so much I got out my camera and took dozens of photos and a video grab. As the ever expanding, ascending eye left the mountains behind, climbing higher over the gulf, it flicked a switch on the day and a series of well-choreographed routines: caiques began to slip quietly out of Koroni harbour, heading perhaps for the Ionian Sea; birds started their languid early-morning flight over the water. I could also hear the first stirrings of the farming family below, the grandfather rounding everyone up for the morning.

A Scorpion In The Lemon Tree

My work was forgotten for a while but the sunrise phenomenon inspired me and reminded me of how, in this corner of the world so racked with crisis, you could see a sight like this, every day, in the immense beauty of this southern region. Nothing much else seemed to matter. Life was bigger than my small problems, and the 'eye' would be back again another day.

One negative consequence of the publishing drama, however, was the fact that we spent too much time at the villa, while there were places in Messinia that we still wanted to visit. The olive harvest had slipped by us this year without us noticing too closely, apart from Svetlana working nearby and the sight of other farmers harvesting on the hillsides, or trucks rumbling by, piled high with heavy sacks of olives, and workers perched on top, holding their harvesting wands high, like tridents.

When we weren't working inside, we walked over the hillsides, which was pleasant in this cooler weather. Sometimes we walked to the small church of the Panayitsa, or stopped by to see Pluto. We had often taken him leftovers and in the year we were there, we had let him try everything from pasta to curries, all of which he downed with gusto. It was possibly his best year ever. He was a rather melancholy creature though and we often saw him sitting at the high edge of his field, behind the fence, staring out to sea. Once in a gale, I saw his long ears go comically horizontal as if he were cleared for take-off. I rather fancied that if he could have, he would have taken a flight to freedom.

One February morning, after getting up before dawn to work, I went back to bed for a few hours, tired from my labours. Jim was sound asleep and Wallace, who now slept every night at the bottom of the bed, was on his back, with his legs straight up in the air. We got up late, around 10am, and were sitting outside in the sun, still in our dressing gowns, when we heard our names being called and sensed some movement along the side balcony. It was Tasos and Eleni, carrying plastic bags.

I realised that we had not seen either them for a few weeks, as they had been busy on their olive harvest in several nearby orchards. Jim and I looked at each other in fright, not because we didn't want to see them but because we imagined we looked pretty ragged. I didn't have time to brush my curly hair but ran my fingers through it, as it has a tendency to stand up in the morning like Einstein's (and that's all we have in common, sadly). Then I gave up when I realised I was making it worse.

It was hard to say who was more embarrassed, us or them, confronting us in our pyjamas, dressing gowns and sheepskin slippers.

"Oh sorry," said Eleni, "you're just out of bed."

"We were working late last night."

"Do you want us to go?"

"No, of course not. Don't be silly. Sit down and have a coffee."

I dived into the kitchen and got out my *briki* to make coffee. I admit that after so many years in Greece I make terrible Greek coffee, always getting the technique wrong, forgetting when to take the muddy mixture off the boil. After so many dozens of times watching Foteini from her *kaliva* doorway, boiling it up on the *petrogazi* cooker, I should have been an expert. I brought out my effort, however, and we all sat at the big front table, enjoying the sudden burst of warm February sunshine. Tasos started to unpack the plastic bags.

"We have brought you some things as I promised," he said. And out came bottles of olive oil, olives, a bottle of his own honey-coloured wine, a jar of capers, a large slab of hard white cheese, and several other items, all from his farm.

"You shouldn't have brought us so much."

"Why not? You are our neighbours. You have to try our products," he said, with a look I have often seen on Greeks

− almost wounded pride. They have such a fine sense of honour and the rightness of things, which is encapsulated best in the unique Greek word *filotimo*.

I brought out some bread and cut some of the cheese, and we had it as our late breakfast. We were thrilled by the gifts and it was nice to think that even though we had been there for less than a year, we had already become neighbours and friends, as you do so easily in Greece.

"You should buy a house and stay here, and then we can always be neighbours," said Eleni.

"I wish we could. At least *ena spitaki* (a small house)."

"Houses are cheap now," said Tasos. "I know a man who can show you some houses around here, if you like. Most will need a little bit of work, though."

Jim and I looked at each other. Was it time to consider a property search finally, just out of curiosity, if nothing else? Tasos gave us the name and number of his friend and told us we could call him any time. There would be no pressure to buy, just to look at the properties. We decided that after both books were safely published, and we had more free time, we would make arrangements to look at a few houses, both in Koroni and the Mani.

"Imagine, Jimbo, if we could find a small place and not have to think about leaving any more. At least for a while."

"You should ease up on the *lotos* fruit, Margarita."

Ease up? No way. I had a real taste for it now.

19

Too old to conjugate

BY February, the Greek class began to develop some teeth, with a little harder grammar and vocabulary. I enrolled in earnest and was given my own textbook, *Learning the Greek Language*, that the others already had. When Christos gave it to me he apologised for its minimal appearance.

"Lack of government funds," he said, with a shrug.

The 'book' was a thick set of what looked like photocopied pages with black and white illustrations. It had been produced by the Institute of Continuing Adult Education, with funding from the Greek government and the EU. On the title page, the book said it was aimed at the education of *metanastes*, migrants, in language, culture and politics. So we were all migrants in Greece now.

The aim of the course was admirable, given that Greek is such a hard language for foreigners. But there was also the shrewd intention perhaps to educate migrants and refugees in certain practicalities, like how to look for work, apply for a job vacancy, secure residency permits and find accommodation – none of which was very useful to a group of people, mostly retired to Greece or with holiday homes, seeking to communicate with real Greeks.

One day, Christos told us to turn to a long passage of conversation about looking for rental properties. Several of us were asked to pick a character and read aloud. We were variously Mohammed, Nadia, Ivan, Stanislav. It prompted a lot giggling around the room but one middle-aged Dutch student was not pleased. Later, out on the balcony during our break, he complained: "I came here to learn about Greek life not the struggles of the *metanastes*." He eventually left the class for good, saying it was not for him. But the textbook was amusing and the vocabulary modern and useful. I am certain I now know how to get a work permit in Greece, should the urge take me, and book a bus ticket for Thessaloniki, and organise a flat share with Boris and Jasmine.

After the elections, there was much vibrant discussion about what Syriza would do first to shake up the Troika. It was obvious that Christos was pleased Syriza had won, especially as there had been a promise to reinstate the national broadcaster ERT again. But we all agreed it was one thing to win and another for Tsipras to carry out all his promises, especially the intention of saying goodbye to the Troika.

"Can Tsipras do that?" we asked him.

"I hope so, but it will not help these language classes."

"What do you mean?"

"The government is struggling to keep funding them. Even if Tsipras can carry out his plan to reject more bailouts and come up with a different way of doing things, there will be chaos for a while. Many things will have to go in the beginning, including these kinds of classes. No-one knows what's going to happen."

Christos still hadn't been paid his salary and the amount owed to him was mounting. It was a miracle really that the classes had lasted this long.

"Why do you come to the classes if this government won't pay you?" asked one of the Germans in a state of indignation.

"It is hard for you to understand this, I know. It is not something you would experience in your country. I love teaching these classes. It is better I go on with my job. Maybe one day I will be paid. *Ti na kanoume*," he said, using the popular Greek expression, 'What can we do?', that seems to set a problem aside for perpetuity. Just as well in this instance.

There was a grumble from behind us. An English couple had joined the classes. They lived in one of the outlying villages and were pleasant enough, if a little like aging hippies on an endless gap year, but then many of the Germans and Austrians also looked like that. Maybe we did as well! As if everyone had come decades ago and hadn't bothered to go home. Lotus Eaters to the max.

A strange dynamic developed in the class, as the Germans sat on one side of the room, the British on the other, and the Jewish guy somewhere in the middle. Perhaps the increasing political dramas in Greece had polarised us all slightly. A rather sexy-looking French woman called Brigitte sat wherever the mood took her. She would float into class like a powder puff in hot pants and all the men would lose their way in a thicket of verb conjugation and accusative stares from partners.

One of the German couples was rather amusing. The man, Hans, was slim, perma-tanned and fit looking for his age and had a very over-emphasised, shouty way of talking his Greek, which made even the other Germans giggle. He also didn't believe in verbs, despite having done the course the year before. I had encountered this problem among British expats as well. When we first went to the Mani in 2010, we rented a house from an Englishman named Desmond. He didn't speak much Greek but what he did speak gave a body-swerve to verbs. On our first day in the village he took us around to introduce us to everyone, which involved pointing at us and saying: "*Ena chrono, spiti mou*. One year, my house."

Before each Greek class started in earnest we usually had a conversational component, where Christos went round the group asking us what we had done in the previous few days. Hans's replies always took much longer than anyone else's and generally involved the same scenario: a drinking session with '*o filos mou*' my friend. It usually went something like: "*Filos mou, spiti, para poli krasi* (my friend, house, a load of wine)," said with a jerking movement of his thumb towards his mouth. One day he delighted everyone by telling us he had a barrel of wine in his house for visits from *filos mou*.

Christos's eyes pinged wide. "A whole barrel?"

"Yes, *poli krasi*!"

His wife slapped him hard on the shoulder, embarrassed no doubt by his tipsy Greek.

"Do you drink, Christos?" I was bold enough to ask him, knowing only too well what the answer would be.

"No," he said. "Only at *paniyiria* and name days. I don't like it so much, but anyway, there is no money for alcohol in Greece now."

"I see lots of Greeks drinking in the *kafeneio*," said Hans. "Plenty *tsipouro*."

"Those Greeks who drink a lot are old ones. They still have pension money. But maybe not for long," said Christos, with a frown.

"They need a drink then, *para poli*," shouted Hans, reducing everyone to gales of laughter as usual.

The classes continued for two nights a week and we tried to attend them all. Much as I liked the lessons, however, there were some rare days when I felt bored with the endless repetition of things I already knew, which was no credit to me as I had been learning Greek on and off for years. Also, hearing other people blundering through the language was not always very stimulating, or having to find out how Ivan or Stanislav would make out trying to find a job in Athens wasn't very exciting either after a while.

One particular afternoon, we were conjugating sets of verbs. It was giving me a headache. Conjugating Greek verbs is no laughing matter. The simplest verb conjugated in all tenses will have around 60 different constructions, and many verbs also have a passive form as well, with a slightly different meaning. Mind-boggling! Ancient Greek, from which the modern is derived, was even more complex, apparently.

Too Old To Conjugate

While Greek is a wonderfully brainy and logical language, I sometimes feel that the ancients must have been linguistic masochists with too much time on their hands.

To give you an idea: the verb *louzomai* means I have a bath or wash my hair. *Louzo* means to give someone else a bath or a hair wash. Why pile in another set of conjugations? It prompted the cheeky Jorgen to comment that he wouldn't bother to learn both forms of this verb and would only ever get other people to wash him. Sorted!

Late in the afternoon that day, I needed to use the toilet, near the front of the building. It was a small bathroom with a locking door, and we always had to ask Christos for the key. I wandered off, taking my time, and on the way back heard some Greek music playing along one of the corridors. I peeped through an open window and saw a group of adults holding hands, about to dance. They were mostly foreigners.

"What are you dancing?" I called out.

An English woman, in her sixties by the look of her, turned.

"The Kalamatianos."

"No kidding!"

There was a door off the corridor, leading to the classroom. I went in and slouched against the doorway, watching the group moving around in a circle. They weren't bad, their movements light and bouncy. I already knew the steps were simple, but it was a case of getting the sequence right.

"Can I join in?" I asked the young Greek teacher taking the class, who seemed quite easy-going.

"Sure," he said.

The group made a space for me and I joined hands with the ones either side. I tried to follow them but my feet were a muddle. It only needed repetition and practice. How many years now had I wanted to learn the Kalamatianos?

The teacher was watching my feet.

"*Pos pao?*" I asked him. How am I doing?

"*Mia hara*, fine." He was lying, obviously.

"Thank you," I said.

"*Parakalo – ligo*," he said with a boyish grin.

The group laughed. It was a humorous, cheeky thing to say in Greek. It meant "you're welcome – a bit". I had heard it from some of the villagers in the Mani, especially those who liked a wind-up.

Round and round we went, my feet trying to obey the rhythm, going in one direction some of the time when I should have gone in another. It was so much nicer than conjugating verbs. Suddenly I heard a loud voice from the window.

"Margarita, what are you doing?"

It was Jim. "Oh hell!" I said, looking at my watch. I'd lost track of time.

"Christos was worried about you. We thought you might be sick, so I volunteered to find you …. and you're bloody dancing!"

The teacher laughed. "More fun than Greek class, eh?"

I nodded and said goodbye to the group.

"Come again," someone shouted.

Jim and I walked back to the class.

Christos looked concerned as I dropped the toilet key back on his desk.

"*Ola kala, Margarita?*"

"Oh sure, thanks. Just needed some air. Bit of a headache."

"It will get worse. We are conjugating some passive verbs now," Jorgen said, shaking his head.

"I don't know why people make such a fuss about Greek grammar. We have difficult grammar too," said the English woman with a frown.

"Perhaps not as hard as Greek grammar," said Christos.

Bravo, I thought. That's why we were all here. Oddly enough, we didn't gel with the English couple at all. They seemed rather insular. During our half-hour break one day, we were all discussing the difficulty of learning Greek. The couple, who had retired to Greece, stood on the sidelines, eating sandwiches from a plastic lunch box. The woman admitted her Greek could have been so much better but she had no-one to talk Greek to in between classes.

"But you live in a village, don't you?" I asked, perplexed.

"Yes, but I don't speak to the villagers. What would I talk to them about? I like to have stimulating conversation in Greek, not talk about goats and tomato yields."

I felt dismayed by the response. Some of us were happy to have any conversations at all with Greeks. I thought of Foteini and our mad conversations, and wondered how we managed to talk so much at times, given that my Greek was less than perfect and we were so very different, but somehow we always had things to communicate. There was common humanity between us; lives lived. That's all it takes.

I decided these two had probably sucked on too much lotus juice, and it was high time they went home.

Home. Where was it anyway? The Greek classes intensified the notion that we were all a rather restless, deracinated bunch of people, who were probably at home everywhere and nowhere. As someone who had been moving back and forth across the globe from the age of nine, like a manic shuttlecock, after my Scottish parents first decided to emigrate to Australia, I had no real idea what constituted home any more. Or where my roots really lay. I had already put down some roots in Greece, but not so deep yet that they couldn't be gently pulled up and relocated out of necessity.

It was a well-travelled Scottish woman who once set me thinking about the importance of roots at all when she said: "Don't worry about roots. After childhood you don't really need them."

Perhaps that was true. It was the change of place that was perhaps more important than sinking anything into it.

There is a Greek *parimia*, saying, that goes: "*Alakse to riziko sou na ideis to ofelos sou.*" Change your fate to see a benefit. In other words, nothing will improve unless you make a move – somewhere.

20

Life on the rogue carpet

THE Ayia Playia taverna that we had begun to visit regularly, in the village of Falanthi, was packed. This was the February night of *tsiknopempti*, a curious date in the Easter calendar, which roughly translates as Barbecue Thursday, as it comes in the last few days before Lent, when it's still permissible to eat meat, and it's usually chargrilled meat that's preferred.

Greeks will fire up barbecues at their homes and invite friends around, turning briefly into Aussies. But many congregate in tavernas where chargrilling is a specialty. Often there will be a party atmosphere, sometimes with live music and dancing, a last fling before the long Lenten period when, if you're devout, you will be lucky to eat anything at all near the end, apart from a plate of boiled greens with a squeeze of lemon. Olive oil is also off the menu, which for Greeks is the biggest sacrifice of all.

We decided to go to the Ayia Playia for its cosy atmosphere, but it was also one of the best places for chargrills, and Yiorgos's usual Saturday *kontosouvli*, pieces of spit-roasted pork, drew punters from the whole area. There was a nice vibe that Thursday night, with long tables of Greek families, music in the background, the 'organ fire' playing a hot accompaniment. There were a few people we recognised from Koroni and one couple from the Greek class with a table of German friends. It was Hans. When he saw us across the room he waved, pointed to the man next to him and shouted. "*O filos mou, para poli krasi!*" (My friend, lots of wine!) So the 'wine' friend really did exist.

Yiorgos was in fine form, moving from table to table, like the perfect host, which he was, and always had a few words for everyone.

This particular evening, he seemed more introspective than usual. While other families were keen to be together, Yiorgos had to live with the reality that he could only see his lovely wife Maria and their young son once a month, if he was lucky, as she had an important government job in Athens and for now they had to work around this challenging routine. They were among a growing band of couples in Greece who had to make big sacrifices to keep their families financially secure, and yet they did it with good grace.

Later in the evening, after he put another pile of olive wood on the fire, Yiorgos stopped by the table we usually took, wedged into the corner, near the fire. He asked us how long we were staying in Greece. We told him we hoped to stay for the summer again but we weren't sure yet.

Like many Greeks, he wanted to know what we made of the crisis and more importantly what people abroad thought about the country, especially after the post-election drama of the new government having to bow to pressure over the terms of the bailout. Despite Tsipras saying he would rip up the agreement with the Troika and ditch austerity, the uncomfortable truth was that the country desperately needed the latest tranche of bailout money worth 7.2 billion euros.

"Don't worry, people around the world are on the side of the Greeks," I told him.

"You think so?"

"We all feel sympathy for the way Greece has been treated by the Troika."

He nodded and stared reflectively towards the fire.

"I hope everyone knows we've been trying to get ourselves out of the mess we're in, but the Troika doesn't make things easy for us. Especially small businesses like mine."

In those months, many Greeks asked the same question: what did the world think about Greece and the Greeks? The question always made me sad. Here was the country that had spawned our western civilisation and all the greatest ideas about politics, philosophy, art and medicine, to name just a few things — the alpha race of Europe — now having to ask what foreigners thought of them. Whenever you reassured them we were on their side, gifts were showered on you, whether you wanted them or not. The owner of a bakery in Koroni gave me a spinach pie and some sweet pastries when I told her we all loved Greece. Another offered me slices of the popular custardy sweet, *galaktoboureko*. I could have dined out for months this way.

Easter in Greece is long and devotional, with many increments of fasting and various church services in the lead-up to the Holy Week, *Megali Evdomada*. Even before the week arrived, we decided to go to one of the great services of Easter known as the *heretismi*, the Salutations, chanted to the *panayia*, Virgin Mary, and performed on four Fridays before Easter. It includes one of the most complex of Byzantine hymns and is very solemn, though on this occasion it was unintentionally slapstick and not part of the usual script at all.

We went to the church of the Eleistria this time, where the previous Easter we had experienced the marathon Thursday service. The young and slightly maverick Papas of that year had obviously not struck a chord with the elders of Koroni because there had been complaints, we were told, and he had been replaced by an older priest who, by the looks of him, poor soul, had been brought out of mothballs to fill the gap, which may have accounted for his slight petulance.

The church was full with the same families we had regularly seen here and at least a dozen children of different ages. Not long into the service, the priest was moving from the sanctuary through the central archway in the ornamental screen, *iconostasis*, when he tripped on the fraying rug, poor man, and nearly swan-dived down the steps on to the floor. The young deacon, standing by the side of the church, was summoned and a lively discussion ensued in front of the congregation that we couldn't quite grasp, while the cantors continued the thread of the service with their chanting. There was much arm waving and orders given by the priest, and the deacon was dispatched out the front door.

A short while later he returned with a short roll of carpet, which intrigued us all. He placed it on the floor near the arch, thinking his duty was done, whereupon the old priest saw it and called him back, giving him another rebuke, telling him, I gathered, not to leave it there but to bring it into the sanctuary. Didn't the boy know the priest had a service to conduct?

The carpet was duly dispatched to the sanctuary via the right-hand door in the *iconostasis* and this was the start of a long segment of rolling out the carpet, shunting down its sides between the pillars of the archway so it was safe. And then the priest did a preliminary amble over it, to see if it would do, while the red-faced deacon sloped around with dropped shoulders, like a magician's rookie assistant in a talent contest.

It was so diverting that we all forgot why we were here, until the service started in earnest. I have always loved Orthodox services for their ritual and their atmosphere, but they are also disarmingly pitched to a human scale as well, when the mood is right. Once we attended a service in a church in Kalamata on a particular saint's day. The church was packed, with rows of school kids as well. A large table had been set up before the *iconostasis,* with baskets of holy bread in hard round loaves.

One of the orderlies had apparently laid out the bread in the wrong manner and he, too, was given a lecture by a very old, grey-bearded priest, who looked like Moses. The minute the orderly had left the scene, the old priest turned to the packed congregation and, in routine worthy of Benny Hill, rolled his eyes dramatically in the direction of the departing orderly and twisted his hand at his temples several times, the Greek sign for 'bonkers'. It made Jim and I giggle, rather loudly, though no-one else seemed to find it funny, or wanted to own up to the comedy perhaps.

For Easter Friday, we went to the main church in Koroni for the service of the *Epitafios* and then the carrying of the flower-decked bier (epitaph), representing the crucified Christ, with his icon laid inside. The bier was taken through the streets and up to the castle just before sunset. We well remembered this service in the hillside village of Megali Mantineia in our first year, when Wallace escaped from the house and decided to join the procession around the village, with amusing results.

In Koroni, the procession of several hundred people behind the epitaph was slow and dignified, moving along the narrow streets of the town, each 'pilgrim' holding a lighted candle. From a distance it formed a moody ribbon of light ascending to the castle's tall, Gothic-style entrance at the top. People spoke in whispers, even the children seemed to have absorbed the sense of solemnity, which was something of a miracle in itself. From the castle gate, a narrow cobbled path leads past the monastery of Timios Prodromos and on to the graveyard spanning the top of the castle area, with views down to either side of the peninsula. On this flat, imposing piece of land, everyone in Koroni has been buried since the beginning of time.

The epitaph was halted several times and the *papas* said prayers for the dead. In between, the procession of light wound its way through the dark graveyard in a sure-footed movement while we struggled to keep up, after our candles blew out. We were rookies and, unlike the Greeks, hadn't thought to bring a torch to help us pick our way over uneven cobbled pathways and around tall cypress and olive trees.

Yet the 'pilgrimage' was compulsive, with the thrill of an ancient mystery play made spooky by the macabre shadows cast against marble tombs and headstones. Amid the drama, I momentarily lost Jim and hung back to look for him as the procession quickly made its way towards the vertiginous staircase that descends to the Eleistria church below, where a huge crowd was gathering for a final service in this church. As I shuffled around in the dark, I felt a hand on my shoulder and jumped. It was Tasos, our neighbour, with Eleni and their daughter Maria. They were huddled together under a tree by the light of a small torch.

"Where's Jim?" they asked.

"Lost, I think."

They all looked amused. I imagined it wasn't the first time a family member had been lost in the graveyard on Epitafios night. I suddenly thought how much fun it would have been if Wallace had come along. It would have ramped up the drama to the max, that's for sure.

"What are you both doing on Sunday?" asked Tasos. Sunday is the traditional day for family get-togethers and the Easter feast.

"Nothing really," I said.

"Come to our house in Koroni, we're having *kokeretsi*. You will like it."

I was delighted with the invitation. Who doesn't relish the chance to have lunch with a Greek family on a festive day. *Kokoretsi* is goats' or lambs' intestines stuffed with various bits of offal and herbs, and barbecued, like a Mediterranean version of haggis. It is something you either like or don't. I did, but earlier in my life it was something I wouldn't have touched if my life depended on it.

During my many trips to Greece, from the first long stay in Athens in the 1970s, I have tried many delightful, and sometimes challenging, meals. I first came across *kokoretsi* while staying in Crete for a few months in the late 1970s. I and a friend had been invited with several Greek acquaintances to have Sunday lunch with a farming family, who lived near our rented house in deep rural Crete.

It was an impromptu visit and the family were embarrassed to have nothing much to offer us, particularly to the foreigners among us, since these were the days when *filoxenia* (love of strangers/foreigners) and hospitality was a more rigidly adhered to doctrine. The family decided one of their lambs must be slaughtered and roasted in honour of our visit. I calculated this would take a good few hours. This was the least of our worries, however. I was horrified at this waste of a good beast, most especially since my friend and I were both vegetarians at that time and were not about to break it, even for a wonderful Greek family.

It took a great deal of persuasion from our Greek friends to convince the family that killing a lamb, for our sakes at least, was not expected. Then we were told that *kokoretsi* would be prepared instead for the *xenoi,* so we could try this delicacy. Again we had to decline. Then finally the offer came for barbecued *tsikles*, thrushes, with their heads left on.

"Now thrushes are just little birds, so that should please you," our hosts told us. These were much simpler times in Greece when no-one had ever met a real vegetarian, and it was assumed we were some kind of strange religious zealots. "Buddhists" was proposed at one stage. It got more and more strange and tormenting as the minutes ticked by but, in the end, they did cook the thrushes for the others and also prepared plates of *horta*, greens, salad and wonderful lemon potatoes, so the day was not lost.

Tasos and Eleni had a small townhouse not far from the harbour. A table had been beautifully set out for lunch, with plates of everything imaginable: pork chops, barbecued chicken, village sausages, spinach pies and, of course, the *kokoretsi,* cooked on a barbecue, which I have since come to like in my post-vegetarian lifestyle. We were thrilled by the invitation to have lunch with the couple and their children Maria and Andreas, who were very much like their parents both in looks and in their sweet temperaments. It was an excellent day, sitting outside with a view down towards the harbour, overlooking other houses, where Greek families were doing just the same as us, sitting at long tables on balconies and in gardens enjoying their Easter feast. It was particularly gratifying as Maria, who worked in Athens, had excellent English and it was lovely to be able to say many of the things to Tasos and Eleni that I hadn't been able to say well enough with my imperfect Greek.

We heard stories about their family and their lives in Koroni and the time passed too quickly. Of all the wonderful things that Jim and I had experienced in our years in Greece, being taken into the heart of a Greek family and shown great kindness ranks as the most rewarding.

21

Walls with a view

WE were in a village we'd never been to before. When we saw a middle-aged woman ambling down the hill with a straggling flock of goats, I just knew she was going to engage us in conversation, but not in the same effervescent way that Foteini had the first time we met her in the Mani.

This woman was rotund, wearing a flowery kind of kaftan, with a long cardigan over the top. Her hair was in a messy up-do, held together by hairpins and combs and other objects of indeterminate usage. She wanted to know why we had come to her village, as it wasn't normally a magnet for *xenoi*.

It was in the north Mani, in the foothills of the Taygetos. It was a rather tumbledown place, with plenty of crumbling buildings, a small but not bustling *pantopoleio*, general store, a *kafeneio* and a couple of locked churches. We had come to this northern area to meet an English couple who were selling their house, as the husband was ill and required treatment back in the UK. The property was going for a good price, with all the furniture in it, which is a common occurrence in Greece when expats need to return home in a hurry. It seemed like a nice village, though noisy at least on the day we visited.

Now that we had stayed the winter and were unsure how long we would stay after that, or where, we finally decided to start looking at properties that friends had recommended. Even if we didn't plan to stay forever, it would give us a small foothold in a country we were obviously besotted with.

A Scorpion In The Lemon Tree

As we sat on the balcony of the English couple's property, we noticed there was some kind of celebration going on in the house next door. The couple explained that their neighbour's daughters had been married that morning and the family were getting ready to depart for a lavish reception on the outskirts of Kalamata.

In the meantime, some of the males in the family indulged in the common practice of firing a few rounds of live ammunition into the air, which is traditionally supposed to remind villagers of the happy event. In this instance, however, one of the men was especially joyful and fired off a semi-automatic rifle at regular intervals, as if defending the hillside from enemy insurgents. It was a frightening sound. We had taken Wallace with us and it set him off on a tormenting round of barking that provoked other dogs nearby to join in. It was pandemonium and the English couple were slightly mortified.

"Is the family always noisy?" we asked, trying not to probe too much.

"Not any more than most rural Greeks," they replied, rather sheepishly. "To be honest, there haven't been that many weddings in this village. Most of the young people seem to have moved away."

Well, that wasn't very hopeful, but a similar situation existed in many of the Mani villages, as people moved away to the towns for work, leaving an increasingly older population, or a few hardy foreigners. We felt for the couple's predicament in wanting a quick sale, but in the end the village felt too remote.

On the way back to Kalamata we passed through a series of small villages and stopped at one to stretch our legs. It was here, on a lane bordered by an olive grove, in the middle of which there appeared to be a 'burial site' for discarded white goods, we met the goat herder called Meropi. Like most rural Greeks, she wanted to know all about us in the first five minutes: where we were from, how old we were, and where we had just been. We made the mistake of telling her we'd been to a village higher up, to see a house.

Her eyes flashed like neon. "You want to buy a house? I have a house. It's very cheap. Only 40,000 euro. Beautiful, traditional stone house with views of the mountains and sea. It's all been fixed up, very nice. Come and look at it."

I wasn't in the mood for another house viewing that day, but translated Meropi's offer for Jim.

He scratched his chin and looked thoughtful. "Hmm. Might be worth a quick look. If it's renovated and 40,000 euros, it sounds like a bargain. What do you think?"

"I don't know, it's getting late. What do you think, Wallace?" I said, looking down at him as he lay patiently on the dusty road, tired after a long day and the drive from Koroni. "Shall we go see the house, or shall we go home?"

"He's a dog, Margarita, not the Oracle of Delphi!"

"Well, not so fast, Jimbo. I say, if he gets up in the next minute, it's a sign and we'll go see the house. If he doesn't, we head for home, okay?"

"This is nuts," said Jim, shaking his head.

Sometimes, when Jim and I were stumped over something, we would look at Wallace and ask him what he thought, because you get like that on occasion and a dog spends so much time with you that it can become the litmus test for life's decisions. It casts the vote. Or was I just overtired?

Meropi was growing impatient.

"*Ti thelete, paidia*? What do you want to do?" she asked loudly.

Wallace suddenly stood up and shook himself.

"Okay, we'll have a quick look," I said to Jim. "The Oracle has spoken."

"*Pame*, Meropi. Let's go and see this house."

Meropi quickly rounded up her herd of goats and waved them through a narrow opening into a field, shutting a wooden gate behind her. We set off at a good pace back down the road, towards the centre of the village, wondering which of the houses was the bijou renovated number.

"There," she finally said, pointing towards a stone house with old window frames and a mass of ancient roof tiles sitting at odd angles. The garden was overgrown and there was another, even more derelict building hanging off one side of the house.

"She's having a laugh, isn't she?" I said.

"Yeah, and so's the Oracle," said Jim, giving Wallace a nippy look.

The woman noted our long faces. "That other place next door belongs to a Greek man who lives in America," she said, proudly, as if that factor gave the rundown neighbourhood a certain cachet.

But if there's one thing in Greece that puts you off, it's a house with a derelict property welded to one side of it, with smashed windows, a collapsed upper floor and nothing probably but rats, rubble, a stink about the place and the knowledge that probably 10 different family members will own it and have fought for years over selling it, which is why it's been abandoned.

She led us through the front gate of her bijou address and stopped at the lower level, which had two tiny rooms, the doors wedged open. One room was crammed with bags of goat fodder.

"This is the kitchen. What do you say?"

How to fit granite benchtops in here came to mind.

"Cooker," she said, pointing to an old brick *fournos* just outside the 'kitchen' filled with cobwebs and mess. The other room had a sink propped up on a table and not much else in its dungeon-like space.

"Bathroom," she said brightly, with the brass neck of someone born to sell real estate, if only fate had dealt this poor woman a better hand.

The top floor was one long, dusty room crammed with moribund bits of furniture. The floor felt like it was sagging under our feet when we walked over it, which she forced us to do, like miscreants on a sappy gangplank, so that we could get to the other side, where a small window with a worm-eaten frame looked down on the gulf of Messinia and the lower part of the Taygetos mountains disappearing towards the tip of the Mani peninsula.

"Views of mountains and sea," she said with a flourish, nodding, and rattling her up-do.

It was a stunning view all right but the whole lot was not worth 40,000 euros. And there was a horrible stink about the place, which we suspected might be coming from the battered American-style fridge leaning against one wall, which didn't seem to be switched on, and was probably heading for the whitegoods graveyard.

"What's in there?" I asked.

"Goat meat."

Oh, time to go!

Even Wallace glared at the mouldering edifice and pulled me back down the front stairs.

"So, what do you think?" she asked when we were standing back in the fresh air.

"It's nice, but a bit small for us," I said, offering a diplomatic let-down.

Meropi looked mortified. "It's big when the furniture's out."

We didn't respond and she gave up the patter faster than you could say 'demolition ball', as if she was used to negativity. I felt slightly sorry for her when she told us a sad story of needing to sell the house to pay tax bills and she planned to move to Kalamata to live with her daughter.

A few days later, with our interest in houses still high, despite our encounter with Meropi's pile, we went to see a few other places in the Koroni area. These were all bargains, a few of them wrecks, but most sitting in large plots of land with olive trees, and sea glimpses. Even when they didn't need total renovation, there was a melancholy, rundown feel about them all and with the same depressing story, of an owner needing to sell for some quick money.

It was a strange window into other people's difficult lives and it would take more than hard work and a lot of money to make them feel like happy homes again. With no suitable properties to buy at that point, we decided to put our house-buying fantasies aside, particularly as the economic and political outlook in Greece once again seemed critical.

After the January election, despite hopes that Tsipras would ease Greece's problems, they seemed only to be increasing. By early March, he was forced to renege on his promise to give the Troika a body swerve and scrap austerity. He had to stick to the terms of the initial 240 billion euro bailout agreed in 2010.

Greece was given an extension to June 2015 to propose economic reforms in order to receive the next tranche of funds (7.2 billion euros) needed to make repayments on its loans, or else the spectre of bankruptcy would rise again. Greeks, even those who supported Syriza, were beginning to wonder if anything had changed and how the continuing merry-go-round of receiving funds from its lenders, only to hand back the money in interest repayments, could be supported indefinitely.

The flamboyant new finance minister and maverick economist, Yanis Varifakis, described the austerity programmes as "fiscal waterboarding", which was one of a slew of popular sound bites he delivered on the state of Greece for international media. Despite the bluster, he was forced to produce detailed reports for Brussels on how Greece would continue to repay its debts if not by austerity measures. Both Varifakis and Tsipras were having to dilute or abandon many of their election pledges. There was tension between the German government, particularly its finance minister Wolfgang Schauble, and Varoufakis.

Varoufakis said: "Schauble has told me I have lost the trust of the German government. I have told him I never had it. I have the trust of the Greek people." But that was slowly ebbing away. The Troika were moaning that Syriza's reform proposals were not specific enough and Varifakis was tasked with creating a better action plan.

It didn't seem to be the right time to think about buying property in a country that continually faced the threat of bankruptcy, but had any time been right to buy in Greece? When we first went to the Mani in 2010, we had toyed then with the idea of buying a modest property, but the country was just entering the maelstrom of economic crisis. Five years later, there was as much uncertainty as there had ever been.

Buying a house in Greece at any time is a minefield. A lawyer friend once told us she'd never buy a house in southern Greece. "The south is full of cowboys," she wailed. "If you're ever thinking of doing it, make sure you've got a lot of money behind you —and I mean A LOT!"

22

In the lap of the dogs

IN early May, Jim returned to the UK briefly to see his parents, who were both very old and not in great health. By now we had relaunched my first book, *Things Can Only Get Feta,* and the sequel, *Homer's Where The Heart Is.* The first book had re-established itself easily and the second book had roared up the bestseller charts in several genres on Amazon. By May, I had finally received some payments from Sir Ambrose but not the amount expected and I was now pursuing the matter by other means. However, I felt ecstatic knowing the books were now in my hands and were not going to be at the whim of anyone else. I would never make that mistake again.

The days were not without their own frustrations, however, as the wi-fi at the villas went on another blinder, with mast problems this time. On the hill at the top of the villa development was an arsenal of masts to relay the signal from Koroni. There were days on end with no wi-fi, which was frustrating while I was trying to promote the books and check their progress. It meant I had to go down to the town regularly and use the wi-fi in the Parthenon taverna, which was not an unpleasant experience. The family were very kind, and felt sorry for my lonely plight. To a Greek with a love of *parea*, being alone, especially at meal times, is the most regrettable circumstance and I found the family more than usually chatty. I had the laptop on the table in front of me as I ate my dinner, the modern version of a paperback leaning against the wine carafe, which was the prop of choice for solo travellers in the 1970s and 80s.

In The Lap Of The Dogs

In between checking emails and surfing the net, it was pleasant to watch the small caiques returning to Koroni harbour for the night and the procession of village life up and down the *paralia*, with no-one in a hurry to be anywhere. After I finished for the evening, I would lock my computer in the car and go on our favourite walkabout in the town, stopping at all the usual places, now reopened for the new season.

Most days I swam and passed pleasant evenings, when I wasn't in the town, sitting on the villa balcony, eating a simple meal, drinking wine and listening to Greek music, watching the light fade over the gulf, the moon rise and hearing small owls hooting in the olive trees. Apart from missing Jim and feeling occasionally an unaccustomed aloneness in a relationship that had always been so warm and loving, with very few times apart, it wasn't too bad.

The only small aggravation was the fact that it was now the start of the tourist season again and a new stream of visitors appeared in the other villas, though not in *Palio Spiti* at least. I even laughed one morning early when I took Wallace out for a walk to see, in one of Yiannis's villas across the road, a couple doing their yogic salute-to-the-sun routine on the balcony and was reminded of Jed predicting yoga nuts and Austrian yodellers. They were yet to arrive, no doubt. And who knew if Jed and Delia would be back for more of their twitching labours – long-term.

I spent a lot of my free time wandering about the hillside with Wallace and often stopped to talk to Tasos and Eleni. One day I found Eleni milking her goats in the field and stopped to chat. I always imagined that goats would be easy to milk by hand because they're small and not aggressive, but it was far from easy, with goats jittering about and goat legs occasionally ending up in buckets of milk.

On the way back to the house on the milking day, a scooter approached on the narrow road. It was a strange sight, as most sights are in rural Greece: a man holding the handlebars with one hand and the other wrapped around a Rottweiler dog, which was reclining on its back in the crook of the rider's arm – like a baby. I recognised Dimitris from the Bogris taverna. He stopped, almost out of breath from holding on to the dog.

"Rex escaped again but this time I found him, and I'm taking him back to the farm."

Dimitris also had a smallholding with olive trees, chickens and a massive pig in a cage, and it was here that Rex was normally chained on guard duty. It seemed like a long time ago that we were in a spin at *Palio Spiti* when the English couple next door had let Rex follow them home and the dog tried to have a bust-up with Wallace. I loved rural life in Greece for its eccentricities and its rule-free environment, where everyone, and the Rottweilers, seemed to live in an unstructured, parallel world, even if it sometimes caused a fuss.

Perhaps it was no more than a desire by Greeks after so many centuries of domination by other countries, and harsh internal politics as well, to have freedom (*eleftheria*) at all costs. In Britain, we have lost many of our personal freedoms to political correctness and over-bearing legislation, which is why many of us are searching for it in other places like Greece, desperately seeking our inner Zorba. But how long Greece will be able to hang on to its maverick sense of freedom before it has to yield to European forces remains to be seen. The loss of it could be the saddest outcome of the crisis overall.

At the end of the second week that Jim was away, despite the comfort of knowing there were friends in the vicinity, I finally appreciated what it felt like to be really alone in a foreign country – which I hadn't felt since some of my earliest jaunts in Greece – when something unexpected happened one morning.

I had planned a trip to Kalamata to meet up with Stavroula at a mobile phone shop to pick up a computer plug-in to connect to the internet because the wi-fi problem was more complex this time and a solution wasn't in sight.

I woke early and opened the big roller shutter on the sitting room windows and couldn't believe what I was seeing. Fog! A pea souper! The whole hillside was wrapped in it, which I'd never seen in Greece this far south. It was so thick I couldn't see the farm below, or even hear the voices of the grandfather chivvying up the others for their morning chores.

The fog had a slightly sulphurous glow about it that looked unpleasant. I was nervous driving to Kalamata at the best of times because of the winding road with edges that often sheered off into olive groves, and drivers who went too fast on the long straight stretches. What would it be like driving in thick fog?

I was due to meet Stavroula mid-morning and needed to leave soon, as the drive took around an hour-and-a-half to the city centre. I decided to call her and see if I could postpone the meet-up and put up with no wi-fi for another day or so. I had taken Wallace out early for his walk and put him outside on one of the balcony chairs, as it was hot despite the fog.

While I was inside, talking to Stavroula on the mobile, I suddenly heard a crashing noise and looked out the window to see Wallace on the ground and walking around with a strange wobbly gait, bashing into things. I told Stavroula I'd call her back.

I ran outside and found Wallace in a distressed state, his head nodding and his eyes flickering from side to side, unable to focus, as if he were having some kind of fit. I picked him up and put him inside in his soft dog bed and called Angelos the vet. Angelos had helped Wallace through a few illnesses and mishaps through the years and was the only vet I had ever met who you could speed-dial at any time and he would get right back to you.

I told him what had happened and he asked a lot of questions and whether I could bring Wallace straight in to Kalamata. Of course I would, but I was worried about the fog.

"You still have fog over there?" he said.

"Yes, you can only see a few yards ahead."

Angelos had a house in the Mani facing the Messinian peninsula.

"When I woke up this morning I looked across at your peninsula and I thought there was a massive bush fire. It was covered in what looked like smoke. I've never seen anything like it."

"I don't really want to drive in it," I told him. "It will be bad on the roads."

"Don't worry, Margarita, I can drive over to Koroni to see Wallace as soon as I have finished the clinic for the day. Only, that won't be for an hour or so, and I am worried about him for now. Let's go over the symptoms once more."

I described them again and Angelos said he was not happy about the way it sounded.

"Look, I am thinking that Wallace could have one of several things and I won't know for sure until I see him. I am thinking he may be suffering from a sudden drop in blood sugar, for some reason, like a diabetic with hypoglycaemia. Or he could be having a seizure."

"Caused by what?"

There was a tiny pause. "A tumour perhaps?"

I gasped.

"I am sorry, Margarita, but we have to consider all these things. Wallace is an old dog and these things happen to the old ones. But I think it's probably something more simple, like blood sugar. So here's what you must do, or else he might go into a coma. You must give him a teaspoon of honey mixed in a little warm water to get his blood sugar back up and try to make him drink as much as you can and call me back in 20 minutes."

In The Lap Of The Dogs

I hung up and checked on Wallace. He was sitting in his bed, looking alarmed, his eyes still flickering madly. I got out the honey jar and mixed a small amount in warm water. But how to get Wallace to drink it? From earlier health problems I knew it was never easy to administer anything to Wallace. He was not a good patient. I put the mixture in a small dish and laid it down in front of him. He didn't want it, so I had no choice but to pour the liquid into the side of his mouth from a teaspoon. It went everywhere, mostly on the floor, so I also rubbed the liquid on his gums and teeth, hoping some of it would stay put.

I did this quite a few times and put him back in his bed. After five minutes he wasn't much different. I was feeling panicky and for something to do I decided to mop the floor where his bowls were lined up against the wall because it was now a sticky mess. The mop was always kept balancing over the low balcony wall, to dry. I picked it up and dashed into the bathroom, setting it against the wall while I ran hot water. When I picked it up, something plopped on to the tiles. A huge beige scorpion.

"No feckin' way!" I exclaimed. That was all I needed now, yet another scorpion. And inside the villa as well. It looked like it was sleeping and I wasn't about to wait for it to rise and shine. I brought the mop down hard on it and heard it crunch like an eggshell. I flushed it down the drain and then manically beat the mop on the tiles, in case there were more of them hiding inside the mop head. There weren't.

Could this morning get any worse? I went back to check on Wallace, who was sitting quietly in his bed with the same flickering eyes and scared expression. I got down on my hands and knees and gave him a cuddle.

"What do you want me to do, Wally?" I said, showing my daft tendency to grill him on all matters, small and large.

He just gave me a panicked look and I made the split-second decision to start the drive to Kalamata. I would be there before Angelos's clinic shut for the day. I dashed about, locking the doors and windows, and got the dog bed and Wallace into the back seat of the car. I took the precaution of tipping some honey water into a glass jar, so I could stop on the way and administer it. Then I set off on the bumpy track towards the farm road below. The fog was still thick and while I could now see the farm, the road ahead was fuzzy. On the main road it was the same, as fog drifted in from the gulf like tumbleweed.

I don't think I'd ever been more nervous driving in Greece where, if a massive pothole didn't poleaxe you, then a driver hogging the centre of the road would, and more so in fog. Ten minutes along the road, and sure enough, I met him, the driver taking up the whole road, roaring out of the fog in a Jeep, like a man with a death wish. I had to pull right over to the right of the road to avoid a collision, and ended up half in the forecourt of a small roadside taverna. It wouldn't be the first time I'd narrowly missed a head-on crash in Greece.

My hands were shaking and I turned round to check on Wallace. He was lying in his bed, looking much as before, his eyes still flickering. What if I'd had an accident? How would Wallace get the help he needed then? I decided to call Angelos again. He picked up the phone straight away and asked for another report on Wallace. I told him how I'd struggled to make him drink the honey mixture, and also that I was on my way to Kalamata.

"No," he said, "forget Kalamata now. There's no time. What I want you to do now is to go home and give Wallace some ice-cream."

"What?"

The idea of treating Wallace to an ice-cream seemed bonkers.

"You must give him ice-cream, riiiight! It must be plain ice-cream, a few teaspoons. It will help him. It will be better than the honey. Easier. Wait 15 minutes or so, and if he's not looking better, a few more, to get his blood sugar up. Call me in an hour unless he gets much worse ... riiiight!"

"Okay."

At least the ice-cream made sense, but I remembered we didn't have any in the house. I waited for a long gap in the traffic and turned the car back towards Koroni, pulling in at the supermarket we used, near the villa road. I rushed down the aisle to the frozen foods but there was hardly any ice-cream. Greeks are very seasonal people. Until the snow is off the Taygetos across the gulf, a sure sign that summer's on the way, they don't want ice-cream. But I did find some miniature tubs of Benny and Jerry's frozen yoghurt with honey. I wouldn't tell Angelos about this. Otherwise, it was perfect! I bought half-a-dozen.

I drove home like a Greek, fast along the olive grove track, without bothering what was coming towards me. Hell, if it worked for them, just for once it would work for me. Anyway, I knew every pothole and serrated edge along this particular road, fog or no fog.

Back at the villa, I followed Angelos's instructions, offering Wallace tiny bits of ice-cream. He wasn't keen to start with, so naturally I had to eat a fair bit of it myself so he could see where we were going with this therapy. It was delicious. After a while, he got a taste for the sweet ice-cream and lapped it up. Half-an-hour later, I was relieved to see his eyes had stopped flickering and he seemed less anxious. I called Angelos and told him the news. He was pleased and told me to give Wallace a few more spoons of ice-cream and that he should come back to normal again. I was to call him again if the situation changed.

I let Wallace sleep on the bed that night so I could keep an eye on him. I didn't get much sleep but at least he did. He seemed peaceful, exhausted. Wallace had had his health dramas over the past five years, most especially in the Mani, when he developed stomach ulcers and we had to take him to an animal hospital in Athens. Wallace was old now, coming up for 14, and he had been with us through the best and worst of times, a wonderful companion. It was hard to imagine any human or animal who could have given us so much hilarity, frustration and frights as Wallace. I spent much of that night reliving many of his finer moments and remembering his great canine ability to always know when we were feeling low and needed some Jack Russell therapy.

I well remembered one bitterly cold winter's night in Scotland when Wallace was about seven and I had come down with a bad chest cold that I feared would turn into bronchitis. It kept me coughing loudly all night and Jim had to decamp to the spare bedroom because he had a 6am start at a Glasgow newspaper. I couldn't blame him, but Wallace had been sleeping on the bed, as he always did when one of us wasn't feeling well. I'm sure I kept him awake as well and wondered how long it would be before he sneaked off and leapt on to Jim's bed for some peace and quiet, yet he stayed.

Some time during the night I must have finally dozed off for a while and woke up feeling a warm weight on my upper back. It was Wallace, jammed in against me, his back to mine, his head on Jim's pillow. And that's where he stayed all night until late the next morning. The warmth was comforting and I had at least stopped coughing. I was convinced that he felt he was doing something therapeutic, and I think he probably did. Although the cold lasted a good few days longer, the bronchitis I had anticipated never came. Now here was Wallace needing my help.

While I had complete confidence in Angelos, who had become as much a friend as a vet, we were still a long way from Kalamata, which was a worry. Angelos told me that this incident might never occur again, or it could be a pointer to a bigger problem, there was no way of knowing for sure until we took Wallace to the surgery for a proper check-up.

In The Lap Of The Dogs

I was greatly relieved the day Jim was due back in Greece. I was longing to see him and I had promised to be at Kalamata Airport at 8pm. The road to Kalamata was quiet and for once it wasn't the usual mad roller-coaster drive. And no fog this time. Everything would be fine now. Or would it?

The first indication I got that the Gods were playing *tavli* with me was when I switched on my mobile after the drive to find six messages from Jim. I couldn't hear them properly. He was shouting over a hellish racket in the background that sounded like he was still in an airport. When I went into the arrivals hall at Kalamata Airport, it all became clear. The flight was showing a delay of three hours. What the hell!

There was a frantic crowd of people around the check-in desk for the outward flight to the UK that was now delayed. Outside the airport building I found a British travel rep trying to placate a group of Brits who seemed to be on a Saga tour. They were either in wheelchairs or leaning on sticks. They were understandably angsty and complaining about the hold-up.

"Are you waiting for the delayed flight back to Gatwick?" I asked the rep.

She signed. "We don't know when it will arrive now. It's been hit by lightning. That's all I know."

My stomach did a queasy back-flip.

"Lightning? Is it still flying okay? My partner's on the flight."

"Oh, I think it's okay, but I don't know where it is. I'm waiting for news myself." And she turned to placate a woman with a Zimmer frame having a panic attack.

I was having one of my own. I took out my mobile and called Jim's number. After a few rings he answered with the same noises going on in the background, like people shouting into metal drums.

"Thank God you're okay. I heard something about a lightning strike. Where are you?"

"Back in Gatwick. Just my luck, Margarita. The flight left on time but just after take-off we hit an electrical storm and the plane was struck by lightning. We heard a loud bang and thought the plane was about to go down. Miraculously, it was okay but we had to return to Gatwick for the plane to be inspected for damage. But it still had a full tank of fuel, which made it too heavy and dangerous to land, so the pilot had to fly around in circles over the south coast for ages, burning up fuel. We're now back at Gatwick, but they said the plane wasn't fit to fly because of the lightning strike, so we're stuck here waiting for a replacement aircraft to arrive."

"What a nightmare!"

"Yeah. The worst. Now the airline's saying we won't leave until about 9 or 10pm our time, so I won't get to Kalamata until the early hours of the morning."

"Do you want me to wait here for you?"

"No, don't be daft. The replacement plane might not leave until tomorrow morning. You better go home. I'll get a taxi from Kalamata when we eventually land there."

"I can't wait to see you, Jimbo. Give me a call in an hour when I'm back, if you can, or send me a text or email."

"Love you, Margarita," he said in a soft voice that seemed so far away. "How is Wally? I've been worrying about him."

"He's better now. But don't think about that now. Just get yourself back here safe and sound."

I couldn't believe this run of bad luck, just after surviving Wallace's funny turn and the fog. What next? A car crash on the Koroni road. At least I wouldn't have sat-nav woman on, moaning about coronaries on the highway. Not yet anyway.

I didn't arrive home until 10pm. I went to bed late but didn't sleep. All night I waited for the sound of Jim's taxi pulling up outside the house. Finally, I heard a car door slam at 4am. I got up to meet him at the front door. He looked exhausted. Wallace was unusually lively for early morning and ran up to Jim with his favourite toy hanging out the side of his mouth, the battered stuffed grouse we'd brought from Scotland.

"How are you, wee man?" said Jim, ruffling the fur on Wallace's head.

Wallace dropped the toy and almost seemed to be smiling.

"He looks fine now. Is he?"

"Yes, I think so. He's an old guy now, that's all."

"I know how he feels. But it's great to be home, I tell you," he said, giving me a powerful hug that brought tears to my eyes. "I really thought the plane wouldn't survive the lightning. It was awesome, like being in the middle of a Hollywood blockbuster about warring Olympian gods, and Zeus having a strop with bolts of lightning. Seriously though, that's just how it felt."

"There's an old Greek saying, Jimbo, that goes: blessed is the man who survives the wrath of Zeus and lives to tell the tale."

"Are you making that up?"

"Maybe. But some Greek, some time, probably said it. And it's got to be true."

We laughed. It was good to have Jim home. It was one of the few rare times in my nomadic life that adventure and risk had little appeal. There was something to be said for predictability and feet firmly on the ground, home comforts, happy dogs, yoghurt and honey ice-cream and, most of all, love.

23

No money, but plenty of Monet

IT was a while since we'd seen Papa Theodoros and I had promised to arrange a visit so we could look at his paintings. I called him on his home phone. I had a mobile number too but I refused to believe that Greek priests used mobiles. He told me to come to his service in the village of Falanthi on the coming Sunday and we would go back to his house from there.

The church service was well underway when we arrived and it was also unusually packed. As we made our way through a log-jam of people lighting candles, I noticed a table laid out at the front of the church, with flowers, candles and a photograph of an old man. It was a *mnimosino*, a remembrance ceremony. The *papas* must have forgotten it. There was no way we could meet up afterwards, as he would have to accompany the family to a nearby taverna or *kafeneio* for the traditional meal afterwards. But we stayed on for the ceremony anyway, as the liturgy was nice and the *papas* had a very sweet voice for chanting.

It's always thrilling to hear a Greek service done with real passion. I didn't understand much of it, as usual, but the constant chanting of a few melodic lines, ending in the words '*eis tous aionas ton aionon*' (for an eternity of eternities), was a very comforting notion.

The essence of eternity in a Greek church, with its ancient aura of stability and permanence, has always appealed to me, but in everyday life it's a different matter, especially where plans are concerned. Plans are bendy things in Greece. I have always known that.

While the service drew to its solemn close, I wondered what we would do about our planned visit to the house of the *papas*. I was thinking all the while about the cake we had brought that was on the back seat of the car and how it would fare on this warm day in May. It would have to be taken home again.

When you are invited to someone's home in Greece for a coffee, there is no pressure to take cakes, even though they are always welcome and most Greeks adore sweet things. But after our last meeting with Papa Theodoros and because of his genial nature, I wanted to take him something as a token of friendship and because I feared that Greek priests lived rather parsimonious lives nowadays. I had gone to a favourite *zaharoplasteio* (pastry shop) in Koroni, where the owner Aristotle had always been kind and chatty.

The shop was crammed with an overwhelming choice: sticky *baklava* in trays, *kataifi* that looks like shredded wheat soaked in honey, chocolate cakes, cream cakes, plain cakes. I wanted to get the choice just right, so I trailed up and down in front of the display counter.

"*Kiria*. You seem perplexed. What are you looking for exactly?" he asked.

I told him I wanted something appropriate for a visit to a local *papas*.

"Which *papas*?"

"Papa Theodoros from Homatero."

He smiled. "I know him – and I know exactly what he likes."

Aristotle was the kind of guy who knew everyone in Koroni and further afield. Sooner or later, everyone buys a big sticky cake for a special occasion.

"I had coffee with Papa Theodoros just the other day and I can tell you he likes this one." He pointed to a round cake on a foil plate. It was *rivani*, a popular cake in this region, but fairly plain.

"Okay, I'll take the whole cake."

It came in a box with a ribbon tied around it, which looked rather grand when it was all finished, and it was placed in a thick plastic bag. I was pleased with the choice, and looking forward to trying a bit of this local treat myself.

"I hope the *papas* likes it," he told me with a wink. "Let me know."

Now here I was in a church doing the manic thing of cogitating over eternity on the one hand and what to do with *rivani* cake on the other. I kept thinking it would dry out and spoil in the back of the car. Dramas in Greece can often revolve around the strangest, smallest things, I have found. After the service we waited outside until the *papas* had finished his Sunday rituals and tidied away the chalice and other items from communion.

A trestle table had been set out in front of the church and two women were handing out small paper containers filled with *koliva,* a ritual food that dates back to ancient times and contains a mix of wheat, nuts, pomegranate seeds, dried fruits and spices. This is supposed to represent the cycle of life and death and it is given out at funerals and memorial services. One of the women handed me some *koliva* and though I took it, I apologised, saying we were *xenoi* and we didn't know the deceased.

"He was my father. It doesn't matter if you didn't know him. He was a good man. I'm sure he would want me to share this."

As I picked away at the *koliva*, I marvelled at the inclusive nature of Greeks and how, because we had been to the service, we were included in the ritual. No rules. No analysis. She then invited us to the village *kafeneio,* where some food was being served to honour her father. It was kind but I felt we'd be pushing the hospitality too far and gratefully declined. Finally, the *papas* left the church to join the others and I managed to catch him before he left. I reminded him of our meeting.

"Yes, of course. I'm so sorry. I forgot about all about the *mnimosino* when you called me. I must go now with the family to the *kafeneio*. It will take a while. Can you come to my house in the afternoon, say, at five?"

It was a slight inconvenience to drive all the way home again, but we had come this far with the arrangement.

Jim sighed as we walked back to the car. "The damned cake is going all over the region."

"We have to get it in the fridge. It will be as dry as the Dead Sea Scrolls in a minute."

I did contemplate giving it to the *papas* to take to the *kafeneio*, but Greek rituals are so strict when it comes to death that I thought I might cause offence. So home we went again, stored the cake away and went out for a long swim at Ayia Triada, where the water was so clear and smooth it reminded me of how sweet May is in southern Greece. Not yet too hot, but still quiet before the tourist hordes arrive. All the trees were bursting with small unripe fruits, the olive groves were full of wild flowers, the swallows were wheeling over the peninsula. It was a grand day.

Later in the afternoon we went back to see the *papas*. His house was compact inside, with one small sitting room, a traditional hard-backed sofa, a table and a large bookcase groaning with books that included some old copies of the Bible and other ecclesiastical books. He had photos of his children on the wall and more piles of books on the table. The *papadia*, his wife, was also there and when we handed her the box of cake finally – which in my mind had now assumed the significance of some kind of sealed letter that I had trudged miles through enemy lines to deliver – I felt lighter. Mission accomplished!

She stood holding it in her arms and when I told them it was *rivani* I felt the atmosphere in the room fizz a bit. They exchanged smiley looks and the *papadia* took the box quickly into the kitchen, where I imagined fat slices would be cut and we would get to try this Orthodox favourite. First, however, coffee was brought out on a tray, and glasses of cold water. I had never wanted a piece of cake so badly. I hoped it hadn't dried up for all its perambulations that day, but time passed and no cake appeared, and instead small dishes of spoon sweets, like fruity jam, were handed out. This is traditional in Greece, favoured more by older people, which you either like or hate. Sadly, the *rivani* stayed in the kitchen. Not that I blamed the priest and his wife for this curious lapse of hospitality. Things were tough in the Orthodox Church, for village priests anyway.

Jim and I smiled knowingly at each other from opposite ends of the table, and when the *papas* got up to fetch something from the kitchen, Jim said: "You and I are daft, aren't we?"

"Yes, you could say that, Jim," I told him as I licked sweet peach syrup from the side of my mouth.

Every time we took someone a cake in Greece we never seemed to score even a crumb. It would disappear into the depths of a fridge or cupboard, never to be seen again. But I had known that to happen frequently in Scotland as well. Maybe we were bringing people cakes of a rather immaculate confection, especially in this particular instance. We would have to scale back a bit.

Cakes were a thing of torment for us, especially with Foteini. She either devoured her share immediately, stuffing cream cakes into her mouth in one hit, or gave our offerings away to passing motorists, for reasons we could never fathom. And her own choice of cakes was sometimes dubious. Once at her *ktima* she made coffee and brought us some cakes wrapped in silver paper. I was always worried about any foodstuff Foteini kept on her farm compound because I don't think she gave a hoot about use-by dates, and the *kaliva* was a refuge for mice. These cakes were like Swiss rolls covered in chocolate, and slightly melty from the heat. She ate one, so we decided to do the same. They tasted okay.

"These are nice. Where did you get them?" I asked her.

"Oh, there was a *yiorti* at one of the village churches yesterday and some food for everyone. There were gypsy girls giving away these little cakes," she said, holding another one up by its wrapper, checking it from every angle and opening it.

Dear God, I felt sick. No-one but Foteini took food from gypsies, as you couldn't tell how old the stuff was or where it came from. And gypsies in Greece never give things away for nothing, as we had discovered. Jim and I looked at each other with queasy faces. But we survived.

The *papadia* was a small, shy woman, dressed in black. She sat at the other end of the room near three walls of paintings that I imagined were the priest's and which I was keen to see later. She hardly said a word but listened thoughtfully while I asked Papa Theodoros a little about his life.

He told me he had been born in this house in the 1940s and after a period of study for the priesthood had returned, working as a priest in the area for 35 years. He was a genial man, easy-going and happy to chat, despite the fact that he would have had a long day. He spoke a little about the hardships of the priesthood in the crisis. Did he like being a priest? I asked him.

"Yes," he said, without a moment's hesitation. "The Orthodox liturgy is amazing, the *psalmodia*, chanting, is beautiful. I like it very much. I never get tired of it. But it's a big job, with three churches to look after, and the monastery."

I had my camera with me and thought it was the right time to show him our photos on the digital display of the Hand of God Tree at the monastery. I showed him how to flick through the photos and he seemed a little unsure of the images at first and called the *papadia* over. They had a discussion and decided it was the old carob tree that had been in the grounds for decades, maybe more.

"What about the shape of the hand?"

He looked at the photos for a long time, running his fingers gently through the end of his beard. "You're right. It looks like a hand, clenched. And there's the thumb. I'm curious because I don't remember seeing this before."

The *papadia* told us they had not been up to the back garden at the monastery for a long time and the hand had not been visible years earlier, or not that she could remember. I decided to push my luck.

"Could it be something mysterious?"

"Like what, *paidi mou*?" he asked.

"Like … the hand of God?"

"*Theos?* God?" He was slightly taken aback. He and the *papadia* had another exchange but I couldn't quite catch it. They were probably wondering if we were a couple of mad people. But after a long pause I was relieved when he laughed quietly and said: "It's a beautiful idea, but the truth is, I do not know what has made this shape. It is curious."

Even still, before he gave me back the camera, he flicked through the pictures yet again. "I will look at the tree the next time I visit the monastery. But that won't be for a few months."

I felt he was in no hurry to go. I couldn't say I blamed him. Given the violent history of the place, maybe the tree unnerved him a little, it was hard to say. And that's as far as we got with it. The mystery remains.

Nevertheless, I felt bold enough to probe a bit further into Orthodox beliefs, as I knew very little about them and we had been to so many services in our time in Greece. He was generous enough to indulge me. It's not always easy to talk to a Greek priest, I'd found. They are too busy, too tired. They don't always open up to foreigners.

"What does the Orthodox Church believe life after death will be like?" I asked him.

"*Einai megalo mistirio*. (It's a great mystery). Even bigger than your mysterious carob tree," he said, with a glimmer of mischief in his eyes. "There is a peaceful life close to God, you can be sure."

"What about the visions we see in some of the frescos? The unbelievers sliding into the hell's fire?" Not unlike our own Christian view of hell. We had seen, in Greek churches, some tormenting frescos, revealing the torrid paranoia of the Byzantine mind: people falling off ladders into the maws of mutant beasts below, their arms and legs devoured by snakes, dragons and fearful fish-men.

He was nothing if not diplomatic. "We will have to wait until we die to find out more. But I can say this to you at least, that by the time we are ready to leave the earth we should have become better people than when we started. We should make a point of it, otherwise what use has this life been, with all its trials?"

It wasn't a complex or original thought, but I liked the way he said it most of all. It had a heartfelt sincerity about it, as if he believed it, strongly. And in his case, I was sure he had reached that blessed plateau, as he seemed a very good man indeed, not withstanding the lapse with the *rivani* cake.

I asked if we could see his paintings and we wandered over to his 'gallery'. He had started painting in the 1990s, he said, because he found it relaxing. They weren't what I was expecting, but neither was the *papas*. The paintings showed more than just a flash of mischief, they revealed a completely different side to his personality from the rather sober, considered one we'd just seen.

The paintings were done in the naïve style and full of humour, with plenty of churches and priests, but also dancing goats and donkeys, reminiscent of the rural whimsies of Marc Chagall. There was a brilliant painting of Einstein with outrageous hair and one of a crazed Van Gogh that made me laugh. Some were surprisingly bawdy, too, featuring copulating chickens, wayward donkeys and a buxom woman, in one, climbing a ladder in a short skirt.

"I like to paint funny images, too. They make me laugh," he said, by way of explanation. And who could blame him? The life of a village *papas* was probably, a lot of the time, no laughing matter, apart from when foreigners swung by raving about trees emblazoned with Godly hands.

Animals featured very affectionately in many of the paintings, including an elephant he said he had copied from a TV wildlife programme.

Levity aside, I asked him if he believed that animals had souls. I had once been told by a surly waiter in Santorini, trying to chase dogs out of a restaurant with a stick, that the reason Greeks mistreat or ignore animals is because they believe they don't have souls.

"They have souls, but not like ours," the *papas* told me, "They are not made in God's likeness."

"Do they go to heaven?" I asked, wondering if heaven would be worth the effort if Wallace wasn't going to be there on our final odyssey together.

He gave me an impish grin. "I don't know. We'll see.... I hope so." So did I.

It suddenly occurred to me that heaven could do with webcam, so we could see who's up there and who's not. I don't think I could have explained that to the *papas* but I'm sure he'd have made a very nice painting of it.

I was very taken with his paintings and asked him if I could possibly buy one. I imagined the sale of his work would be helpful in the crisis, yet I was surprised and a little disappointed when he told me he didn't want to sell any of them. I think I liked him even more because of that.

"I like to look at them and I get pleasure when other people like them," he said. However, he gave me a charming sketch to keep of the Byzantine church at the monastery.

We passed a delightful hour with the priest and before we left he told us to come up to his third church at Mistraki, a small village in the hills above the monastery, for the feast day of Ayia Triada in June.

"It's a nice service and you'll like it. You won't need to bring a cake this time," he said with an indulgent smile. Perhaps he had some insight after all into our cake anxieties.

@@@@@

In May, we finally admitted to ourselves that we couldn't really stay in Greece for the whole of summer. Buying a 'bargain' house was a fine idea but not on the edge of a possible Grexit. And we didn't have the energy to search out another rental. By the following month there would be the spectre of summer bookings for Villa Anemos, which meant that while it all seemed quite sudden, it was time to tell Stavroula and her family when we would be leaving.

We had put our lives on hold in a sense, even though we had begun to feel that being in Greece was our life, or the only one we wanted for now. There were other compelling reasons, however, that made us decide to return to the UK, and with a heavy heart we fixed a departure date for the end of June and set about telling everyone, including Christos at the Greek classes.

"But if you like it here, why not stay?" he said.

We had heard this so many times before and began to imagine that other people had fewer obligations and less complicated lives than we had. Or else we lacked their sense of maverick risk-taking. Christos told us he wasn't sure the classes would continue the whole year anyway, and that turned out to be the case by late summer, in which time we heard that he had lost his job, with no assurances he would get all the pay owing to him. He began to teach Greek privately.

On one of the last classes in June, when we were tackling the intricacies of passive verbs, I needed a toilet break, and on my way back, I was delighted to find the dancing class was again doing the Kalamatianos with the same young teacher. I asked if I could join in again, and round and round we whirled to the strains of a popular folk song played on a CD player. After five minutes of dancing I started to get the sequence of lefts and rights sorted.

"I think you've got it, finally," said the teacher.

"Really?"

"You've just learnt the Kalamatianos."

The others cheered. I felt elated. It was something I had always wanted to do, even if my offering was slightly rudimentary.

"In the summer we're going to be dancing at the local festival in Koroni. If you want, you can join us. It's nice. You will get dressed in the regional costume," the teacher said.

The others muttered their encouragement. I felt bereft. Imagine being able to get up with the others and dance the Kalamatianos in Koroni. I felt a little tear tremble at the corner of my eye. The things I was going to miss now.

"I won't be here," I told him. "I have to go back to Britain for a while."

"Oh, that's a shame. But you will return, surely?"

"Of course, but I don't know exactly when."

I felt a sudden pang of envy that the others would continue their dance in this school, set on a clifftop, in this mythical swathe of land, linked to the King of Asine. It couldn't get any better. But not for me. For four years I thought I held Greece tightly in my hands, but I had not. It was as illusive to me now as it ever was, like the glorious past of this country that even Greeks torment themselves trying to keep hold of.

"Could that be the King of Asini we've been searching for so carefully on this acropolis
Sometimes touching with our fingers his touch upon the stones."
(George Seferis, *The King of Asine*)

When I got back to the Greek class, 20 minutes later, my cheeks flushed with the effort, Christos smiled.

"You've been dancing again, haven't you, Margarita?"

Jim sniggered from his miniature desk in the front row. I shot him a devilish look.

"Ah, Jim told you, didn't he?"

Christos made a funny gesture, drawing a finger across his lips.

"Yes, but I will keep a *fermouar* on it," he said. And then wrote the word on the blackboard.

It was the Greek word for zip, and everyone burst into hoots of laughter. I kicked Jim under the table. I hoped it hurt. I felt slightly bruised myself from the realisation that we would not sit in this funny old room again, with this motley crew of foreigners. It had definitely been worth all the effort. My conjugations might have still been duff but I had the Kalamatianos in the bag.

24

Day of lost souls

WE set off one June morning for the service that Papa Theodoros had invited us to. It was the important feast day of the Ayio Pnevma, the Holy Spirit, at the church of Ayia Triada in Mistraki village. It was also a national holiday and would be the last great feast day before we left Greece.

We aimed to get there by about 8.45am for the last hour of the service. It was a pleasant drive on a glorious sunny day up through the hills behind Koroni, where there are only a few scattered villages with views down to the Messinian Gulf, where the waves were diamond-tipped in the sun. As we have often found on our travels in the southern Peloponnese, villages are often not what you expect. This one seemed unnaturally quiet and while it may have been a feast day of souls, there was not a single one about. Only two dogs were lying across the road, the dust raked about them. All the houses were shuttered and there was no church in evidence, not even a kafeneio. No sign of life.

We parked the car and wandered around from one end of the village to the other. It was a small settlement, with old, rather patrician-looking houses, mostly dating from the early 18th century, though there is said to have been Byzantine settlements on this hill in the past, hence its name, meaning Little Mystras, after the Byzantine city near Sparta.

Many of the houses had been restored to their original state but others lay in ruins, with crumbling walls and wild fruit trees hunched against them, as if to save them from falling down completely. In derelict gardens occasionally we saw a tethered goat. But where was the church?

It was past 8.45 when we began to walk up dirt tracks out of the village, looking for signs of a church dome peeking up from the trees, listening for the sound of chanting. But every path yielded nothing, except more houses and small farms. This was curious. Had we got the name of the village wrong? Was the church hidden deep in the folds of the surrounding hills?

After nine o'clock, we were still wandering about, convinced that having come all this way we would miss the service, and the small *yiorti* (gathering) we anticipated afterwards. We were disappointed.

"Let's hope the Holy Spirit's looking out for us and we'll get a sign," said Jim, trying to make light of it. On our odysseys in Greece from the start of the crisis, we had always tried to undercut the difficulties and frustrations we encountered with some daft humour. It had always served us well. We trudged around a bit more. It was getting hot and we decided we'd have to give up soon and retreat. Jim suddenly stopped and cocked his head slightly.

"I can hear a tractor in the distance."

He started running through the village, scattering dogs and dust, with me trotting on behind, trying to avoid potholes in my Sunday shoes. Sure enough, I could hear it too and we sprinted the last bit to the 'main' road just as a tractor with two men aboard was rumbling by. We shouted and waved our arms and thankfully the tractor stopped. The men gave us squinty looks when we asked where the church was.

"It's just through there," said one guy in overalls, "Five minutes' walk away."

They pointed to the only dirt road we hadn't tried yet, unsignposted, but with the remains of an old spring water outlet on the corner, which should have alerted us to a church nearby. We rushed along the track until the church appeared, in a clearing amid tall trees. The faintest sounds of chanting reached us.

"Well, Margarita," said Jim, as we jogged along. "Did the Holy Spirit come to the rescue or what?"

I laughed. "Probably! It was a nice touch though, wasn't it, sweeping in on a tractor. Very moderno."

We burst into the church a bit out of breath. Heads swivelled our way, and we were surprised to find a big turnout of locals in this old, restored church with some lovely icons. And Papa Theodoros, dressed in his ornamental white and gold robe, was in fine voice again.

This is an important service and celebration, coming on the day after the *Pentakosti*, the Pentecost, which falls 50 days after Easter Sunday and commemorates the descent of the Holy Spirit on Christ's disciples. After the service the congregation gathered in the forecourt. These were locals from several outlying villages too, who were among some of the friendliest people we had met in this part of Messinia. They wished us *chronia polla*, many years, and a good month, *kalo mina*. They were chatty and keen to know where we were from and what our impressions were of Greece. They were at least able to explain why Mistraki seemed deserted. There are now, sadly, only seven permanent residents left in this village, and they were all at the service.

At the edge of the forecourt, two men had set up a trestle table with a whole roasted pig on top, complete with head, and a set of scales nearby. The meat was not all destined for this venue, however, as the pair with their 'roaming roasts' would visit other locations today for other *yiortes*.

I was reminded of our experience of the roast *gourounopoulo* at the previous summer's *paniyiri*. The air was full of the succulent aroma of spit-roasted meat, yet there were no other signs in the forecourt of a *yiorti*: no chairs, tables or ecclesiastical bunting. The *papas* came strolling out of the church dressed down in his black cassock, carrying a bulging plastic bag.

"You managed to get here then; that's good. *Elate*, come," he said, putting his hand lightly on my arm to direct us over to the low wall around the church forecourt under the trees. The others followed. Perhaps because we were the only foreign 'guests' there that day we were asked to sit down first on the wall, which we did while we watched the curious proceedings. The *papas* unscrewed the top of a large plastic bottle filled with honey-coloured wine and put a liberal dash in our plastic cups.

There was a lot of banter and laughter from the rest of the congregation behind him, watching as he pulled things from his bag like a magician: paper plates, serviettes, chunks of bread, sweet tomatoes and goat cheese, carefully wrapped in tin foil. Someone was summoned to collect a steaming wedge of roast meat, wrapped in thick paper, from the pork handlers. It was placed on the wall and opened up for everyone to help themselves, while the wine was shared around.

It was an impromptu feast, and one of the nicest *yiortes* we had ever been to for its spontaneity and warmth, and its Biblical simplicity. Papa Theodoros was the very best kind of priest for his ability to be warm and inclusive, reaching out to ordinary Greeks and inspiring them. In these difficult times, priests like him were appreciated more than ever in rural areas. Historically, it has been the Greek Church that has kept faith with the culture, protected the language, education and rituals during the Turkish occupation, the world wars and the German invasion. In my mind, Greek priests were often the unsung heroes of this country.

Papa Theodoros also had an impish sense of humour, as we discovered from his paintings. One attractive, well dressed woman had been chatty, asking what we had been doing in Greece. I asked her where she came from.

"Falanthi," she said.

The *papas* laughed. "Irini always says that because she thinks it's posher than Homatero, where she really comes from." These are two similar villages, very close together, with hardly a whisper of difference between them. She laughed graciously and the two of them bantered for a while.

The time passed all too quickly and people started to leave. "*Kai tou chronou*," they chorused to the *papas*, meaning, "here's to the same thing, next year".

We thanked the *papas* for the invitation to the *yiorti*, and for his friendship that, even though it had come late in our stay, was no less joyous for that.

"*Kai tou chronou*," he said, giving us both a warm handshake that felt like a blessing as much as a farewell.

25

I was born under a wandering star

THERE was one important thing to do before we left the region and that was to say goodbye to Foteini – not for the first time in our lives.

She came up to the gate to meet us dressed in her usual mismatched layers of clothing. I didn't see any trace of the new socks though, festooned with sheep, or the addition to her figure of a push-up bra. I wondered if she ever did go back to Kalamata to finish that part of her shopping.

We sat outside her *kaliva* on the rickety chairs and drank Greek coffee. I had put Wallace on one of them to keep him away from critters. She was always amused when I did that. She stood with her hands on her hips, staring at him, as if he were a circus act. It was the equivalent of us watching dogs dancing on their hind legs in tutus on *Britain's Got Talent*.

We talked about our imminent departure and she became rather mournful, just as she had the last time we left Greece, but this time I had brought her no farewell gift, like the one-eyed cat called Cyclops that she was tasked with looking after, but which had disappeared long ago. I told her I regretted the lack of a small gift for her this time.

"You gave me the book, Margarita!" Her eyes blazed with pleasure.

She got up, went into the *kaliva* and came out with a small cardboard folder. In it was the book, wrapped in thick plastic. She also pulled out a ragged collection of photos, some that I had given her, and there were clippings from newspapers:

farming stories the local papers had written about her over the years. There were also clippings of some of the interviews I had given to Greek papers about the first book, which I had sent to her.

"It's great, Foteini, that you've kept all these things."

"I'm famous, Margarita. That's what you said. America, your country, and Australia. Everyone knows Foteini now."

I laughed. "Yes, they do. And I've written a second book, too."

"With me and Riko on the front?"

I explained that it had a different cover, but there were more stories about her life in this sequel.

"There's no-one like me."

It was something she often said, and no less true now. There was no-one quite like her in the Mani, which proved to me that uniqueness, in Greece at least, didn't require wealth, position, or even precocious intelligence. It was something more precious: a few simple and eternal qualities refined in the crucible of this country's history and nurtured on verdant hillsides. That was Foteini.

I promised to send her a copy of the second book when I returned to Britain.

We decided not to stay too long talking in the *ktima;* it would make us sad. I scanned the familiar scene around us, wondering if I'd actually miss this ramshackle place. Then I saw sweet-faced Riko tied up near the gate in front of his big feta tin. It got me thinking.

"You know, Foteini, as we're leaving, there's one favour I'd like to ask of you."

"What is it, *Margarita mou?*"

"Well, I've always wanted to ride Riko. May I?"

"What, right now?" she said, anxiously, because Riko to her is irreplaceable; almost a minor deity in her life.

"What are you asking?" said Jim, not sure of the Greek but aware that the mood had altered slightly.

"I asked Foteini if I could ride Riko. It's something I've always wanted to do."

"Have you lost your marbles? First dancing, now donkey riding."

"Relax. It will be fine."

I had ridden horses in Scotland for a number of years, but I'd never tried a donkey. It wouldn't be so far to fall at least.

Jim tapped his watch face anxiously. "We should be going really."

"Chill, Jimbo!"

I turned to Foteini, who looked preoccupied, scraping her top teeth nervously over her lower lip.

"So, what do you say, can I ride Riko, just for a bit, Foteini?"

She continued to worry her bottom lip. It was mental, as if I'd asked her if I could take Riko back to Britain. But in the end she gave in, as I was sure she would.

"Okay, but just around here, for a bit."

We walked up the rough stone steps to the top, where Riko was tied to an olive tree. He already had his traditional wooden saddle on because Foteini would be riding him home later. I had to climb on a small rock to get on him, even though he was small. I got a leg either side of his broad saddle. It felt bulky, unyielding. Foteini untied the rope attached to his head collar and led us into the adjacent field of olive trees, walking around its perimeter. I remembered the field well from years past when we had helped Foteini here with the olive harvest. Jim trailed along behind us, swatting at bees as he went.

"Are you happy now, Margarita?"

To be honest, I wasn't. It was all too slow and I had an urge for something a bit more spirited.

I said to Foteini: "This is *para poli oraio*, but what if I just ride him along the road for a while, just to the end of the *ktima*?"

She stared at me hard. "On the road? Out there?"

"Yes, just for 10 minutes. You know I won't let anything happen to Riko."

She scratched at her face, worrying a curly grey hair hanging from her chin. We had now walked back to where we started, beside Riko's feta tin.

She sighed. "You'd be careful wouldn't you, *koritsara mou*?"

"Yes, of course I will," I said, wondering if she felt this nervous when she took him on the road, or did I just seem like a total rookie.

Jim was watching me with narrowed eyes. "What's going on, Margarita? I'm having a Greek breakthrough moment. I'm making out words and I'm not well pleased."

"I've asked Foteini if I can take Riko along the road for a proper ride."

"Oh no way! You know how people drive in the Mani. A car will hit you and Riko."

"Shhh! Stop fussing. Can a woman not have a moment of madness in her life?" I said, remembering Zorba's appeal for getting in touch with your inner rebel.

Jim shook his head. "Margarita, you have not been a woman bereft of mad moments, I seem to recall."

"I won't be long, I promise."

"Okay, *Margarita mou*," Foteini said at last as she led the donkey through the main gate.

She handed me the lead rope, which was all I had for reins and for a crop she gave me a thin piece of whittled olive wood.

"Don't worry, Foteini. If there's a problem I will get off and walk him back. I promise."

"*Endaksi*, Margarita. Take him. You're always giving me things. This is my gift to you. Enjoy it, and don't be long."

"What about your hat. It'll blow off," said Jim, pointing to my battered straw hat with the floppy brim that I always wore it in the summer at Foteini's to keep the hornets and bees off my head.

"No. I want my hat," I shouted, as I brushed my legs over Riko's sides to move him quickly down the road. As I went I could hear them both grumbling together, and Wallace whining. It was like a Greek chorus.

When I was a few yards ahead, I glanced back at them and waved. Foteini was standing with her hands on her hips. Jim stood beside her, looking oddly defeated, and Wallace was straining on his lead, poor little mite. He wanted to join us. I had a strange, dislocated moment seeing this little group in front of the *ktima,* imagining that this is how we must have appeared to Foteini the first day we met her as she loped along this road on Riko. And from a distance it was true that Wallace looked like a baby goat with a black face.

After a steady walk, I got the donkey into a kind of trot, which was a small compact movement that made me feel the hard wooden saddle under my bum. I would suffer for this tomorrow. By the time I was level with the end of the *ktima,* I was just hitting my stride. I felt good: the sun on my arms, a warm breeze tickling the brim of my hat. I could smell the aroma of herbs and wildflowers wafting up from the road as Riko crushed them underfoot. I felt so good I even turned into Lee Marvin briefly from *Paint Your Wagon*, singing: "*I was born under a wandering star.*"

We trotted on like this for a while until I saw a pick-up truck roaring around a bend in the road, coming straight towards us. It pulled up sharply, with a crunch of gravel. The driver waved. It was a farmer called Leonidas, who had befriended us in our first year and helped us with some of the more challenging rural issues. He had startling pale blue eyes and a gentle manner and he was someone we had never managed to see enough of while we'd been in Koroni. He got out of his truck and came over, looking somewhat startled.

"Margarita, is that you?"

"Of course," I said with a chuckle.

"I saw the donkey in the distance, the straw hat and I thought at first it must be Foteini."

He started to laugh. I thought it was pretty funny as well. Me being mistaken for Foteini.

"But tell me, did Foteini really let you take the donkey out?" he said, stroking Riko's muzzle. He knew Foteini well. Did he think I'd hijacked the poor beast?

"Yes, of course, she did. It was a favour to me. For years I've wanted to do this." I laughed nervously, thinking how mad that would sound to a rural Greek. On the scale of things to do before you fall off the twig, riding a donkey wouldn't be one of them.

"Well, that just proves it, Margarita. You're a *horiatissa* (village woman) now. I keep telling you and Dimitris you should find yourself a house and settle here."

"Ach! Maybe one day but right now we have to go back to Britain. And there's the crisis here, with more trouble ahead, I imagine."

He made the windmill gesture with his arm. "But it will pass. Look, we Greeks have had more than a few crises to deal with, but they never last," he said with a wink. "So, make a plan and we'll see you again before too long, I hope."

He shook my hand and wished me a safe journey. "*Sto kalo*", "Go to the good". He walked back to his pick-up truck and drove towards the village.

Make a plan? Was he kidding? I want to follow the Greek philosophy. I don't want to do plans any more. As Foteini in her rural wisdom would say about plans: "Might as well comb the clouds, or wash a brick."

After Leonidas left, I should have turned back to the *ktima*. Foteini would be getting frantic, but I couldn't bring myself to do it. Not yet. I continued to trot down the road, feeling a sense of freedom that I hadn't felt for months. We were approaching the point on the road where it intersected with a narrower track leading towards the hills behind Megali Mantineia. I cursed myself for not having thought of riding Riko before when I had more time, when I didn't have two people waiting for me. I wanted with all my heart to go up the track and ride on and on, just Riko and me, but he came to a dead stop by the roadside just before the intersection. Nothing I did would persuade him to go further. Not this time. Wise, good donkey. So I turned him around.

We made easy progress on the way back. I let myself relax into the saddle, enjoying the ride. All around me were glorious, familiar horizons: the Messinian gulf, with the sea rising into gentle peaks from a hot southern wind; to the right, the rounded, inverted bowl of Mount Kalathio, with its switch-back road ascending to a high village. Either side of the road was a tumble of olive groves – row after row of small trees, their lush, sticky-up branches like morning hair.

As I took in these familiar images, I had a heightened sense of happiness and well-being. Life was sweet. All the disparate experiences we'd had in our years in southern Greece seemed to be distilled in this one perfect moment on a Mani road. It would be something I would recall in the years ahead and would never forget.

When I got back, Foteini and Jim were still standing where I left them. Wallace was yapping and jumping around the donkey's legs. Foteini rushed up to Riko and took the lead rope, rubbing his ears and whispering endearments, as if they'd been separated for days. It was strangely endearing. She tied him to the olive tree again and topped up his feta tin with fresh water, offering him a few cremated *haroubia*, dried carob pods, that passed for treats.

"Well, Margarita. You were away a long time. Did you enjoy your adventure?" she asked.

I put my arms around her and gave her a hug.

"Thank you, Foteini. That was a marvellous gift. I'll never forget it."

A Scorpion In The Lemon Tree

She smiled coyly and gave Jim a conspiratorial wink, as if the pair had been standing at the gate the whole time analysing the 'riding' situation.

"I hope you enjoyed your donkey ride as much as your Kalamatianos extravaganza. I'm wondering what will be next," said Jim.

He looked at Foteini. *"Margarita, poli treli!"* Margarita's completely bonkers!

Foteini laughed heartily until her lovely blue eyes sparkled with tears, but I knew her well now and they weren't tears of amusement. She wiped them with the back of a big sweaty hand. She gave us both a farewell bear hug. I tried not to think of this as a goodbye but just a temporary break from someone who had been such a unique part of our odyssey, even if we hadn't seen her as much this time.

"Don't forget to come back," she said, as we made our way towards the parked car.

"You know we will. I wouldn't want to miss another donkey ride, perhaps, or even a shopping trip in Kalamata."

"An iparho," she said. If I exist.

"You will. You're a tough *Maniatissa*."

As we started to drive away, I heard her shout from the front of her *ktima*.

"Kali andamosi." Till we meet again.

26

Margarita's inheritance

THERE was much to do in the couple of weeks before we left, and we wanted to make sure we had time to say goodbye to everyone.

We had asked Tasos and Eleni to join us on our balcony, late one afternoon, for a final meal. We made *keftedes* with lemon potatoes, Greek salad, and sizzling slices of the spicy *loukaniko* sausage that everyone loves in this part of Greece. We drank wine while the sun went down. It was an entertaining evening but overshadowed by our imminent departure.

"Why do you have to leave?" asked Tasos. "If you love it here, then stay." It was that common refrain again for which there is never a proper answer.

"Yes," said Eleni. "Stay and we can still be neighbours. We can have many more meals together."

"Nothing would please us more, but for now it's impossible."

Tasos had been a great support in our final weeks when we needed to get the car serviced for the long drive back to the UK and recommended a local garage. He escorted us on his motorbike and helped us to haggle with the garage owner over a fair price when we discovered that at least one engine part needed replacement – not surprising, as the little Fiat had done thousands of miles since 2010 and had criss-crossed southern Greece, taken us up perilous mountain tracks and on rough-hewn village roads in all weathers.

We hugged our friends goodbye and watched their pick-up truck rattle down the narrow track from the villas for the last time. It was a sad moment.

A few days before we left, Stavroula and her husband drove down from Kalamata to say goodbye. We strolled around the garden, remembering some of the more diverting moments we'd had at the villas, the 'mouses', the snake, the loud holiday-makers.

"You won't miss all the scorpions, will you, Margarita?" she said, laughing.

Actually, I thought I would miss the little devils. As Jim had once said, it was the scorpions that constantly reminded us where we were – living on the edge in Greece. And isn't life more intense on the edge?

"You know you can come back any time. Come in the winter as well, when you need a break from the cold weather. You will stay as our guests. And you can bring Wallakos, too," Stavroula said.

"Thank you. That's very generous, but if we come for a short break we can't take him on the plane," I pointed out, wondering if she knew that. I had visions of Wallace in his own seat causing mayhem, requesting chicken and leaping up and down on take-off.

Jim looked at me, his eyebrow twitching with pleasure at the thought of being able to come for short breaks when we wanted.

"Will we stay here, in Villa Anemos?"

We had come to like the villa, with its awesome views, and we had spent many hours working in the small garden, enjoying our modest harvest.

"No, this will be booked most of the summer, and in the winter we will close it now, I think. But there is a place you can stay."

I thought of Yiannis's villas across the road and on the top of the hill, where we had first stayed last spring.

"Up there?" I said, pointing towards them.

"Not there, Margarita. I mean the old house," she said.

I gulped and worked hard to stop my face from betraying terror. She wasn't fooled, and laughed.

"Okay. Yes, I know the old house isn't your favourite, but I will fix it up more at the end of summer. I will have time. It will be very sweet. It will have new doors and new paint. Some new furniture. You will see. You will like it then."

I wasn't won over. I had no urge to live again in the cramped old cottage, with the memory of mouses and *kounavia* tap dancing above us, even though I was sure they had long gone.

"And we will give it a name, and put it on our website now with the other villas."

Out of jest, or irony, I said: "Why not call it Margarita's Cottage?" What could be more ironic than that?

She beamed with satisfaction. "Yes, I like that. We will call it that. You know why? Because if it had not been for you and Jim wanting to have a house, and quickly, we would have left it in a bad state, forever. So it makes sense. We have you to thank for that."

Later on, when Jim and I were back in Villa Anemos, we dissected our day over dinner on the balcony.

"Honestly, can you believe it, Jimbo? All those months and years we've talked about owning our own house in Greece one day, and then looking at those old village wrecks, and we've finally got one, named after me. But it's the last house on earth I'd want to live in again. Is that not bloody incredible? Doesn't it make you want to cry?"

"Oh, don't, Margarita. Have another wine instead. It's not that bad. It could be cute, if it's properly fixed up."

"It was an amazing gesture, of course. And they are a nice family. We have been blessed with many good people in Greece, as always. But I draw the line at falling in love with the old house."

On the morning we left, we struggled to squeeze all our belongings into the Fiat and still leave a space for Wallace's bed on the back seat. We wanted him to be comfortable after his recent illness. We had taken him to see Angelos not long after Jim returned, for a check-up, and although it didn't show anything seriously wrong with him, we were mindful like never before that Wallace was showing his years, finally.

For the trip back, we wedged his bed on top of a suitcase so he could look out the window and not go too stir-crazy. However, it was a struggle to get everything into the car. The boot was crammed with more bags, and a five-litre can of olive oil given to us by Tasos and Eleni, as well as bags of lemons (no scorpions included) jars of olives and herbs, one oregano plant in a small pot, as if we could somehow take a swathe of Greece away with us.

Just as we were putting the last items into the boot, something caught my eye and I looked up to see Pluto standing at the top of the driveway watching us. The cousins must have let him out of the compound. This summer we had seen him a few times, running free through the olive groves, his big ears flying out behind like wings. He rarely came to the villa, though, but always watched us from afar.

A wild dog at heart, he seemed to know his place in the pecking order, and here he was, coming for a farewell glance. He was a sweet dog and I'd miss him as much as this verdant hillside. I knew he'd miss his chicken korma and spaghetti bolognaise leftovers.

Yiannis came past the house to say goodbye, dressed in his striped trousers and battered straw hat.

"Come back any time, remember. And Stavroula told you about the old house – Margarita's Cottage?" he said with a chuckle.

I must have given him a pained look. He burst out laughing.

"You don't like the house, Margarita, we all know that. Remember when we first went to see it that day, when it was *hamos*, a mess?

I nodded.

"And we said to you and Jim, 'don't worry it won't look like this when we finish'. Well, I knew whatever we did with it, you wouldn't like it."

"Did you? Why so?"

"I don't know. It wasn't just the mess inside. It's an old place, with a lot of history. A lot of happiness, but struggles too. It's the history of every Greek house."

He patted me on the shoulder. "And now you've got some history in the old house, to add to all the others."

I glanced at the squat structure, the front balcony on which we'd had our breakfast in the summer because it was the only place to catch a morning breeze. The trees that offered so much fruit. I had a soft spot at least for the small study bedroom, where I had written most of my second book. So, in effect, I had left a small piece of my soul here.

"One day, we will take up Stavroula's generous offer. We will stay a few days in Margarita's Cottage. How could we not?" I said.

I'm not sure if I meant that, but finally I liked the idea of inheriting a house, even if it wasn't mine. It was a small bit of Greece — for now.

But I preferred to think my Greek inheritance went beyond bricks and mortar. As Dimitra, the nun at the Koroni castle monastery, had once told me: "When you really love a place, it doesn't matter if you're far away. It's always in your heart. It's yours."

As we drove down the bumpy villa road towards Koroni, Jim beeped the horn and I waved from the passenger window. The slim figure of Yiannis, in his *kipos*, waved back. Wallace barked at all the commotion and the old farmer who lived across the way — whose life and seasonal toil we had witnessed every day from our villa balcony – got up from his white plastic chair under the fluttering Greek flag and waved.

He would have known we were leaving because everyone in rural Greece knows everything, even before it has happened. We hadn't spoken very much to him in our year in Koroni but, true to his Greek character, he struggled towards the road as we passed, waving and shouting loudly: *"Kali andamosi! Kali andamosi!"*

Καλή αντάμωση

Till we meet again.

THE END

Acknowledgements

SINCERE thanks to the people of Koroni, Messinia, for their friendship and for allowing me to rattle about in their hitherto quiet lives, and also the villagers of Megali Mantineia, in the Mani, some of whom reappear in this book. Thanks to the families: Tsirolias, Bossinakis, Sipsas, Blanas and Kosteas. Thanks to Maria Vinieratou for her guidance in Greek language and history of Falanthi and surrounding villages.

Grateful thanks to other Greek friends for advice on Greek expressions and aphorisms, especially Margarita Nikolopoulou. Any mistakes are mine alone. Thanks to Papa Theodoros of Homatero for offering insights into his unique world, and Eleni Kostea for being an original *Maniatissa*. Grateful thanks to our Kalamatan friend and vet, Angelos Papadimitriou, for allowing us to keep him on speed-dial.

I am hugely indebted, as always, to friend and mentor, Scottish author Peter Kerr, for his publishing advice and wisdom.

Most importantly, thanks to my partner Jim Bruce for navigating the sometimes rocky shores of our Greek odysseys. I am grateful also for his expertise in editing and designing this edition through www.ebooklover.co.uk. Thanks also to artist and designer Anthony Hannaford for his vibrant cover illustration www.anthonyhannaford.co.uk.

Hugs to crazy terrier Wallace for making us laugh, as always, and gratitude to his inimitable breeder, Anne Milne, of Edinburgh, who kept me on the right track from the beginning, reminding me that a Jack Russell can never be a poodle. How right she was!

East Sussex, England, 2016

The prequels

If you enjoyed this book, you might also like to read *Things Can Only Get Feta* and *Homer's Where The Heart Is*, the first two books in the Peloponnese series. These insightful and humorous memoirs explore Marjory, Jim and Wallace's adventures from the beginning, as they settle into the hillside village of Megali Mantineia in the Mani, in 2010.

The books chart their attempts to assimilate into Greek like as the economic crisis deepens, with an unforgettable cast of local characters, particularly the irrepressibly unique goat farmer, Foteini. The Kindle and paperback versions are available on Amazon worldwide.

Praise for Things Can Only Get Feta

"Honestly, you won't be able to put this book down." – Maria Karamitsos, reviewing in *The Greek Star* newspaper, Chicago.

"A book to relax into, a wonderful record of Greece's uniqueness, written with wonderment, admiration and wit, all in equal measure." – Anne Zouroudi, award-winning author of the Greek detective series of novels.

"I respectfully suggest to all wannabe authors of an 'expat life' type of book that you read this book before putting pen to paper. It's an object lesson in how it should be done. Congratulations, Marjory!" – Peter Kerr, best-selling author of *Snowball Oranges*.

"Marjory is a very talented storyteller, and many descriptions of events and turns of phrase she used in this book actually made me laugh out loud while reading silently to myself, a feat that until now was only achieved by Douglas Adams and P.G. Wodehouse." – Gry, Good Reads reviewer.

"Marjory McGinn's style of writing is totally captivating. However, this book is much more than just the adventures of a couple and their dog. It is also a loving and caring approach to Greece at the beginning of the worst economic crisis the state has witnessed since the Second World War." – Spyros Litsas, newspaper columnist and Professor in International Relations, University of Macedonia, Greece.

"A tale full of adventure and wit, delving into the heart of the communities in this area (Mani)… This book might become a future reference source about life in 'unspoilt' Greece." – Stella Pierides, author of *The Heart And Its Reasons*.

Praise for Homer's Where The Heart Is

"Beautifully written, at times funny and always insightful, it entertains and at the same time gives us a unique perspective on an indomitable country coping with crisis. What more could you ask for?" – Richard Clark, author of the *Greek Notebook* series.

"Through her stories, sentiments and humour, we see and feel her love for Greece. Put this at the top of your summer reading list." – Maria A. Karamitsos, founder and editor of *Windy City Greek*, Chicago.

"Marjory takes us on an odyssey with mind, heart and great skill. I loved reading this book." – Pamela Jane Rogers, author of *Greekscapes*.

"Another wonderful book by Marjory McGinn. The ending tugged at my heart." – Linda Fagioli-Katsiotas, author of Greek memoir, *The Nifi*.

"Marjory writes at a level that sits with the best of the travelogue genre. Her depth of characterisation and turns of phrase are outstanding." – Amazon reviewer.

"Beautifully written. Her historic insight gives this book a gravitas far beyond its genre without taking anything away from a charming read." – Anthony Hooper, author of *The Glass Lie*.

"A fascinating and heartwarming memoir. I absolutely loved this book and had a huge lump in my throat at the end of it." – Valerie Poore, author of *Watery Ways*.

Praise for A Scorpion In The Lemon Tree

"This book is rare within the travel genre. It cleverly combines a travel narrative with enlightened observations about Greece." – Peter Kerr, best-selling author of *Snowball Oranges*.

"If you enjoyed Marjory McGinn's first two memoirs, you will love *A Scorpion in the Lemon Tree*. This book is her best yet, and that is saying something. McGinn's deeply-held affection for Greece always shines through. She has a lightness of touch that even makes reading about the dark shadows cast by the current crisis a joy. Her empathy with Greece and refusal to lapse into sentimentality makes this a witty and poignant book." – Richard Clark, author of the *Greek Notebook* series.

"I could read this series forever." – Amazon reviewer.

"I absolutely love all three books in this series ... written with warmth and with humour." – Dawn, *Goodreads* reviewer.

"Fun and enlightening." – Expat Bookshop website.

Marjory McGinn's new novel

A Saint For The Summer
A compelling story of heroism, faith and love

This novel, set in the wild and beautiful Mani region of southern Greece, is a contemporary story, with a cast of memorable characters. It is set during the economic crisis and combines family drama and a gripping narrative thread going back to a Second World War mystery, during the little-known Battle of Kalamata, which has been described as 'Greece's Dunkirk'.

It's also a love story between the protagonist, journalist Bronte McKnight, and the charming, enigmatic doctor, Leonidas Papachristou, with a heart-warming conclusion.

Available in paperback and Kindle on Amazon.

Printed in Great Britain
by Amazon